THE
PROFESSIONAL
FENCE

THE PROFESSIONAL FENCE

Carl B. Klockars

THE FREE PRESS
A Division of Macmillan Publishing Co., Inc.
New York

The Free Press
A Division of Macmillan Publishing Co., Inc.
866 Third Avenue, New York, N.Y. 10022

Collier–Macmillan Canada Ltd.

Library of Congress Catalog Card Number: 74–483

Printed in the United States of America

printing number

1   2   3   4   5   6   7   8   9   10

To the memory of Rayna Sue Moskovitz,
who, as dear friend and fellow student,
shared in almost all the trials of *The
Professional Fence*

and

To Joan,
who, during the years it took to write it,
gave me love, encouragement, and a son

CONTENTS

FOREWORD

This is an unusual book which has had an unusual history.

When the young scholar, who was a doctoral candidate, first approached me with the topic which is the thesis of this work, I at once admired his enthusiasm and courage and admonished him about the difficulties of doing what he hoped to accomplish. In fact, I tried to dissuade him and to turn his interests elsewhere, for fear that he would never accomplish the tasks he assigned himself and in hope that he might undertake a more facile, rapid dissertation.

But he was persistent and persuasive in his enthusiasm to investigate sociologically an area not systematically studied and about which we had, as yet, only anecdotal accounts.

The fence is one of the least studied and most firmly recognized agents of subterranean economies in this and many earlier societies. Until now, no one has organized the information, analyzed the social structure, and examined the status and proficiency of the receiver of stolen goods. Carl Klockars has performed for us a most valuable analysis which English social history has only alluded to but never accomplished.

My bias is admitted. I supervised the doctoral dissertation which was received for this publication. But I am prepared to say that this is one of the most delightful supervising experiences I have had as a professor of sociology and criminology. The chief character of this work, named Vincent for this account, is surely the king of his territory and stands in equal posture with Edwin Sutherland's Chic Conwell, who was the classic professional thief. Hence, this current study is in the tradition of the old Chicago School, represented by Clifford Shaw, and in the current mold of the best of ethnography and ethnomethodology. With sociological insight born from erudition and experience, the author adds a prelude of history and a coterminous analysis that closets us inside the mind of the true fence. Henry Fielding, Arthur Hayward, Jerome Hall and others gave us stories, character sketches and socio-legal references. But Klockars gives us chiaroscuro, a depth study, and analytic insights gained from hundreds of hours of congenial conversations and social psychological observations that have not been previously recorded. In the style of Oscar Lewis, this author has captured the essence and existence of the real fence—his aspirations, motivations, rationales, goals, and achievements.

The fence provides services and transfers of goods. His is an economic function. Read carefully the *Apologia Pro Vita Sua*, for here is indeed the rationale, the defense, of all of us for the parasitism of our labor in a society not totally geared for production designed by central planning.

As I came to the conclusion of my own involvement in the production of this study, I came to realize how unusual this work is, how carefully documented is the historical and contemporary analysis. And I recall with joy my acquiescence to the perspicacity of the author who has produced a most fascinating documentary story of the professional fence.

Marvin E. Wolfgang

Professor of Sociology and Law
University of Pennsylvania

ACKNOWLEDGMENTS

The researcher who undertakes to work directly with criminals inevitably incurs debts for assistance which cannot be acknowledged publicly. For some quite obvious reasons and others not quite so obvious, at least half the people who have helped me over the past four years must bear the contradiction, here at least, of a public but confidential acknowledgment of their participation. Appearances notwithstanding, I wish it could have been otherwise.

There are others who have also helped but have not contracted for confidentiality. The members of my dissertation committee—Marvin Wolfgang, Leon Higginbotham, and Norman Johnston—are to be thanked for their guidance and wise supervision. I am particularly grateful to Norman Johnston, who managed to be my close friend, informal teacher, sharpest critic, and Department Chairman, with no visible signs of role strain.

From many of my colleagues at Beaver College I received free and frequent editorial assistance. I profited especially from the many hours of careful attention that Steve Miller gave to various drafts of the manuscript, and I must also thank Barry O'Connor, Bette Landman, Howard Robboy, Pat Hazard, Loretta Bulow, and Pradyumna Chauhan for their critical readings.

Three Beaver College students—Janice Krenkel, Marilyn Rafkin, and Angela Schneider—are to be thanked for technical as well as substantive contributions to my research.

Eleanor Wilson gave most careful attention to the typing of the manuscript. Like much of the rest of the work which went into *The Professional Fence*, hers was partially supported by National Institute of Mental Health grant #RO 3 MH 21819, "The Professional Receiver of Stolen Goods."

Finally, I thank Hutchinson Publishing Group Ltd. and St. Martin's Press, Inc., for permission to quote from *Thief-Taker General* by Gerald Howson.

Carl B. Klockars

THE
PROFESSIONAL
FENCE

Chapter 1

THE CAREER OF
JONATHAN WILD

*Little research has been done on fencing despite its central
role in professional crime. More information is needed about
the nature of the market for illicit goods and the extent to
which the demand for various types of goods affects the incidence of theft. More should be learned about the relationship of legitimate and illegitimate markets. Little is known
about the pattern of distribution of stolen goods. . . . The
redistribution of goods through theft might constitute a
significant subsidy to certain groups in our society; its cur-
tailment might have significant side effects which should be
explored. Finally, it would be desirable to have more information about the organization and operations of large-scale
fencing operations, to aid in the development of better law
enforcement.*[1]

With the paragraph above, the President's Crime Commission's
Task Force on Assessment completed the half page on which they
chose to discuss the subject of the fence. In their footnotes they
remarked that Jerome Hall's *Theft, Law, and Society* was the only
systematic study of fencing ever published, but added that Maurer,

1. President's Crime Commission on Law Enforcement and the Administration of Justice, Task Force on Assessment, *Crime and Its Impact—An
Assessment* (Washington, D.C.: Government Printing Office, 1967), p. 99.

Sutherland, and Martin provided some additional descriptive and analytic material.[2] While one could fault the Task Force for not doing a bit more homework (or, at any rate, not reporting all they did do), their claim that little research has been done on fencing is true, and their mandate for more information raises some excellent questions.

This book is the case study of a single fence, a man whom I have chosen to call Vincent Swaggi. Vincent is one of the best-known fences in the city in which he does business. He has worked successfully at buying and selling stolen goods for more than twenty years. This portrait of his life and criminal career cannot answer all the questions that the Task Force on Assessment asks, but it can answer some and may suggest others.

Although names, dates, and certain details and descriptions have been changed so that Vincent cannot be identified by what is written here, these changes have not altered the essential characteristics of his life and work. Some aspects of Vincent's methods of doing business, however, have been omitted, because Vincent considered that a detailed description of them might endanger his security or the security of others. He offered me the choice of an edited account or no account at all, and I chose the former.

Because the account of Vincent's criminal career is edited in certain ways, however, it cannot stand alone as a description of the way in which a professional fence runs his business. It must be supplemented by other accounts not subject to the same limitations. Such supplementary information has been included, in part, by reference to testimony about professional fences available in the biographies and autobiographies of thieves. The observations of others who have studied the lives and behavior of fences—reformers, jurists, historians, and criminologists—have also been noted. Such testimony and observations have been used throughout the text and especially in the analytical chapter, Chapter Seven, not only to supplement Vincent's edited account but to suggest

2. Jerome Hall, *Theft, Law, and Society*, 2d ed. (Indianapolis: Bobbs-Merrill, 1952); Edwin H. Sutherland, *The Professional Thief* (Chicago: University of Chicago Press, 1937); David W. Maurer, *The Big Con* (New York: Pocketbooks Inc., 1949) and *Whiz Mob*, (Gainsville, Fla.: Publication of the American Dialect Society, 1955); John Bartlow Martin, *My Life in Crime* (New York: Harper and Brothers, 1952).

historical, economic, and sociological similarities between the way Vincent and other professional fences do business.

The third and possibly most important means by which it has been possible to augment Vincent's edited account occupies the remainder of this introduction to it. It is a summary of the criminal career of Jonathan Wild, the only other fence I know of whose life has been studied in detail. Wild was without doubt the most powerful and prominent fence in history. He controlled the London underworld for more than a decade in the first quarter of the eighteenth century. He published pamphlets defending his reputation and gave a version of his biography to Defoe.[3] Henry Fielding wrote a satirical novel on his life,[4] and John Gay's popular *Beggar's Opera* (1728) features Wild, in the character of Peachum, as the chief antagonist. If anyone deserves the dubious distinction of being the "Father of Professional Fencing," it is undoubtedly Jonathan Wild.

Although nearly two and one-half centuries, a different culture, different laws, and different law enforcers now separate Jonathan and Vincent, Wild's solutions to the problems of becoming a professional fence still stand as archetypes for those who follow him. This does not mean that fences after Wild study what he did and adapt his methods to their own contemporary circumstances. Rather, it means that Wild's spectacular success as a prominent dealer in stolen property bears a special relationship to the essential elements of the type of crime which brought him enormous wealth and power. Wild solved the problems of becoming a professional fence correctly and efficiently, *elegantly*, in the way mathematicians use the term. As the closest historical approximation to an "ideal type" among professional fences, Wild betrays both the legitimate and illegitimate bases upon which the operations of all professional fences are variations. Therefore, time, culture, different laws, and

3. Daniel Defoe, *The King of the Pirates, Including the Life and Actions of Jonathan Wild* (New York: The Jenson Society, 1901). Defoe's work was originally published in 1725 under the title: *A True & Genuine Account of the Life and Actions of the late Jonathan Wild, Not made up of Fiction and Fable, but taken from his Own Mouth, and collected from PAPERS of his own Writing.*

4. Henry Fielding, *The Life of Mr. Jonathan Wild The Great* (Oxford: Basil Blackwell, Publisher to the Shakespeare Head Press of Stratford-upon-Avon, 1926). Originally published in 1743.

various law enforcers notwithstanding, the reader who understands what Wild managed to do ought to have a good idea of what and what not to expect from Vincent.

MR. JONATHAN WILD THE GREAT
(1682?–1725):
A CASE STUDY IN MINIATURE[5]

Jonathan Wild was born in Wolverhampton, Staffordshire, about the year 1682.[6] His family was poor: his father worked as a carpenter and his mother sold fruit at the Wolverhampton market. The family consisted of three sons and two daughters, with Jonathan the first born. His education was limited to attendance at the village free school, where he was taught to read and write. At about age fifteen, Wild was apprenticed to a buckle maker. Almost nothing else is known about Wild's life before 1710, when at about age twenty-five he came to London. Here, it seems, his extravagant disposition resulted in his falling into debt, and, "some of his creditors not being endued [sic] with altogether as much patience as his circumstances required, he was suddenly arrested, and thrown into Wood Street Compter (debtors' prison)."[7]

During his stay in prison, Wild cultivated the friendship of a great many thieves, from whom he undoubtedly learned much about their way of life and occupation. Of his incarceration, Wild himself says that "by misfortunes in the world, he (Wild) was

5. This study of Jonathan Wild was written in collaboration with Rayna Moskovitz.

6. The literature on the life of Jonathan Wild is extensive. Chief among the sources used in the construction of this review of his career is Gerald Howson's *Thief-Taker General* (New York: St. Martin's Press, 1971). Howson's text is unmatched for its thoroughness and is a model of historical scholarship. Additional sources we have found helpful are George Borrow, *Celebrated Trials*, Vol. 2 (New York: Payson and Clarke, 1928); Arthur Hayward, ed., *Lives of The Most Remarkable Criminals*, vol. 1 (London: George Routledge and Sons, 1927), originally published in 1735; William Robert Irwin, *The Making of Jonathan Wild* (New York: Columbia University Press, 1941); *The Newgate Calendar* (New York: Capricorn Books, 1962); and two works by Patrick Pringle, *Hue and Cry* (Great Britain: William Morrow and Co., n.d.) and *The Thief-Takers* (London: Museum Press, 1958). We have also made use of Frank W. Chandler, *The Literature of Roguery*, vol. 1 (Boston: Houghton, Mifflin Co., 1967); Henry Fielding, op. cit; Jerome Hall, op. cit.; and Sir Harold Scott, ed., *The Concise Encyclopedia of Crime and Criminals* (London: Rainbird, McLean, 1961).

7. Hayward, op. cit., p. 248.

subject to the discipline of the Compter for above the space of four years during which time he was, in some measure, let into the secrets of the criminals there under confinement; of which afterwards he availed himself."[8]

In the Compter, Wild worked his way up to the position of a "trusty," a prisoner charged with the management of other prisoners. He earned the "Liberty of the Gate," which allowed him to leave Wood Street to deliver prisoners to nearby magistrates, and it may well have been on one of these trips that he met Mary Milliner, a prostitute who became his mistress. In 1712 an act was passed which permitted prisoners who appeared unlikely ever to repay their debts to be released from debtors' prisons (10 Anne c. 29). Wild's petition to be released under this act was granted in December of 1712.

Upon gaining his freedom, Wild

> . . . seems to have returned to his old trade of bucklemaking, but at first Mary was the main breadwinner. It would perhaps be misleading to say that he lived on her immoral earnings, for the normal rate was only sixpence for a short time and there was no premium in that. Besides, Wild did his bit. Like many of her colleagues on the game, she was, in the crooks' slang of that time, a buttock-and-file. The first word meant whore and the second pickpocket, and the reason for the hyphens is that she did both jobs at the same time. Most whores did their business standing in the street, and a girl with a light touch was in a good position to pick her customer's pockets when he was likely to be somewhat off his guard. The main danger was that he would discover the theft before she had time to get away, so most girls liked to have a boy-friend lurking in the shadows. He was called a twang. When he was not making buckles Wild went out as Mary's twang.[9]

By means of this employment, they were successful enough to move from their small brothel in Lewkenor's Lane to a tavern in

---

8. Borrow, op. cit., p. 517. The quotation is from a pamphlet which Wild had published in 1718; it was probably in part the work of a ghost writer. Wild exaggerated the length of his stay in the Wood Street Compter; he actually spent only two years there.

9. Pringle, *The Thief-Takers*, p. 21.

Cock Alley, where Wild opened a small brandy shop. It was at this location that Wild expanded his receiving operations from simply disposing of the pocketbooks, watches, and snuff boxes his buttock-and-file had stolen to fencing goods brought to him by thieves who frequented his small shop. His growing success in Cock Alley, also brought him into contact with Charles Hitchen, an Under City-Marshal, who was then the city's largest dealer in stolen personal property.

WILD AND HITCHEN: THE THIEF-TAKERS' SYSTEM

At the time of the first meeting between Wild and Hitchen, the City of London was a virtual crazy quilt of corrupt, inefficient, and ineffectual police forces. There was one force for each ward within the city, and one for each parish outside of it. By "police force" I mean an appointed constable and perhaps one or two poorly paid deputies. The authority of these forces stopped at the boundaries of the ward or parish, and to escape arrest a thief could on occasion cross the street. However, while there was no central, organized police force, the two chief posts of Upper and Under City-Marshal gave those who held them power of arrest throughout the city.

Hitchen had bought his office at auction for £700. It was common practice to sell such offices in eighteenth century London (the cost of the post of Keeper of Newgate went for £5000),[10] and it was understood that those who bought them would use the position to recoup what they paid for it, and more. The practice led to horrid abuses, but in the absence of funds to otherwise finance the positions, there seemed to be no alternative to this "eighteenth century tradition of exploiting private greed for the public good."[11] Hitchen, though, went too far. In a pamphlet published by Wild in 1718, a form letter of the kind Hitchen sent to recent victims of theft is printed:

10. Howson, op. cit., p. 29. The sum is roughly equivalent to $100,000 in modern currency.
11. Pringle, *The Thief-Takers*, p. 23.

To Mr. A— Merchant,

Sir,

I am Inform'd that you have lately had the Misfortune to be Depriv'd of your Pocket-Book. It is not long since I labour'd under the same Calamity, and perhaps to a greater Degree than you, I having Notes for very considerable Sums enclos'd in the same; but upon applying my self to Mr. C—s H—n, in St. Paul's Church-Yard, whom I was inform'd was the greatest Proficient in the Business of Thief-Taking in England, he took care to serve me effectually. There is no doubt but he will serve you likewise to the Extent of his Abilities, and I can assure you he has universal Acquaintance with, and Influence over all Persons in the Town Employ'd in Thefts of this Nature. But I must give you this Caution, that you go to him with your Pockets well lin'd, or He'll have nothing to say to you.

> I am, tho' unknown,
> Your Friend Etc.
> A. B.[12]

The letter itself was not outrageous by the standards of the time, but Hitchen's prices were. So much so, that within a year of his taking office a dozen charges were filed against him at the Court of Aldermen. The court reviewed the matter, but repeatedly postponed its decision to suspend Hitchen for fear that no one else would fill (i.e., buy) his office if it seemed that the money paid for it could not be earned back. In June of 1713, Hitchen was tem-

---

12. The letter is quoted in both Pringle, The Thief-Takers, p. 23, and Howson, op. cit., p. 52. Howson suggests that in publishing the pamphlet to discredit Hitchen, Wild probably added the last sentence himself. The pamphlet, published in response to one Hitchen had published attacking Wild, was entitled: An Answer to A late Insolent LIBEL, entituled, A Discovery of the Conduct of Receivers and Thief-Takers, in and about the City of LONDON: presumptuously Dedicated to the Lord Mayor, Aldermen and Common Council. Written by C—s H—n. Wherein is prov'd in many particular Instances, who is Originally the GRAND Thief-Taker: that a certain Author is Guilty of more flagrant Crimes, than any Theif-Taker [sic] mention'd in his Nonsensical Treatise: and that he has highly Reflected on the Magistracy of the City, in the said Scandalous Pamphlet. Set forth in several Entertaining Stories, Comical Intrigues, merry Adventures, particularly of the M—l [Hitchen] and his Man the Buckle-Maker [Wild]. With a Diverting Scene of a Sodomitish Academy.

porarily suspended from his office, but he retained his powers of arrest. His trusted assistants had been arrested during the investigation of his activities and his business in stolen articles was disrupted. Jonathan Wild, small-time fence of Cock Alley, appeared to be a promising replacement.

Hitchen approached Wild with the offer of a profitable partnership (with Wild as the junior partner), and Wild accepted. In order to appreciate the importance of Hitchen's offer to Wild, and the dispatch with which Wild accepted it, it is necessary to review some of the changes in the law that made fencing a different business from what it had been in the seventeenth century.[13]

Until quite late in the seventeenth century, buying or selling stolen goods, even with the knowledge they were stolen, was not a felony.[14] This does not mean that buying stolen property could not have gotten one hanged, although the almost open trading in stolen property during most of the seventeenth century suggests

13. The first fence about whom we have found any detailed information is Mary Frith, alias Moll Cutpurse. Moll was an outrageous woman who dressed in men's clothes, claimed to be the first woman to smoke tobacco, and ran the largest clearinghouse for stolen property in London. She was born sometime in the 1580's or '90's, and could well have continued her business of returning stolen property to its owners until she died in 1659. However, Moll, "The Queen of Receivers," was a fanatic royalist and spent her later years in plots against the Roundheads to avenge the execution of Charles I. Her literary legacy is not as great as Wild's, but she was the character upon whom Middleton and Dekker based their play The Roaring Girle (1610). Moll's legacy to fencing is a system quite similar to that of Wild's: restoring property to its rightful owners, controlling thieves under the threat of informing on them, running a central clearinghouse for stolen property, tutoring thieves, and currying the favor of the judiciary. I believe the most complete account of Moll's life is to be found in a small rare book entitled: The Life and Death of Mrs. Mary Frith, commonly called Mal Cutpurse (London: Printed for W. Gilbertson at the Bible in Giltspur Street without Newgate, 1662). Its author is unknown. A copy of the book is held by the British Museum. More accessible accounts of Moll's life may be found in Ronald Fuller, The Beggars' Brotherhood (London: George Allen and Unwin, 1936) and Charles Whibley, A Book of Scoundrels (New York: E. P. Dutton and Co., 1912).

14. The most thorough modern study of the growth and development of laws affecting criminal receiving is Hall, op. cit., esp. pp. 52–62, 70–79, 155–232. We have also found helpful some sections in Leon Radzinowicz, A History of English Criminal Law and Its Administration From 1750, 2 vols. (New York: Macmillan Co., 1957). An excellent review published not long after Wild's time appears in [P. Colquhoun], [A Magistrate], A Treatise on the Police of the Metropolis (London: Printed by H. Fry for C. Dilly in the Poultry, 1796), pp. 183–199.

that the chances were slim. What it does mean is that if you were hanged you would be hanged for being an accessory after the fact to theft, not for receiving stolen goods. One had to be proven "a receiver of men" rather than a receiver of stolen goods.[15] Furthermore, because receiving was understood by English law of the seventeenth century as an extension of theft, one could not be brought to trial unless the thief had been convicted first.

This situation prevailed until 1692, when the purchase or sale of stolen goods was made a felony (punishable by death) by 3 & 4 William and Mary c. 9, IV.[16] While this law removed the obstacle of having to prove that the receiver aided or abetted the thief, the requirement that the thief be first convicted was not completely abolished until 1706 (5 Anne c. 31). Until then, if the thief was not captured, the receiver could be prosecuted only for a misdemeanor (punishable by branding, shipping, or transportation to the colonies). These measures made receiving a dangerous business in the early eighteenth century, and the wide-open fencing of the seventeenth century became a memory.

A different occupation, however, one that mixed blood with stolen property, grew to take its place. "Thief-taking," as this occupation was called, was nurtured by three provisions of the Highwayman Act of 1692 (4 & 5 William & Mary c. 8, 7, 6). The first offered a reward of £40 (roughly equivalent to $2,000 today) to anyone who captured a thief and provided evidence that led to his conviction. The second allowed the thief-taker to keep the

15. Hall, op. cit., p. 53, cites the decision in Dawson's Case, 80 Eng. Rep. 4 (1602)
    . . . where an action in slander was brought for the words: "*Thou art an arrant knave, for thou hast bought stolen swine, and a stolen cow, knowing them to be stolen.* And adjudg'd against the plaintiff, for receipt or sale of goods stolen is not felony, nor makes any accessory, unless it is joined with a receipt or abetment of the felon himself."
16. The language of the act suggests how ineffective the control of receiving was in the seventeenth century:
    And forasmuch as thieves and robbers are much encouraged to commit such offences, because a great number of persons make it their trade and business to deal in the buying of stolen goods; be it therefore enacted by the authority aforesaid, That if any person or persons shall buy or receive any goods or chattel that shall be feloniously taken or stolen from any other person, knowing the same to be stolen, he or they shall be taken and deemed an accessary or accessaries to such felony after the fact, and shall incur the same punishment, as an accessary or accessaries to the felony after the felony commited.

thief's horse, guns, money, and just about anything else he had that was not stolen. The third gave a Royal pardon and a £40 reward to anyone except a convicted felon who informed on at least two other thieves and secured their convictions.

The effect of these provisions was to produce a small army of mercenaries and bounty hunters who employed blackmail, "protection," perjury, false witness, and receiving stolen goods in the vicious combination that was thief-taking. The reward of £40 gave them reason to follow their trade, and the Royal pardon gave them protection against the charge of receiving if they informed on thieves; and those, like Charles Hitchen, who held police powers as well were virtually immune from prosecution. In the early eighteenth century the safest way to be a successful receiver was to be a thief-taker too. It was this offer by Hitchen, to be taught the trade of thief-taking and enjoy the power and influence of Hitchen in the meantime, that Wild accepted quickly in 1713.

The partnership lasted about a year. As Hitchen's man, Wild dealt with hundreds of thieves and pickpockets from whom Hitchen bought stolen watches and diaries, and also bank bills too large for thieves to pass. He learned of Hitchen's methods of extorting money from small merchants by threats of arrest and the use of false witnesses. He learned how Hitchen blackmailed those who lost their watches or purses to a "buttock-and-file," and learned that blackmail could be used as well on some who had lost these articles in completely innocent positions. Chiefly though, Wild learned that Hitchen made most of his money not from £40 rewards available for the arrest and conviction of thieves, but by using the life-and-death power he held over thieves to force them to sell their goods to him at a fraction of their value.

By 1714, when Hitchen was reinstated as Under City-Marshal and had, therefore, less use for Wild, the latter had learned all he needed to know from Hitchen and had, therefore, less use for him. The two quarreled, and Wild, with some better ideas of his own, went into business for himself.

JONATHAN WILD'S SYSTEM

Where Hitchen had seen receiving as a protection racket, Wild saw it as a business. The motive in both is profit for the dealer, but the distinction between them is that a business depends upon keeping customers satisfied, while protection succeeds by keeping them scared. Wild changed the face of receiving by presenting an image of what he was doing that attracted both thieves and customers and satisfied the law as well. Thus, it is best to see Wild's system as a mixture of two images: the one presented to his thieves, and the one presented to his customers.

Howson reports a contemporary account of the presentation Wild made to a gathering of thieves shortly after he left Hitchen:

> "You know, my Bloods" (quoth he), "that as Trade goes at present, you stand but a queer Chance; for, when you have made [taken] anything, if you carry it to the Fencing-Culls and Flash Pawnbrokers, these unconscionable Dealers in contraband Goods will hardly tip ye a quarter of what it is worth; and, if ye offer it to a Stranger, it's ten to one but you are hobbled [arrested]. So that there's no such Thing as a Man's living by his Labour; for, if he don't like to be half-starved, he must run the Hazard of being scragg'd [hanged]—which, let me tell ye, is a damn'd hard Case! Now, if you'll take my Advice, I'll put ye in a Way to remedy all this. When you have been upon any Lay, and spoke to some Purpose [stolen something worth while], let me know all the Particulars; and I'll engage to pay-back the Goods to the Cull that owns them, and raise ye more Cole [cash] upon that Account, than you can expect from the rascally Fencers. And at the same Time take Care that you shall all be Bowmen [successful thieves]."[17]

The thieves were undoubtedly impressed with Wild's offer. His language was simple and straightforward; by his presence and his manner, he was clearly one of them. He understood the hard times a thief was dealt by men like Hitchen and the "rascally Fencers" and he offered to pay far better than they did. The thief who was skeptical of Wild's promise of better prices was persuaded, too. Wild did not even want the goods until he sold them; all he wanted were the details of the theft. If he could not keep his

17. Howson, op. cit., p. 67, takes the quotation from *Select Trials at the Session House in the Old Bailey*, 2 vols. (1742 ed.). The quotation in slightly different form appears also in George Borrow, op. cit., pp. 518–19. This work, *Celebrated Trials*, is a later, abridged edition of *Select Trials*.

promise of better prices, the thief could take his goods elsewhere. Where Hitchen had forced thieves to deal with him by threats of arrest and hanging, Wild appealed to their economic interests. With Wild there was apparently nothing to lose; his offer simply could not be refused.

Moreover, Wild was able to keep his promise of better prices by making presentations like this one to the people his thieves told him they had robbed:

> I happened to hear that you have lately been robbed, and a friend of mine, an honest broker, having stopped a parcel of goods upon suspicion, I thought I could do no less than give you notice of it, as not knowing but some of them might be yours; if it proves so (as I wish it may), you may have them again, provided that nobody is brought into trouble, and the broker has something in consideration of his care.[18]

On occasion, a victim so approached would question Wild about his association with thieves, perhaps accusing him of being nothing but a common fence. Wild would feign outrage and take his leave after saying:

> Sir . . . , I come only to serve you, and if you think otherwise, I must let you know, that you are mistaken. I have told you, that some Goods being offered to pawn by a suspected Person, the Broker had the Honesty to stop them; and therefore, Sir, if you question me about Thieves, I have nothing to say to you; but that I can give you a good Account of myself, my Name is Wild, and I live in *Cock-Alley* by *Cripplegate*, where you may find me any Day of the Week; and so, Sir, your Humble Servant.[19]

Standing before an honest man, Jonathan Wild became a legitimate citizen, a permanent resident, the friend of an honest broker who wanted no trouble with the law. Thus Wild was a man with two images. Before a thief, he was a fellow thief; before a gentleman, a gentleman. When challenged as the cohort of thieves, Wild became indignant, as a gentleman should.

18. Borrow, op. cit., p. 519.
19. Howson, op. cit., p. 68, takes the quotation from *Select Trials* (see note 17), pp. 240–41. The quotation also appears in Borrow, op. cit., pp. 519–20.

These two images, always joined, were the central elements of Wild's system. As long as he sustained them, his power over and control of the eighteenth-century underworld grew. When they lost their reality Wild's system failed, and he ended up on the gallows.

Of course, images are only part of reality, and no criminal system would survive if it left the one who ran it unprotected. With respect to the law of his time, Wild's images left him most secure. His thieves kept possession of the stolen property until it was sold. Wild did not receive it; he only received descriptions of it. (Although thieves hid their stolen merchandise, Wild undoubtedly learned of their hiding places in the course of dealing with them.) Perhaps most important of all, the information thieves gave Wild was enough to hang them. In brief, the thieves took all the risks.

Wild was equally secure as he, a gentleman, stood before his gentleman victims. He could not be forced to return their property; he did not have it. He was not an accessory to theft; he was only helping an "honest-broker" friend. He did not ask for money for himself; he was returning stolen goods, not selling them. He was doing the true owner-victims a "favor," and the owners usually wanted to be helped. His story to victims was sound. It rested firmly on his thieves' legal risks and their victims' private interests. From the perspective of the law, Wild, standing between his images, was nowhere to be seen.

BUILDING A BUSINESS

Almost immediately after leaving Hitchen in 1714, Wild began to use the system we have described above. By 1724, when he reached the peak of his power, he ruled the eighteenth-century underworld. He owned a cargo ship which transported stolen goods to Europe and returned to smuggle dutiable items back into England. According to Defoe, he employed some 7,000 thieves. In less than a decade, Wild took a small but brilliant swindle and turned it into the greatest criminal corporation in history by preserving the images he created for himself in his first few weeks away from Hitchen. His spectacular growth depended upon streamlining his system and solving the administrative and organizational problems which came with expansion. On the eve of the industrial revolution, Wild adopted the methods of modern business.

ADVERTISING. If Wild's trade were to grow, it would not do to have every sale require a personal visit to the victim's home. A natural businessman, Wild decided to advertise:

> Lost on Friday Evening 19th March last, out of a Compting House in Derham Court [i.e. Durham Ct.] in Great Trinity Lane, near Bread Street, a Wast Book and a Day Book; they are of no use to any one but the Owner, being posted into a Ledger to the Day they were lost. Whoever will bring them to Mr. Jonathan Wild over-against Cripplegate Church, shall have a Guinea Reward and no Questions asked.[20]

Wild placed hundreds of similar advertisements during the next few years on behalf of victims of theft he approached. Each described the property which had been "lost" (stolen). Each offered a reward, and explained where the property could be returned, "no questions asked." Such advertisements were common in the papers of Wild's time, and one has little trouble finding their modern equivalents today.[21]

If Wild already knew who had stolen the goods, advertisements like the one above served to divert suspicion from him as a confederate of thieves. If he did not know who had stolen the goods, the advertisements brought him new thieves who could then be recruited to work for him. In both cases, such advertisements kept the name of Jonathan Wild before the reading public. His reputation as the man who could successfully recover stolen property

20. *The Daily Courant.* May 26, 1714. Quoted in Howson, op. cit., p. 66. The analysis of advertising which follows is taken exclusively from Howson.

21. The first *Philadelphia Daily News* I looked through (June 28, 1973) listed twenty-three Lost and Found ads. Two of them were exactly what I was looking for. "LOST: ANYONE KNOWING THE WHEREABOUTS FIFI 3 yrs. fem. Beagle. Severe rash, sore bald back, needs med. Birthmark on lips. Sick owner grieving. ALL INFO STRICTLY CONFIDENTIAL." The second was less desperate, but it ended with the phrase which has had the same, lightly veiled meaning for at least three centuries. "LARGE REWARD Lost: 2 diamond rings. 1 engraved with date. No questions asked." Such advertisements are prohibited under modern English criminal law. See Section 23, Theft Act, 1968.

grew large enough that he no longer had to call on victims; victims came to him.

By 1715, Wild had moved from his brandy shop in Cock Alley to a large, respectable office in a street called Old Bailey. He was in business now, and charged a consultation fee for meeting with those who had been robbed. At such meetings, he would carefully collect detailed information about thefts, suggest appropriate rewards, and offer to "see what he could do." Because he knew not only what the victim would be willing to pay for the return of his property, but also what the thief would sell it for, he was in an exceptional bargaining position:

> When they came according to appointment, and desired to know what success he had met with? why [sic] indeed says Jonathan, I have heard something of your goods, but the person I sent to inquire tells me that the rogues pretend they can pawn them for more than you offer, and therefore, if ever they make restitution, it must be upon better terms. However, if I can but once come to the speech of the rascals, I don't question but I shall bring them to reason.[22]

There was no way Wild could lose. If the client offered more, Wild made more. If the client refused a greater reward, Wild's reputation as an honest businessman was enhanced when he recovered the goods at the client's firm price. On occasion, Wild would return goods at a price even lower than his client's offer, and his reputation profited handsomely.[23]

PERSONNEL. Because the economics of his system were superior to those of his competitors, Wild's army of thieves grew steadily. Clients were required, as we indicated in the quotation above, to make appointments to meet with Wild. It became clear to him that he would need assistants to administer this growing concern.

22. Borrow, op. cit., p. 521.
23. Max Weber, in *The Protestant Ethic and the Spirit of Capitalism* (New York: Charles Scribner's Sons, 1958), pp. 47–78, remarks that the spirit of capitalism is a particular blend of rationality and restraint. This lesson is as essential to the successful business of fencing as it is to legitimate corporate success. The irony of the Calvinists, as of Vincent and Jonathan, is that they took in as much as they did because they took out less than they could have.

Because such assistants would of necessity possess enough information to hang him, however, he would have to choose them very carefully. The Crown, as if to come to Wild's aid in deciding whom to hire, passed the Transportation Acts (4 George I c. 11 and 6 George I c. 23) in 1718–19.

These acts provided for the transportation of felons to the Colonies and added that if they returned before their time was served, they could be retransported for twice as long, or hanged. As it happened, many felons did escape the slavery of the Colonies and became employees for Wild, whose needs they fit perfectly. If they became difficult, Wild needed only to reveal them to the authorities to have them immediately retransported or hanged. If Wild had employed members of his own family, he could have found no more dependable assistants.

ORGANIZATION AND PUBLIC RELATIONS. As Wild's business grew, his competition suffered. His system permitted him to pay as much as half the market value of stolen goods, twice what his competitors had usually paid. Because of Wild's better prices, thieves flocked to him, and he received them readily. In exchange for his better prices, he imposed an organization on them. He divided London into several separate sections, and assigned a deputy (an escaped transportee) to govern each. Wild also encouraged specialized theft and was able to order bands of thieves and pickpockets to work when and where he wished. Although Pringle's designation of Wild as "director-general of a corporation of thieves"[24] invites a somewhat too formal understanding of his position, Wild certainly held unequalled influence in London's underworld.

From another point of view, however, Wild's success at recovering stolen property might easily have become an embarrassment of riches. His system depended upon his maintaining a respectable public image; he could hardly sustain such an image as the director of a corporation of thieves. In order to sustain the balance upon which his system depended, Wild had to counter the claim that he was nothing but a fence. He did so by emphasizing that integral part of fencing which most strongly contradicts the charge of being too intimate with thieves. He proclaimed him-

24. Pringle, The Thief-Takers, p. 23.

self to be "Thief-Taker General of Great Britain and Ireland," and proceeded to earn that puffed-up title.

Although Wild, like Hitchen and the other thief-takers of his time, had used the provisions of the Highwayman's Act to see that recalcitrant thieves were arrested and convicted, he was not obliged to do so in order to force thieves to trade with him. Wild's system was so economically superior to the systems of other thief-takers that thieves came to him willingly. But, as we observed, his system did require thief-taking in order to sustain his image as a friend of justice. This image was easiest to maintain, of course, when his business was still a small concern:

> . . . in a short time he began to give himself out for a person who made it his business to procure stolen goods to their right owners. When he first did this he acted with so much art and cunning that he acquired a very great reputation as an honest man, not only from those who delt with him to procure what they had lost, but even from those people of higher station, who observing the industry with which he prosecuted certain malefactors, took him for a friend of Justice, and as such afforded him countenance and encouragement. . . . And so sensible was Jonathan of the necessity there was for him to act in this manner, that he constantly hung up two or three of his clients [thieves] in a twelve-month, *that he might keep up the character to which he had attained.*[25] [Italics mine.]

As the image and reality of Wild as one who could successfully recover stolen property grew, the image and reality of Wild as Thief-Taker General grew with it. In 1716 Wild captured an especially brutal gang of murderers whose crimes had outraged London. For this, Wild was "universally and justly praised."[26] The press carried frequent reports of his courageous acts of thief-taking. Howson reports that many news items similar to this one were published during Wild's career:

> Last Saturday Night, Mr. May, a 'Change Broker, was set upon by a single Highwayman against the Men hanging in

25. Hayward, op. cit., p. 251.
26. Pringle, *The Thief-Takers*, p. 34.

Chains upon Holloway, who took his Watch, Rings and Money. But the Place being immediately alarm'd, it happened that Jonathan Wild and one of the Turnkeys of Newgate, were drinking on Horseback at the Three Foxes in Holloway. Jonathan took to the Road, and fir'd a Pistol at the Highwayman, who got clear off; but they track'd him beyond Highgate by the Blood, the Slugs having wounded either him or his Horse. [*Applebee's Original Weekly Journal*, 28 January 1721.][27]

Wild continued his thief-taking throughout his career. By 1720 he had destroyed most of the major gangs in London. By the time of his death in 1725 Wild had brought to justice (i.e., transportation and execution) more than 100 felons. He publicized his thief-taking widely, carried a small scepter as the symbol of the power of his fictional office of "Thief-Taker General of Great Britain and Ireland," and was consulted by the Privy Council in 1720 for his advice on controlling crime. In 1723 he audaciously petitioned the Lord Mayor of London to award him the Freedom of the City for his services to law and order:

To the Rt. Hon. the Lord Mayor & Court of Aldermen,
    The Humble Petition of Jonathan Wild,
    SHEWETH:
    That your Petitioner has been at great Trouble and Charge in apprehending and Convicting divers Felons for returning from Transportation since October 1720 (the Names of whom are mentioned in the Account hitherto annexed). That your Petitioner has never received any Reward or Gratuity for such his Service. That he is very desirous to become a Freeman of this honourable City, wherefore your Petitioner most humbly prays that Your Honours will (in Consideration of his said Services) be pleased to admit him into the Freedom of this honourable City. And your Petitioner shall ever pray Etc.

JONATHAN WILD[28]

27. Howson, op. cit., p. 117.
28. Ibid., p. 211.

The petition was never granted, but the public-relations value of making it was its own reward.

Just as Wild had understood the need for dependable (i.e., disposable) deputies, the subtleties of advertising, the economics of receiving, and the necessity of organization, he also understood the critical role his thief-taking played in maintaining his public image. He knew his system depended upon a symmetry of success in thief-taking and taking from thieves. For more than a decade he maintained that symmetry against repeated attempts to discredit and destroy him. Then, in 1725, he was arrested, tried, and hanged before a giant crowd which stoned him as he rode to the gallows. What is of interest here about his end is that his public image had to be destroyed before Jonathan Wild could fall.

THE UNMAKING OF JONATHAN WILD

In June of 1724, William Kneebone's drapery shop was robbed. He immediately suspected Jack Sheppard, who had once worked for him. Kneebone advertised for the return of his goods and went to Wild for help in recovering them. Wild sent for William Field, a known associate of Sheppard and a man indebted to Wild for having saved him from the gallows. Field confessed that it was he, along with Sheppard and Joseph "Blueskin" Blake, who had robbed Kneebone. Field also told Wild where both Sheppard and the stolen cloth could be found. With the information given him by Field, Wild and two assistants captured Blueskin while another of Wild's assistants captured Sheppard. Field gave testimony which convicted both, and the court sentenced them to death.

Sheppard's story, however, differed from Field's. Although Sheppard did not deny that he had robbed Kneebone's shop, he claimed that Field had no part in it. Rather, he asserted, he had told Field about the burglary only when he asked him to act as receiver for the goods. According to Sheppard, Field then decided with the help of Wild to give evidence against Sheppard and Blueskin, secure their convictions, and collect the reward. Despite this testimony, the prosecutions against Sheppard and Blueskin were successful, but Wild suffered greatly.

His problems began with Blueskin, who had trusted Wild and

worked with him for many years. Wild came to Blueskin's trial, and although it was Wild who had captured him, Blueskin asked Wild to help him. (It is possible that Wild could have used his influence to do so.) Wild's reply to Blueskin's request was that he would see to it that he got a sturdy coffin, and was not used as an anatomist's cadaver.

> All this put Blueskin at last into such a passion that though this discourse happened upon the leads at the Old Bailey, in the presence of the Court then sitting, Blake could not forbear taking a revenge for what he took to be an insult on him. And therefore, without ado, he clapped one hand under Jonathan's chin, and with the other, taking a sharp knife out of his pocket, cut him a large gash across the throat, which everybody at the time it was done judged mortal. Jonathan was carried off, all covered with blood. . . .[29]

Wild survived Blueskin's assault, but Sheppard proved to be an even greater problem. At the time Wild captured him, Sheppard enjoyed a small folk-hero's reputation. He had once broken into prison to rescue his mistress, but it was breaking out of prison which finally earned him acclaim. While awaiting trial for the drapery shop robbery, Sheppard escaped from Newgate twice. The first brought attention not only to Sheppard but also to Blueskin, who had not as then been hanged. The second, after Blueskin's death, made Sheppard a national hero.

It was truly a miraculous escape. Although loaded down with dozens of restraints, leg irons, handcuffs, and bars and bolts of all description, Sheppard managed to free himself from them. He then broke through six iron doors that stood between the most secure section of Newgate and his freedom. For ten days, Sheppard roamed the streets of London until he was finally arrested, drunk, in a gin shop.

When Sheppard was returned to Newgate, he was the most celebrated man in England. Hundreds of visitors came to see him in his cell, and the daily press faithfully reported all he had to say. He gave Defoe his life story, and he railed against Jonathan Wild. Almost overnight, Wild's public image withered. The anger that the people normally felt for thieves was turned on Wild and Field

29. Hayward, op. cit., p. 263.

for bringing down the dapper Jack Sheppard. "Probably nothing Wild did in his life so lowered him in the public esteem."[30]

Just when Wild's image as a thief-taker was being turned inside out, his system developed an internal flaw of major consequence. In August of 1724, one of Wild's most trusted thieves, Roger Johnson, had successfully stolen a large amount of jewelry from the English nobility. Instead of delivering it all at once to Wild, Johnson began selling it to him piece-by-piece, finding that he could get more money that way; Wild paid more because his clients offered more as they became impatient for the return of their property. Johnson strung out the return of the jewelry over many months, and by February of 1725, when Wild was arrested, most of the jewelry had not been returned. Needless to say, Wild's reputation with the nobility suffered. Not only did he seem a bloodthirsty thief-taker to the general public, who by then were singing ballads about the escapades of Jack Sheppard, but he also appeared an ineffective agent to his wealthy clients, who were still waiting for their missing jewels. It is within this atmosphere of hostile sentiment towards Wild that his arrest and trial must be understood.

Ironically, it was for helping Johnson that Wild was arrested. Johnson, who was the captain of Wild's ship, became involved in a quarrel with a certain Tom Edwards, with whom he had been enemies for many years. Edwards subsequently procured some information with which he managed to have Johnson arrested and fined for smuggling. When Johnson was released, Edwards captured him again and this time held a warrant against him on a felony charge. Johnson managed to get word to Wild before Edwards could locate a constable, however, and when a constable did arrive he proved to be a friend of Wild's and arrested Edwards on a phony charge. Johnson escaped, and Edwards spent the night in Wood Street Compter before he was released on bail.

Still undeterred, Edwards obtained a warrant against Wild as the owner of a warehouse full of stolen goods. Wild claimed that the warehouse belonged to Johnson and that Edwards was his fence. Wild backed up his claim with a warrant, and this time Edwards found himself in Marshalsea prison.

Again released on bail, Edwards continued to search for John-

30. Pringle, *The Thief-Takers*, p. 45.

son, whom he finally captured in February of 1725. This time Edwards had a constable with him. But before Johnson could be brought to prison, Wild arrived with an assistant and Johnson escaped from Edwards again. Wild, aware he could be charged with helping Johnson to escape, went into hiding for about three weeks. On the day he reappeared in public, he was arrested for helping Johnson escape and committed to Newgate.[31]

Shortly after Wild's arrest, two unsigned articles were published in the *British Journal* which further stirred the public sentiment against him.[32] These articles later appeared as the first two chapters of Bernard de Mandeville's *Enquiry into the Causes of the Frequent Executions at Tyburn*. They were a direct attack on Wild, explaining the reverse side of his image to an already hostile public:

> As soon as any Thing is Missing, suspected to be stolen, the first Course we steer is directly to the Office of Mr. *Jonathan Wild*. If what we want is a Trinket, either enamel'd or otherwise curiously wrought; if there is Painting about it; if it be a particular Ring, the Gift of a Friend; or any Thing which we esteem above the real Value, and offer more for it than Mr. *Thief* can make of it, we are look'd upon as good Chaps, and welcome to redeem it. But if it be plain Gold or Silver, we shall hardly see it again, unless we pay the Worth of it.[33]
>
> It is highly criminal in any Man, for Lucre [money], to connive at a Piece of Felony which he could have hinder'd: But a profess'd Thief-Catcher, above all, ought to be Severely punish'd, if it can be proved that he has suffer'd a known Rogue to go on in his Villany, tho' but one Day, after it was in his Power to apprehend and convict him, more especially if it appears that he was a Sharer in the Profit.[34]
>
> It is possible that a dextrous Youth may be esteemed, and

31. The events leading to Wild's arrest are quite complex and the description offered here is a highly truncated account. See Howson, op. cit., pp. 227–36.

32. *The British Journal*, 27 February 1725 and 6 March 1925, as noted in Irwin, *Making of Jonathan Wild*, p. 15.

33. Bernard de Mandeville, *An Inquiry into the Causes of the Frequent Executions at Tyburn* (Los Angelos: Clark Memorial Library, 1964), p. 3.

34. Ibid., p. 9.

be a Favourite to the Superintendent a great while, but when he grows very notorious he is hunted like a Deer, and the Premium on his Head betrays him. . . . A Thief bred must be hang'd if he lives.[35]

With this new image, Wild was brought to trial. City Recorder Sir William Thompson produced a detailed warrant of detainer (denying Wild bail), which we shall quote here because it is an excellent summary of Wild's criminal career:

1. That for many years past he had been a confederate with a great number of highwaymen, pick-pockets, house-breakers, shop-lifters and other thieves.

2. That he had formed a kind of corporation of thieves of which he was the head or director, and that notwithstanding his pretended services, in detecting and prosecuting offenders, he procured such only to be hanged as concealed their booty, or refused to share it with him.

3. That he had divided the town and country into so many districts, and appointed district gangs for each, who regularly accounted with him for their robberies. That he had also a particular set to steal at churches in time of divine service; and likewise other moving detachments to attend at court, on birth-days, balls, &c. and at both houses of parliament, circuits, and country fairs.

4. That the persons employed by him were for the most part felons convict, who had returned from transportation before the time for which they were transported was expired; and that he made choice of them to be his agents, because they could not be legal evidence against him, and because he had it always in his power to take from them what part of the stolen goods he thought fit, and otherwise use them ill, or hang them as he pleased.

5. That he had from time to time supplied such convicted felons with money and clothes, and lodged them in his own house, the better to conceal them; particularly for counterfeiting and diminishing broad pieces and guineas.

6. That he had not only been a receiver of stolen goods,

35. Ibid., p. 16.

for near fifteen years past, but had frequently been a confederate, and robbed along with the above-mentioned convicted felons.

7. That in order to carry on these vile practices, and to gain some credit with the ignorant multitude, he usually carried a short silver staff, as a badge of authority from the government; which he used to produce, when he himself was concerned in robbing.

8. That he had under his care and direction several warehouses for receiving and concealing stolen goods; and also a ship for carrying off jewels, watches, and other valuable goods, to Holland, where he had a superannuated thief for his factor.

9. That he kept in pay several artists to make alterations, and transform watches, seals, snuff-boxes, rings, and other valuable things, that they might not be known, several of which he used to present to such persons as he thought might be of service to him.

10. That he seldom or never helped the owners to the notes and papers that they had lost, unless he found them able exactly to specify and describe them, and then often insisted on more than half the value.

11. And lastly, it appears that he has often sold human blood, by procuring false evidence to swear persons into facts they were not guilty of; sometimes to prevent them from being evidence against himself, and at other times for the sake of the great reward given by the government.[36]

Although the events of Wild's trial are quite complicated, it will suffice here to say that in general they reflected the efforts of various law officers to convict Wild by whatever means could be arranged. Wild was arrested on one charge, detained in prison on others, and convicted on yet a different one. Howson suggests that the warrant of detainer submitted by City Recorder Thompson

36. The warrant issued by Thompson can be found in many sources, including Borrow, op. cit., pp. 502–04; Howson, op. cit., pp. 238–40; Irwin, *The Newgate Calendar*, pp. 84–86; and Luke Owen Pike, *A History of Crime in England*, vol. 1, 2d series (London: Smith, Elder and Co., 1873), pp. 256–58.

could not have been so thoroughly prepared in the few days after
Wild's arrest; Thompson had probably prepared it well in advance,
so that he could submit the impressive document whenever Wild
was arrested.[37]

On the day before his trial Wild distributed a printed pamphlet
to the jury and to observers in the courtroom.[38] It listed seventy-
five names of felons Wild had captured, and added that some who
had escaped him in his diligent pursuit of justice were now trying
to convict him. The pamphlet was an obvious attempt to recon-
struct his fractured image as Thief-Taker General—so obvious, in
fact, that the prosecution used it against him. The King's Counsel
explained that Wild had used the provisions of the Highwayman
Act to convict only those criminals with whom he had quarrels,
and had distributed the pamphlet in an attempt to discredit prosecution witnesses and influence the jury.

Jonathan Wild was brought to trial on Saturday, 15 May 1725;
among those on the bench was none other than City Recorder
Thompson. There were two indictments against Wild. The first
charged him with stealing fifty yards of lace from the shop of an
elderly blind woman. His defense was that he had not entered the
shop and, therefore, could not have taken anything from it. Although Wild had in fact engineered the theft, he had not actually
stolen the lace. The first indictment was dismissed.

The second indictment came under 4 George I c. 11, sec. 4,
which read:

> And whereas there are several persons who have secret
> acquaintance with felons, and who make it their business to
> help persons to their stolen goods, and by that means gain
> money from them, which is divided between them and the
> felons, whereby they greatly encourage such offenders: be it
> enacted by the authority aforesaid, That wherever any per-

37. Howson, op. cit., p. 241.
38. The pamphlet was entitled: "A List of Persons discovered, apprehended, and convicted of several Robberies on the Highway; and also for
Burglary and Housebreaking; and also for Returning from Transportation: by
Jonathan Wild," (ibid., p. 258). Howson corrects errors in Wild's list of 75,
and estimates that if one added all those convicted by others on behalf of
Wild and the women whose names Wild omitted from his list for reasons of
discretion, "a total of 120 or even 150 would seem quite reasonable." (p. 311).

son taketh money or reward, directly or indirectly, under
pretence or upon account of helping any person or persons
to any stolen goods or chattels, every such person so taking
money or reward, as aforesaid, (unless such person doth apprehend, or cause to be apprehended, such felon who stole
the same, and cause such felon to be brought to his trial for
the same, and give evidence against him) shall be guilty of
felony....[39]

This Act had been passed in 1718 as a section of the Transportation Acts (see p. 16). It was so obviously directed at Wild
that it acquired the nickname "Jonathan Wild's Act." Although it
was directed at putting an end to Jonathan's business, some minor
adjustments in Wild's operating procedures had rendered it completely ineffective. Its author was Sir William Thompson.

Under this Act, Wild was now charged with receiving ten
guineas from the blind shop woman for the return of her property
without discovering, apprehending, or causing to be apprehended
the felon who had stolen the lace. Wild was found guilty and Sir
William Thompson pronounced the sentence of death.

Wild's last hours were particularly brutal. On the eve of his
execution he attempted to commit suicide by drinking laudanum
(a mixture of opium and alcohol). He was unsuccessful and,
though barely conscious, was judged well enough to attend his
execution:

He went to execution in a cart, and instead of expressing any
kind of pity or compassion for him, the people continued to
throw stones and dirt all along the way, reviling and cursing
him to the last, and plainly showed by their behaviour how
much the blackness and notoriety of his crimes had made
him abhorred, and how little tenderness the enemies of man-
kind meet with, when overtaken by the hand of Justice.

When he arrived at Tyburn, having by that gathered a

39. Quoted in Hall, op. cit., p. 74. On p. 76 of the same work, Hall con-
cludes: "... the correlation between Wild's elimination and 4 George I c. 11,
sec. 4 (1718), is direct and positive." Such a statement seems precipitous. Cf.
Howson, op. cit., p. 266: "... it is almost certain that had the prisoner been
anyone else but Wild, or even Wild at an earlier time, he would have got
away with it." One must remember that Wild's system operated smoothly for
six years while this Act was in force and that some matters quite unrelated to
it finally brought Wild down.

little strength (nature recovering from the convulsions in which the laudanum had thrown him), the executioner told him he might take what time he pleased to prepare his death. He therefore sat down in the cart for some small time, during which the people were so uneasy that they called out incessantly to the executioner to dispatch him, and at last threatened to tear him to pieces if he did not tie him up immediately. Such a furious spirit was hardly ever discovered in the populace upon such an occasion. They generally look on blood with tenderness, and behold even the stroke of Justice with tears; but so far were they from it in this case that had a reprieve really come, 'tis highly questionable whether the prisoner could ever have been brought back with safety, it being far more likely that as they wounded him dangerously in the head in his passage to Tyburn, they would have knocked him on the head outright, if any had attempted to have brought him back.[40]

THE HERITAGE OF WILD

The immediate result of Wild's execution was a dramatic reduction in the rate at which thieves were apprehended and convicted. That irony was brief; within two years, the number of hangings per month was restored to previous levels, and the criminal justice system thereby proved it had adjusted to the loss of the Thief-Taker General. The reward remained the standard means by which police were paid, and, consequently, thief-takers flourished. For a short time people found it difficult to recover what had been stolen from them, but new entrepreneurs soon filled the gap left by Wild. Crime waves continued in their curiously eternal crests. In Howson's words, "Just and necessary though it might have been, Wild's death taught no lessons, brought no reforms, and alleviated no suffering."[41]

And surely, Wild himself had always known it would be so. If one thing alone is clear about his life, it is that he knew very well the groups whose needs he served:

40. Hayward, op. cit., pp. 270–71.
41. Howson, op. cit., p. 283.

For do I not, quoth Jonathan, do the greatest good when I persuade these wicked people who have deprived them of their properties, to restore them again for reasonable consideration. And are not the villains whom I have so industriously brought to suffer that punishment which the Law for sake of honest subjects, thinks fit to inflict on them–in this respect, I say, does not their death show how much use I am to the country? Why, then, added Jonathan, should people asperse me or endeavor to take away my bread?[42]

His customers wanted their property back; his thieves wanted money for what they had stolen; the forces of justice needed to hang highwaymen at a rate that would satisfy London's crowds. Indeed, the needs of all of these groups were the cornerstones of Wild's system. And, by and large, these same groups with these same needs survive today. Thieves still have property to sell and still seek the best price they can obtain for it. The courts and the police are under continuous pressure to solve those crimes which the public conscience finds offensive; and although there is no longer a quota of hangings per month, the most commonly used measure of police performance is the rate at which crimes are "cleared" by arrest. People who have their property stolen are now often covered by theft insurance, so that (with some notable exceptions, which will be discussed later) their needs are not what they were in Wild's day; but the attraction of a "bargain" ("a steal at that price!") serves to replace those who fed his system with an equally willing group.

But our age is surely different from Wild's. Our laws are more complex; our police are better trained. We are, in fact and image, far more subtle. The portrait of his modern counterpart that follows requires closer strokes and more detail. They are not necessary to describe the elements of Vincent's system, which with almost inconsequential substitutions, are identical to Wild's. They are needed only to capture the modern meanings and impressions that continue to make Wild's ancient system work.

42. Hayward, op. cit., p. 252.

Chapter 2

VINCENT'S EARLY YEARS: DEVELOPMENT OF HUSTLING SKILLS

There is some question about the year of Vincent Norfior Swaggi's birth. Records of the Federal Bureau of Prisons and the FBI indicate 1919, his probation case folder bears 1912, and the meager official records of the orphanage where he spent three early years state 1910. For as long as he can remember, Vincent himself has claimed 1913 as the year of his birth. To my arguments for the probable authority of the orphanage records his response was a half-joking "But that would make me an old man." Just to be sure, the following day he sent $2.50 to the city's Bureau of Statistics for a copy of his birth certificate.[1]

1. For reasons unclear to me Vincent first requested a search only of the years 1911 and 1912. A second search of birth-certificate files returned a certificate bearing 1914 as the year of Vincent's birth. Since Vincent had always reckoned from 1913 and I was arguing for 1910, he welcomed 1914 triumphantly. (All my estimates of his age are based on the Bureau of Statistics' date, 1914.)

Vincent was the third son and fourth child of Joseph and Lucy (Cella) Swaggi. Joseph had come to the city from Sicily. On his arrival he wore a cape, carried a cane, and bore the masculine dignity appropriate to the son of a prosperous Sicilian merchant. Joseph was a desirable husband. The feather-importing business which he started allowed him to comfortably support a wife, a stepson, and eventually 5 of his own children. Like Joseph, Lucy was of Sicilian heritage, although she was born in the United States. Her father was an immigrant, who earned his living in this country by practicing Black Hand crafts. Lucy saw fit to give Vincent her father's first name—Norfior. In 1914 Vincent was born into a family of five: Joseph (26), Lucy (26), a half brother, Bennie (8), Tony (3), and Marie, a little more than a year old.

To Vincent his early years are an object of uneven recollection and questionable clarity.

I've seen pictures of Pappa Norfior. Everything he wore was black: shoes, suit, hat, and a big black moustache. Real old country style. My mother and Hoppo [Vincent's paternal uncle] used to talk about him. He was Mafia, in those days they used to call it Black Hand. He was in protection. He'd go into your store, take what he wanted, and if you squawked, he'd smash things up.

Pappa Norfior could write with his foot. He'd put a pen between his big toe and the one next to it and write a letter. They'd put the Black Hand on after.

I was his favorite, you know. I guess because we had the same names. He was a good man. Bennie and Tony knew I was his favorite so they'd tell him I was gonna be a cop when I grew up. He'd pretend to get angry and tell me to get out of the room. He'd yell, "Get that little cop outta here." You see, I don't think I remember that but Tony tells that story so that's what I remember.

You're asking me to go back fifty years.

When I try to think about when I was a kid, some things I'm sure I remember. Other stories I don't know whether I remember them because they happened to me or because I heard about them later when I was older.

I don't know how my mother and father got into the feather business. I know that they used to have peacock feathers and also bird of paradise. They were very popular in those days. The Black

Hand knocked them out of business when I was still a baby. They must have been up to something. I still have some of their bill-heads around somewheres.

My father was a very intelligent man. He could do anything. All he'd have to do is read something in a book and he could do it. Like if some men were digging a well and my father was there. They'd ask him what he thought they ought to do. If they didn't listen to him nine times out of ten they'd get themselves in trouble.

The Swaggi family did well in their feather-importing business. Joseph owned his own carriage and two horses to draw it. The Swaggis incurred the disfavor of Italian organized crime, however, and before long found their business bombed and Anna, Vincent's younger sister by two years, kidnapped. For some reason Pappa Norfior could not intercede, and the business was lost. Anna was returned, but the message was clear that the feather business was no longer a wise venture for the Swaggis. Joseph was a resourceful man, quick to learn. He became a plumber for a large contractor. There were schools, hospitals, and offices to be built in the city, and a willing and intelligent worker could find his way.

When Vincent was three Joseph died, leaving Lucy with five children of his and one she had brought to their marriage.

My father died in 1917 at the age of 33. He had dropsy. He would swell up like a balloon and go into a coma. He was on a plumbing job at the baseball stadium when he took sick. They rushed him to the hospital, where he died.

Later, when I was thirteen or fourteen, my [maternal] Uncle Paul told me a different story. You see, Paul was the one they called to the hospital to identify my father's body. He said that he still had clumps of his own hair in his hands. You see, sometimes he would go into a coma and his pulse would be very weak. Some stupid intern probably declared him dead and put him in one of those drawers in the morgue. I think he woke up before he suffocated. They killed him.

Joseph's death cut the economic supports out from Lucy. Her father, Norfior, and Vincent's uncles, Paul and Hoppo, helped out, but six children weighed heavily. Soon Bennie, Vincent's half brother, left home and went to Mid-City. In July of 1918, Tony, Vincent's older brother, was placed in a convent home. He

stayed there for six months until January of 1919. When he returned Lucy managed to take care of her five children by Joseph
for almost a year. She offered a hiding place for thieves who
needed a place to disappear. Her father and uncles would direct
suitable tenants to her.

In October of 1919 her youngest daughter, Josephine, less than
two at the time, died of diphtheria. Her death prompted a further
readjustment in the family. This time Vincent, now age five, was
sent to the convent.

*I remember when my mother took me up there, she brought
me into a room with a nun, then turned around, closed the door,
and left. When she shut the door I started to cry. The nun
slapped me and told me to shut up. I was only five then but I
knew that this place was gonna be no picnic.*

*For the first couple of months they would get you dressed up
on Sundays so that if anybody came to visit you you'd look nice.
After a while when they saw that nobody was gonna come they
couldn't bother dressing you up anymore.*

*I was probably very good in school there. You know that today
I can do mathematics with the best of 'em.*

*I remember problems with food mostly. They never fed us
enough. I used to smuggle bread under my shirt into the dormitories. The nuns could tell because they'd find the crumbs. Also
the nuns told us that it made pimples come on our stomachs. We
used to eat the white inside the corn cobs, too, after the nuns ate
the corn. The only time they'd ever feed us enough is when the
societies came to look over the operation. Then all of us kids
would eat enough for a week.*

*We slept in dormitories. Each kid had his own iron bed.
Everybody would have to make his own bed. I remember they'd
get all the bed wetters up at two in the morning to pee. I never
had that problem.*

*I ran away a couple of times. I never got farther than the farm
next door. Where the hell was I gonna go anyway?*

*I used to wear out one shoe on the pavement. I'd rub it back
and forth until I made a hole in it. Then they'd have to give you
a new pair. The nun in the shoe shop looked at it and saw what I
done. She hit me on the head with the shoe I wore out.*

*They had us on our knees every day. We'd scrub the church.
We had mass every day and benediction on Wednesday nights.*

One day I ate a whole package of communion wafers. When the nun caught me my mouth was so full and dry I couldn't even talk. Ooo, did I get it that time.

I remember I liked Sister Diaz and Sister Immaculata. Sometimes they'd put their arms around you and be nice to you. When I got out of that place I swore I'd never go into another church again. And I haven't.

Some of the kids who came outta that place did awright. One guy who I was friends with there became a big cartoonist in New York, another guy was a big shot in the D.A.'s office.

You know, even though I got rotten treatment there, there's not a nun in this city who doesn't think the world of me. I've given so much to charity you wouldn't believe it. Nuns come in my store all the time. When I was in prison I got letters from nuns, scapulars, rosaries, all that stuff.

When Vincent was discharged from the convent in August of 1922 his mother arrived to take him home. He was brought to a room and told that the woman who stood before him was his mother. Vincent, who had last seen his mother at age five, did not recognize her at age eight.

The nun said, "Here's your mother." I said, "That's a lie. I ain't got no mother." She came over to me and tried to hug me and all, but to me she was just a strange woman. I remember on the train home she told me all about the sisters and brothers I had so that when we got home I'd know what to expect. I believed her after a while and when we got home she introduced me to Tony and my sisters. I didn't recognize any of them.

Those first few weeks home were really hard. I kind of withdrew. I wouldn't eat or anything. I don't know if I was just scared or if I hated my mother for sending me away. Instead of eating at home I begged for stuff on the streets and in the shops. I didn't want to take nothing from my mother.

The neighborhood to which Vincent returned provided ample opportunities for a willing young boy to earn his meals. There were butcher shops, tailor shops, bakeries, and corner stores. Stock could be loaded, floors swept, and errands run. Three years in an orphanage can teach independence and self-reliance to a boy of eight. They can also teach him to deal with strangers and make decisions.

The neighborhood was mostly German. They were good, hard-

*working people. They kept things clean. People weren't poor
either. Most of the people around us had steady jobs like plumbers,
carpenters, tailors, bakers, store owners, jobs like that. It wasn't
really poor but nobody was rich. Just honest, down-to-earth, working people.*

*It was a clean neighborhood, you know. Not like neighborhoods
today. A lot of Germans. They're some of the most decent people
I ever met. Our street had a lot of Italians on it but mostly everybody was German in my neighborhood. Jews owned a lot of the
shops though. They'd let me sweep or run errands and little jobs
like that. Pretty soon I began bringing stuff home from my jobs—
meat, bread, milk. My brother, Tony, never worked. Every day I
brought something home.*

Vincent's insecurity at home was soon to be reflected at school.
He was for some years a quiet student of average ability. It was not
long, however, before his success in the independent world of the
streets made him uncomfortable with the discipline imposed in the
classroom. By the seventh grade Vincent had acquired the label of
"troublemaker" and found himself transferred to three different
schools within a year.

*After I got switched around to the other schools they finally
sent me to P.S. 89. It was a school for discipline problem kids. It
was the toughest place I ever been in. A lot of fighters came out of
that school. You had to fight in there to stay alive.*

*I remember two teachers I had there. One was Mr. Toomey.
He was a tough man. One day he gave me a couple of whacks
with a stick he carried. I probably deserved it. I didn't cry but I
told him I was gonna kill him for that. After school that day I
went down to a corner near the school where a lot of hoods hung
out. I tore my shirt and told them that he had beat me. I wanted
them to kill him. They drove down to the school but Mr. Toomey
never came out. Later we became friends.*

*The other teacher I had was Miss Robinson. She was a wonder-
ful woman, a striking woman. She took a real interest in me.
When I was in 8B she came to visit my mother. She told her that
I should go to college and that she would help pay for me to go.
(At that time I was making more money than she was.) I didn't
want to go to school any more. I was already too advanced for that.
So I'd joke with her and say things like, "I wanna work in a*

vegetable store and carry big sacks around." She would say, "Oh Vincent, that's not the life for you. You must go on to college and make something of yourself."² I *wonder what would'a happened if I did. Maybe I'd a been a college professor today.³*

Vincent completed 8B and, at Miss Robinson's urging, started the first semester at Washington High School. He left before the semester was over. The life of a schoolboy could not compete with the action Vincent was able to manage before and after school hours.

I guess it began with Paul and Hoppo. They were both hustlers.⁴ They'd sit around in the kitchen at night and talk about the scores they made that day. One guy they stuck for fifty dollars, another for forty-five, things like that. They always had their merchandise around, so I'd take some of it with me to school. I peddled it on a different route each day before school and after school.

My first item, I'll always remember, was Parker pens. They weren't really Parkers, they were actually Barker pens but they made the "B" funny so you couldn't tell. Hoppo got 'em for three dollars a dozen. They were in nice boxes and the boxes said $15 on them. I started out just selling 'em straight. You know, "Hey Mister, you wanna buy a pen?" People used to ask me, "Where'd ya get this, kid?" So I started making up stories. At first I said I found it but nobody believed me. Then I started

2. Here Vincent speaks in a high-pitched, woman's voice.

3. Reference to me.

4. By "hustler" Vincent means one who sells inferior merchandise under the pretense that it is of high quality but can be had at a bargain because it is stolen. This is a particular use of "hustler," which in general refers to one who earns money in shady but nonviolent ways which legitimate society would be unlikely to consider "work." "Hustler" is probably most commonly applied to pool sharks and prostitutes; in its general sense it is widely used in the young, black, drug-using subcultures. See Ned Polsky, *Hustlers, Beats, and Others* (Chicago: Aldine Publishing Co., 1967). Harold Finestone, "Cats, Kicks, and Color," in *The Other Side*, ed. Howard Becker (New York: The Free Press of Glencoe, 1964), pp. 281–97; H. L. Ross, "The 'Hustler' in Chicago," *Journal of Student Research* 1 (1959): 13–19; James H. Bryan, "Occupational Ideologies and Individual Attitudes of Call Girls," *Social Problems* 13 (1966): 441–50; Henry Williamson, *Hustler!* (Garden City, N.Y.: Doubleday and Co., 1965); Iceberg Slim, *Pimp: The Story of My Life* (Los Angeles: Holloway House Publishing Co., 1969); Iceberg Slim, *Trick Baby: The Biography of a Con Man* (Los Angeles: Holloway House Publishing Co., 1967); and Theodore Isaac Rubin, *In the Life* (New York: Ballantine Books, 1961).

saying I worked for such and such a company and they wouldn't miss an extra one. Sometimes I told 'em I was a delivery boy and I got an extra one I didn't want to return.

Hoppo bought 'em from a little store in the West End that all the hustlers bought stuff from. At first he started bringing me the pens to sell. Later I went to the store myself. That damn Hoppo was making a buck a dozen off me! He bought 'em for three dollars and sold 'em to me for four dollars. Now when you went to this store the guy would give you the labels and sell you the pens separate.

In the summer after 8B I hustled real well. I was bringing in seventy or eighty bucks a week when grown men weren't making forty dollars. When Washington High came around in September I was earning twice as much as my teachers. I was just too advanced for that stuff.

I got a job in a tailor shop when I quit Washington. I was a delivery boy. It let me get into real high-class joints. I quit on the pens and started with perfume. Same story with that. Phony perfume and fancy bottle. It was called Christmas Night. I'd sell [to] all the servants in those big places. I also had another deal going with that job. When I made pickups (the tailor did cleaning) I'd go into the apartment next door if it was open. I'd call out the right name in the wrong apartment. You could always clip something small. Most of the time nobody'd even miss it.

I remember one time the tailor got a call from somebody about a tablecloth I picked up. I denied it but he told me he had suspicions about me. He said, " 'Talian boy, since you been here my pressers don't find no change, no checks,[5] not even no dust in the suits. I got my eye on you."

He was right. You see I had a little Gem razor blade I kept in a cork in my pocket all the time. I'd cut a small hole in the lining on the edge of the coats and get the change that fell through the pockets.

The one mistake that tailor made was to give me the keys to his warehouse. You see, he shared a big basement warehouse with a general merchandise store, Mandelbaum's, next door. One day he

5. The "checks" referred to are rental keys for which one could get seventy-five cents if they were returned to the company. Vincent reports this anecdote in a Jewish accent.

tossed me the keys and I went downstairs through the basement and out the delivery entrance to a shop on the other side of the street and had my own set of keys made. Now I owned that warehouse. I gave him back his set of keys and I was in business. I never took much from the tailor. But poor Mandelbaum's really got stung. I had an arrangement with a taxi driver. He would pick me up after work. I'd go in the delivery entrance and bring stuff out. This was on the West Side and so we'd drive home with it and sell it on the East Side where we lived. Pretty soon Mandelbaum thought the tailor was stealing from him and the tailor thought Mandelbaum was trying to pull a fast one so they built a big fence across the middle of the place. That stopped me.

Vincent's family welcomed his money and his gifts, and his donations of money, groceries, and goods were received with full knowledge of their illegitimate source. For Lucy had been living from the profits of criminal or quasi-criminal enterprises for most of her life. Vincent explains:

She would give thieves who were on the lam a place to stay in our upstairs. She brought them food and took care that nobody know they were with us. She also would take care of alcoholic women. They were society women and their husbands knew that when they were on their binge my mother would see to it that they didn't get hurt. You'd be surprised the big people's wives my mother took care of.

It would have been simple hypocrisy for Lucy to say anymore to Vincent than "Be careful."

Vincent's hustling talents and their lucrative rewards, the family's needs, the unexciting alternative of school, and the drama of "the score" gave Vincent sufficient reason to embrace his illegitimate entrepreneurial career. Success came on many fronts.

I always dressed nice, you know. Like the society boys. I was a polite kid. When I took a girl out their parents always liked me. They weren't too sure at first. You see I dated mostly German girls. Their parents told them to stay away from Italian boys because we all were supposed to be carrying stilettos and might stab them.

The first girl I ever had sex with was named Elsie Albricht. She would wait for me after school. I'd take her to have an ice cream soda or something. I had the money to do that. I'd always bring

her home and talk to her parents; they liked me a lot. I dressed
nice and was very polite to them. I guess I was about 14 then.

I never hung around on corners or at pool rooms or dance halls.
I never could stand that. It's just a lot of bullshit. I was working
and I didn't have time for that stuff.

It is not easy to separate the facts of Vincent's patently difficult
childhood from the meaning it had to an aggressive adolescent and
the retrospective evaluation of it that Vincent makes today.

I never had a childhood. I mean I never played baseball or
basketball or football like other kids. All I ever wanted to do was
work. I always wanted to be able to buy anything I wanted to. I
used to watch what we used to call Park Avenue Boys. They would
get taken to school in a limousine, they'd have nice clothes, any-
thing they wanted. That's what I worked for. I set a goal, you
know, I always liked nice things.

All I was ever after was money. I tried to get myself in a posi-
tion where I could have what I wanted. But it's funny, you know,
after I bought something then it meant nothing to me. It didn't
mean a thing after I had it.

I wouldn't say I had a happy childhood. I had very few friends.
The one friend, Bennie Bellini, I did have was killed by Dutch
Shultz (his real name was Fliegenheimer), 'cause he stole his one-
armed-bandit slot machines. You know, the kind with the cherries
and lemons. He'd go into a place and yell out "Repair man." Then
he'd pretend he was fixing it and he'd take it out and move it
somewhere else. I was a loner. I would get very enthusiastic about
things but that would wear off. Then I'd get depressed.

It would be inadequate to say that Vincent had an unhappy
childhood, however. His observation that "I never had a childhood" is a retrospective judgment made against his current notions
of the sequence of experiences one follows in becoming an adult.
While Vincent's games were not baseball or football, his street
hustling provided the drama and action of genuine competition.
His games were complex and required planning and innovation.
They were not team efforts, however, and Vincent was not only
the star player but also the umpire and scorekeeper. When the
game was completed only Vincent knew who had won.

Hustling taught me how to read people. I was a great bull-
shitter, a good con. I could tell nine times out of ten who I could
sell.

I knew I was doing wrong—larceny by trick—selling under false pretenses. But I was twelve years old and I was outsmarting men five times my age. I would get a kick every time I clipped somebody. I never got pinched. I even sold detectives. I'd say something like: "Gee mister, I don't wanna get in no trouble. My mother owes the rent and if you turn me in I'll lose my job sure."

Some people would even pay me the money for stuff but not take it. They'd say:

"Why don't you take it back, Sonny, before you get into trouble."

I'd say, "My mother needs the money real bad." Everybody's got a mother, you know. Then they'd give me the money I would'a made on the sale and I'd promise to take it back. I was "rehabilitated" already. My promise meant nothing. A sale like that was pure gravy. Only certain types of guys would ever do that, milkmen sometimes. Real honest, hard-working people.

Anything I'd say I'd believe myself. If I said my mother needed the money, I'd believe it. I'm still that way today. If I tell you something and I say it strong, I really believe it. Another thing, after I sold you, the deal was over and I'd forget you. I could see you two hours later and I wouldn't remember you.

I had another habit too. Now suppose I had perfume and I paid fifty cents a bottle for it. If I missed a sale, say I wouldn't sell it for two bucks, now that perfume cost me two bucks and I'd have to make it up on my next sale. I'm funny that way but I really believed that perfume cost me two bucks now.

By the time Vincent had reached the age of fifteen, he was, by all critical social criteria except age, an adult. He earned money at adult enterprises; he supported a family; he could be depended upon; he had enjoyed sex; and his knowledge of worldly affairs was anything but childlike. Vincent's ability to assume his childlike role for hustling purposes was, if anything, further testimony to his adulthood.

At age fifteen Vincent left the city and his family, with perhaps slightly less confidence than he now admits.

I didn't like all the hustle and bustle in [the city where he grew up]. It was too much. Hoppo was in East City and doing pretty good. I was ready to go. My mother couldn't say nothing about it.

When I came to East City I was only fifteen. I knew Hoppo was doing OK there. When I got there I stayed at the old Bailey

Hotel on Ring Street. That's where all the hustlers stayed, Hoppo, everybody. It was a good place to be if you were hustling. You got all the news, who was working where, who to watch out for, that kind of stuff.

Most of the hustlers traveled around. They'd work one city, then move on. They were a great bunch of guys. Every so often they'll come into my store today. We talk about the old days, when we were working the streets. Some of 'em made it real big. One guy, Jocko Keenan, is a betting commissioner in Boston; another guy, Harry Fox, owns his own plumbing supply business.

They were characters, you know. Let's see, there was Little Red Gleason. He was kinda weird. One day I saw him crying his eyes out on his bed. I asked him what was the matter and he just kept bawling. Later I found out that every time he had sex with a woman he'd cry for hours. There was Willie the Wop, Cigar Face Joe, Marble Head, Abe the Louse, Big George, Al Pratt, Two Bits, Four Bits, Six Bits (they were brothers), and Harry "Pissy" Abrams.[6] He was kicked in World War I and he would wet himself. He couldn't control it. He wore one of those pads that women wear. All the guys used to put cheap cologne on him so he wouldn't smell.

When any of those old-timers come in my store today, they don't even have to ask if they need money.

I used to listen to those guys talk at night. All they'd ever talk about is hustling. I'd listen close and try to improve on their technique. Like, for example, they'd try to force a thing on you. I never did that. I'd always be polite and have a good story. My delivery-boy cap was an improvement on them. Most of them were careless with their money, they were gamblers, all of 'em. They'd earn a hundred bucks one day and blow it that night gambling.

Right off when I got to East City I needed transportation so I got a phony driver's license. It's easy, you know, just get somebody to give you his and he sends in and says he lost it. No trouble. There was also the problem of a peddler's license. Your license was your cover, you see. It made you a legitimate businessman. Now in East City in those days there was two kinds of

---

6. Question: "Can we put that in the book, 'Pissy'?" Answer: "Sure."

licenses you could get. One was for street selling and that cost you a hundred bucks. The other was a door-to-door license and that only cost you seven fifty. So I figured why pay all that money when you didn't have to.

I got my first arrest over that license but no conviction. You see, I would drive up to people and stop them on the street. One day this cop watches me do this and after I make my sale he comes over and asks me if I got a license. I says, "Certainly, Officer." He looks it over and tells me it's the wrong kind of license and brings me before a magistrate.

I explained to the magistrate that I really worked door-to-door but sometimes when I see somebody come out of a door I stop him on the street after he comes out. It don't make no sense to go knock on his door if he's already outside, does it? The magistrate dismissed me and told me to be careful. After that a lot of the hustlers got door-to-door licenses like me. It was a good story and it always got you off.

Vincent's way into the East City society of street hustlers was cleared by his Uncle Hoppo, for whom Vincent had respect and admiration.

I had the highest respect for Hoppo. He was a kind man. Nobody could want a better man for an uncle. I buried him when he died. And I got his wife for him when I came back to East City years later. They called him Hoppo because he had infantile paralysis as a kid. His right leg was like a seven-year-old's from the knee down. He was strong, though; a big chest, powerful arms, not an ounce of fat on him. He was the one who gave me my first phony furs to sell. I'll tell you how it happened:

One day it's about four o'clock, Hoppo and me and Cigar Face Joe are sittin' in Horn and Hardart's having coffee. They had done all right that day so they decided to knock off early. So the truck's parked outside, and I know he's still got a couple of pieces on it. Now this knocking-off-early stuff was never for me no matter how good I done, so I asks Hoppo if I can use his truck. He asks me what I'm gonna do with it and I tell him I'm gonna work. He says OK.

I took the truck out and sold three silver foxes in about an hour. When I get back to Horn and Hardart's Hoppo and Joe can't believe it. I made ninety bucks in one hour. Hoppo couldn't be-

lieve it. Of course he wanted to split fifty-fifty with me. He said it
was his truck and his merchandise. Well, I wouldn't do it. I gave
him ten bucks apiece for the furs. After that he let me hustle the
furs with him whenever I wanted to. In those days I worked perfume mostly, some furs, and some cloth.

The cloth was a cheap material that had a gold sticker we put
on it. It said "Leeds, England." It was supposed to be an English
tweed.

I worked mostly the good areas in East City. In the morning
I'd get people going to work. Then I'd go down to Dock Street
where the trucks came in. I'd look for out-of-town trucks. Those
hillbilly drivers were a pushover. I'd always tell 'em it was an overload or a broken case. Then I'd go back to center city and work
lunch hour. Afternoons mostly I'd get people shopping, people
sitting in squares, things like that. At five o'clock you could always
pick up a few sales from guys who wanted to bring their wives
something. In East City I sold mostly perfume and some furs.
Later I had the suits.

I stayed in East City maybe three or four months. Every week
I went home to see my mother. Hoppo and me went up together
a lot. I'd bring her a hundred bucks a week. I was a good hustler,
the best in East City and I didn't have no bad habits. I didn't
drink or gamble. Most of the hustlers like Hoppo made a lot of
money but they'd throw it away on gambling or drinking. It was
stupid, see. They'd be having a very good day, two, three sales in
one morning. Then what do they do? They knock off for the rest
of the day and spend their money, put a pile on some number, get
drunk, gamble. At the end of the week they'd be borrowing money
even though they made five hundred. That's the whole secret to
that racket, you can't throw your money away or you'll always be
just a street hustler. It's like a regular business, you know, if a guy
drinks or gambles or fools around and blows his money on women,
he's gonna go bankrupt. Me, I always got up early and started to
work. I been doing that since I was eleven. Before school and
after school. I still get up at five-thirty and I'm at my store at six.
I been that way all my life.

You had to work from a truck if you were gonna sell furs.
Sometimes you could work on the street but a truck lets you move
around. The way we used to do it was we'd see an expensive car

and we'd pull up beside it. If you were working with somebody he could talk out his window to the guy in the other car. The idea was to make it look suspicious but not too much. Anyway, you'd pull up beside him, see, and say, "Hey, Mister, would you be interested in a silver fox fur?" Sometimes they'd shake their heads or ignore you but mostly they'd say, "I don't know" or "How much?" or "You got one?" Then you tell 'em, "Pull over," just like a police car. After he pulls over you park behind him and jump out. I would be wearing my delivery-boy hat. Later I improved on that in Mid-City.

So you come over to him and you're lookin' around like there might be cops watching. You say, "Sir, my buddy and me, we were makin' deliveries this morning and we see that they gave us an extra fur package. We can use the money more than those Jews[7] who own the place, so if you're interested we can do some business." Now the guy usually says, "Let me see what you got," so you hand him the box, which is a real nice box with a delivery address on it. Now in my hat I got a pile a bills and I pull one out and say, "See, I got the bill right here, one Canadian Silver Fox Fur to Miss Dorothy Chambers, Sheraton Hotel. One hundred thirty-five dollars." Then the guy says, "Well what do you want for it?" Then I know I got him. I say, "Well, we gotta get at least seventy-five dollars for it." The guy then says, "I'll give you fifty." I look disappointed but I say, "Well, I dunno," then I look around like I'm lookin' for cops. Sometimes when I'm doing that the guy'll say "OK, how 'bout sixty," or sometimes even the seventy-five. If he don't then I give it up for fifty.

Now if he pulls out a big bankroll to pay me, I say to him after I takes his money, "Mister, if you are interested I got the match to that one on the truck. I'll let you have 'em both for a hundred and a quarter." Now you can see that guy calculating, "One fur that really cost a hundred thirty-five, a second one at the same price, both for one twenty-five." "It's a deal," he says. "OK," I say, back to the truck I go. I get the other fur and take off the delivery label.—Dorothy Chambers ain't getting two furs, you

7. Vincent's comment on reading the manuscript: "Are you gonna put "Jews" in there just like that?" "Why not?" I asked. "Well," he said, "you know them Jews ain't gonna like it." "But it's true, isn't it? I mean, that's the way you said it," I replied. "Yeh, but they still ain't gonna go for it."

know—I give it to him and he checks it over and I'm gone. I paid six fifty apiece for those furs. They make them out of the skin of some Chinese goats. So for thirteen dollars I clear a hundred and twelve. Now that's hustling.

To me East City was the end of the world. Squares everywhere. It was a dead town, you know. No entertainment. No nothin'! In those days they had a cop on Main Street with a damn umbrella; he'd turn it one way to tell cars to go, then turn it another way to tell 'em to stop. No traffic lights in those days. It was a dull place, I didn't want to hang around there too long.

Vincent's decision to leave East City and his choice of destination were influenced by factors other than the boredom he experienced there. Hustlers are travelers, by and large, and choose to work a city for a while and move on after their con is made public; naturally the police pressure on them mounts as more suckers are taken. Furthermore, hustlers from western cities who stopped at the Bailey Hotel would talk of their successes and the relative advantages of one place over another, and Vincent listened carefully. In addition, Vincent's half brother, Bennie, ran a small hustling business in Mid-City. Finally, for a young man there may have been some romance to "going west" in 1929, even if it were only as far west as Mid-City.

Bennie, Vincent's half brother, had been successful in Mid-City. He had organized a small but prosperous organization of twelve to fifteen hustlers whom he supplied with phony furs, suits, and clothing. The arrangement called for a fifty-fifty split of profits and, although rarely honored, provided quite a reasonable income for Bennie. When Vincent arrived at the train terminal in Mid-City, Bennie, whom Vincent had not seen since he was five, was there to meet him.

Bennie wrote me in East City that if I came to Mid-City he'd make me a rich man. He said he had got good reports on me—that I was a good hustler and all. He met me at the station in a pretty new sedan delivery.

As we're riding along he tells me about his operation and how he's doing real good and all that. He shows me his merchandise, which is pretty good stuff. All the while I'm watchin' the street and I say to him, "This looks like pretty good territory, slow down." "What?" he says. "Slow down," I tell him, and I take my delivery-boy's hat from my suitcase. "What's that?" he says. "You'll see," I says. So I spot this guy on the street and I yell, "Could you ford on touk for the bedeek for the asfay?" "What?" the guy on the street says. So I gives it to him again, "Could you ford on touk for the bedeek for the asfay?" He still don't know what I'm sayin' so I wave him over to the truck and give him the overload story. He flashes a big roll and I stick him for a matched pair. Two for a hundred thirty-five.

Meanwhile, Bennie don't know what to think. He's never seen nobody work like me. After I make the sale he says, "What's that you was yelling out the window?" I tell him, "Look you just can't go yellin', 'You wanna buy a silver fox fur?' to everybody on the street. You gotta get 'em over to the truck to make your pitch." Well, between the train station and his house I sold six pieces and made four hundred twenty-five dollars. It couldn't't'a been more than forty-five minutes. When we got home he told his wife about how much I done. She couldn't believe it either.

Now you see, he expected me to go fifty-fifty with him on that merchandise. You see, that's the deal he had with the guys who worked for him. They were supposed to split fifty-fifty. Which, anyway, they were all liars. Well, I told him I didn't work that way. Instead I let him make five bucks on each piece of merchandise. If a stole cost him five dollars, I'd buy it off him for ten dollars. In the beginning I used his car and he paid for gas and that kind of stuff.

You see, I wasn't going to go for no fifty-fifty deal. For one thing, every week I was sendin' a hundred dollars to my mother. Also I knew that I was gonna get my own truck pretty soon. Now it wasn't more than two months and I saved enough for my own truck. I always paid cash. I never went for no credit deals. Even today I don't have no charge plates, no nothing. Well, when I got my own truck it was no more five-dollars profit on each piece. I let him make a buck on each one he sold me, but that's all. You see, I could'a cut him out of the picture entirely but I didn't because he got me started and all that.

Vincent stayed for only a day or two at Bennie's home. He moved to a hotel nearby and registered under the name of Vincent Arnez. Arnez was Bennie's last name and Vincent considered it politic to emphasize his family ties as well as protect his real name in case of an arrest, an eventuality Vincent didn't have to wait long for.

I never took no convictions in Mid-City. In fact I only took two convictions all my life, but I got my first hustling pinch there. I'm standin' by my truck on Main Street about eight-thirty in the morning. It was a new sedan delivery. On the side I got painted in gold letters "Alaska Fur Trading Company—New York, Paris, Mid-City." By this time I got my hat, a jacket with a patch which says "Alaska Fur Trading Company" on it, leggins and those high leather boots. I really look legit.

Well, this guy comes down the street and he's real class. See, he's got a vest, bowler hat, cane, you can just see he's loaded. Anyway, he walks by me and I tell him I've got an extra matched pair of silver foxes. He looks at me, then at my truck, and says, "Are they yours, son?" I say, "Well, sort of." He says, "What do you mean?" I say, "Well, I was given some extra cartons by my shipper," and I pulls the bill out of my hat. (Old Dorothy Chambers is gettin' more furs.) "You see," I say, "they sent a double order." "Why don't you return them?" he asks. "Those Jews'll never miss 'em," I say. (I can tell he ain't Jewish.) "Well," he says, "what do you want for them?" I say, "The matched pair cost two twenty-five, I'll give 'em to you for a hundred thirty-five dollars, sir." "Well," the guy says, "I don't have that amount of money on me at the moment but if you will come with me to my bank around the corner I will get it." I tells him "OK," and we both go down to the bank.

Meanwhile, I'm suspicious because he never really looks at the fur. Anyway I figure nothing can happen to me because I'm legit, right? Well, in we go to the bank and what does he do right off, he tells the bank guard to arrest me. This old guard pulls out his gun and points it at me. I can tell he's nervous so I says, "Look Pop, just calm down, I ain't going nowhere." So I sit down on the floor right in the middle of the bank. That old guy don't know what to do. Everybody's watching me and the guy I tried to sell calls the police. Well, they come and lock me up for a couple of hours.

They book me on fur theft and bring me before a judge. Well the rich guy is there, the D.A. is there, and the rich guy's got his lawyers with him. The magistrate asks the rich guy what happened and he tells him. I stay quiet all the time. I was really a gutsy son of a bitch in those days. Anyway, the magistrate says to me, "Son, do you have anything to say in your defense?" I say, "Yes, Your Honor, I have a question. Is there any law in the city against selling merchandise?" He says, "No, not if it's yours to sell. You can't steal them from your employer, however." "Well, Your Honor," I say, "how can I steal them from my employer if I'm my employer?" "What?" the magistrate says. "I am the Alaska Fur Trading Company. Here's my papers, my license, and my bills." Well, in a minute everybody's screaming. The rich guy's screaming his lawyer's screamin', the D.A.'s screamin', and I'm just sittin' there nice and quiet. The magistrate lets me go and tells me to get outta town.

Next day in the paper's front page is the whole story. See, this rich guys turns out to be the city editor of the Mid-City News. That whole week there was editorials every day about fur fakers. I had to ease off business for awhile, work perfume and suits. In a couple of weeks it was just as good as ever.

Vincent did well during the year he spent in Mid-City. Within a few months he was independent of Bennie: he had purchased his own sedan delivery truck and had begun to save his earnings. The year was 1930, and although the country was in the midst of the Great Depression, it apparently did not affect Vincent. He claims to have easily cleared $300-a-week profit and to have saved $10,000 during that year. Early in 1931 Vincent, now seventeen, decided to leave Mid-City for home.

In '31 I left Mid-City and came back home. I had been away a year and hadn't seen my family at all. I left five thousand with Bennie to hold for me and took back about the same amount. I had my sedan delivery, which I paid cash for, and almost a thousand dollars worth a clothes. I had three steamer trunks and a couple a suitcases. In those days I traveled like Humphrey Bogart.

When Vincent arrived home, his car, his clothes, and his money were evidence of his success. Lucy Swaggi was proud of her son's fortune and referred to him regularly as "my rich son, Vincent." For almost three months Vincent did not work. He stayed at home with his mother, visited his family, saw some of his friends, and took himself a wife.

When I got home I didn't work. I didn't like to hustle there. I never liked it. Well, I had money so I just relaxed.

When we were back home Donna and I decided to get married.

See, she was a Cella, my cousin. I knew her ever since I was a little kid. I never thought anything about her, you know. Well, when I saw her then I couldn't believe it. She was just beautiful, blonde hair, big blue eyes; she was just like an angel. Well, we started to see each other. Nothin' fancy, just going out to places, sittin' and talkin', that kind of thing.

Her father didn't like me seeing her. He was an old-style Italian. He was always on top of her. He thought I was a gangster. Actually, he was more of a gangster than me. He was in real estate in New Town. He'd sell land that was under water half the time. So we saw each other anyway. We talked about getting married and we knew that her father would never go for it. So one day we decide to run away to Mid-City so we just left.

When we got there we were married by a judge who was a friend of Bennie's. I got a place in a furnished elevator apartment. We paid a hundred twenty-five dollars a month. Donna kept it and never worked after we were married.

Now when I left Mid-City I left five thousand with Bennie to hold for me. He was my brother and I figured I could trust him. It turns out I was wrong. I asked him for the money and he says that he can't give it to me 'cause I don't know how to handle money. I spent the five grand I took to home and that shows I can't handle money. Well, I hit the roof and we had a real fight over it but he doesn't give back the money. Well, I burned his car, I burned his garage, I did three times the damage to him that he owed me. He never gave me that money back.

Donna had her savings and we used that to get working again. I bought stuff on consignment and I hustled like I never hustled before. I improved my technique and I started my own systems. In a month you couldn't hold me.

One thing I did was to start working bars. It was my own idea and I worked it out this way. I kept a book of every bar I went to so I wouldn't go to the same place twice. Well, I'd walk into the bar and I'd be dressed in my delivery costume. I'd order a beer and look around for the license. Every bar has a license and they gotta show it. So you look at the license, see, and you find the guy's name who owns the joint. Then I'd say, "Is Tony here?" or "Is Mister Sullivan here?" The bartender would say something like, "Who wants to know?" I'd explain that I was makin' deliveries in the neighborhood and I got an extra piece and I saw another driver who said that Mr. Sullivan might be interested in the silver fox stole I had. Well, sometimes it'd turn out that the bartender was Mr. Sullivan or if he wasn't I usually could sell him anyway.

Now that was a good hustle. I made a very high percentage of sales that way, but I had to be careful not to work the same street twice so I kept my book and I used a map.

My other improvement was hustling women. For some reason most of the hustlers stayed off women. I guess it was their technique which was too strong. Anyway, I did real well with women. My uniform helped and I was always very polite. I'd even take checks from women. Really. I'd have a phony bank account and phony I.D. I'd always say something to them like, "Ma'am, you're not going to turn me in for this or get me into trouble are you?" They'd say, "No, young man, you needn't worry about that." You see, in my experience women have just as much larceny in them as men. Maybe more.

Now all this time Donna never knew what I was doing. She only knew I was buying and selling. She never asked and I never told her. She didn't know until 1952, when I got arrested and went to jail. Even when I was running trucks from Wisconsin with bootleg whiskey and I'd get up early like one or two in the morning. I'd just tell her it was business and that's all. Even with Bennie. All the time we were having our fight she never really knew what was happening. She stayed good friends with Bennie and his wife. I was burning his car and she was shopping with his wife. It's funny to you, but that's the way it was.

Now in Mid-City I saved my money. Everybody thought you couldn't really trust the banks in those days, so I put money every day in postal savings accounts, just like when I was a kid. The only thing though was that you couldn't put in any more than twenty-five hundred. So I opened one up in Donna's maiden name and in my real name and different things like that.

Vincent had managed to recoup quickly the financial loss he had incurred by trusting his half brother with $5,000. Aided by his wife's savings, he built a business, paid for a new sedan delivery truck, and began a daily savings program. He maintained the full-day, every-day work schedule that he had initiated at age fifteen, and improved his hustling techniques with skill and imagination. From his wife's perspective he was a good and steady provider who worked very hard and had no bad habits. Although she enjoyed

the company of Bennie's wife, her major objection to Mid-City
was that she was separated from her family. Later in 1932 she became pregnant and asked Vincent to take her home to her
"people." He did, and they stayed for more than a month. The
visit was good for Donna and she returned to Mid-City to have
her baby, wishing that she could have stayed home longer. After
Vincent's first daughter was born in 1933, Donna again requested
visits to her family until 1936; then Vincent, for several reasons,
consented to move East permanently.

*Donna was pregnant again in '36. She wanted to go back home.
I was in some trouble and I figured that if I stayed in Mid-City
any longer I was gonna get killed. A lot of the guys I knew out
there were getting killed. I started in on hijacking trucks and driving bootleg whiskey in from Wisconsin. I took a couple of arrests,
which got fixed by the guys I was working for, but it just wasn't
my thing. So when Donna wanted to go back to New Town I
said OK.*

Once back in New Town, Vincent, Donna, and their two-year-
old daughter, Linda, lived for a few months with Donna's parents.
Vincent had saved a substantial sum of money in Mid-City, and
within a short period of time he decided to purchase a small auto-
supply store and gas station.

*With the money I brought with me from Mid-City I bought
this small auto-supply place. It had gas pumps right in the sidewalk and inside I sold auto supplies—like a Pep Boys. In fact I was
a Pep Boys, only Pep Boys didn't know it. See, I made contact
with this manager of a Pep Boys warehouse only ten blocks from
my store. I had a real good thing going. I had a better stock than
Pep Boys. I would get anything I wanted: tires, batteries. I even
had Pep Boys brands, Cadet batteries. I had the Motorola car
radios, everything.*

*I should tell you for the book that you have to "open a guy up"
so he'll do business with you. Like you can't just go up to somebody who is managing a warehouse and tell him you want him to
send you hot merchandise. I started out with this Pep Boys guy
buying dented stock, dead merchandise, overloads, anything I
could steal.[8] Once he got to know me he started sending me cur-*

8. By "steal," Vincent means here "buy very cheaply." It is a small irony,
but one related to the consumer psychology that nurtures fencing, that a good
bargain is commonly referred to as a "steal."

rent stock at real good prices. Then after we was doin' business good for a couple of months he knew I'd take whatever he could get with no questions.

I got into trouble with a loan deal I worked. You see, one day this lawyer came into my store and he asked if I was interested in setting up a credit program. I would give credit up to five hundred but I'd have to call the company and check. They'd call me back in half an hour. I would make ten percent on the loan. Well, I went for it but I got into a little trouble. Every time hustlers came by I'd tell 'em they could have credit; all they'd need to do is sign. They'd give phony addresses and phony names and I'd write 'em up for double of what they actually got. Sometimes I'd write one up and there'd be no customer at all, no hustler, no nothing, just me.

Well, in those days I didn't know anything about law, and it turns out that these papers have what's called recourse on them. That means if the finance company can't collect, it's my problem and I gotta get back the merchandise. Well, in about six months I had about eight to fifteen thousand dollars worth of phony loans, which that loan company was not going to collect. They got the sheriff after me and stuck a lien on my business. I dumped it on a guy who I told I had to sell it 'cause the smell of gas made me sick. The guy bought it cheap, until he found out he owed the finance company ten thousand dollars.

Then I moved to East City. I wanted Donna and the kids to stay in New Town till I got settled and started a business, but she wanted to come with me.

When Vincent moved in 1937 to East City, the city in which he would remain for the rest of his life, he was twenty-three years old. His wife was twenty-four and his daughters, four years and nine months. At twenty-three, Vincent had already spent a decade at criminal enterprises in four cities under two names. He had bought, managed, and sold a business, married and had two children, supported his mother and family through depression years, and, in his opinion, contributed imaginatively to an occupation that was chiefly the vocation of men more than twice his age.

Chapter 3

GETTING INTO BUSINESS

When Vincent returned to East City in 1937, he found at the Bailey Hotel almost the same group of hustlers he had left eight years earlier. They had all felt the weight of the Depression, and Vincent was struck not only by their degenerate condition but also by their seeming lack of interest in recovering themselves.

The old-timers were all broke; they [had] lost their cars, their merchandise, everything. You never seen such a broken-down bunch. They'd just sit around, you know, not even trying to work. When I got there I was the only one with any money. I started hustling myself but also gettin' merchandise for them. I got things going and pretty soon everybody was working again.[1]

1. Vincent's observation here raises some interesting questions about the interrelationship between criminality and economic conditions. In general, the depression of the thirties is thought to have (1) decreased the incidence of theft of very valuable items, and (2) increased the incidence of petty theft. The explanation given for this effect is that "the depression limited the market

Vincent developed a position as supplier to the East City hustlers; by 1938 he had outgrown the basement room in the Bailey Hotel that he rented to store merchandise. He bought a home in a comfortable East City neighborhood and used the basement as a warehouse for his hustlers' supplies. Vincent was still pressed for space, and late in 1938 he bought a store/warehouse in an East City business district. In 1939 he expanded further and added a second small warehouse to his property holdings. Vincent's growing business was due, in part, to his development of a subtle recruitment and training program. Vincent explains:

Most of the hustlers were old. They were shot, over-the-hill. Drinking, gambling, that kind of thing; they just didn't have that desire. They weren't aggressive. So what I did was to start buying cars and renting them to the hustlers. Six bucks a day and I pay for the gas. That got some of 'em going.

I had a consignment program. I'd give 'em the merchandise in the morning. They'd pay me that night and give me back what they didn't sell. Never more than one day, though. If they didn't show up after work I'd be knockin' at their door that night. Sometimes twelve, one o'clock at night.

But my best idea was with the young guys I started as drivers. You see, what I did after I started buying cars was I'd find some young guy who was makin' maybe fifteen or twenty dollars a week

---

for stolen property with the result that large scale thefts committed for the purpose of sale decreased whereas unemployment and poverty increased the number of thefts committed to secure goods for consumption." (Jerome Hall, *Theft, Law, and Society,* 2d ed. [Indianapolis: Bobbs-Merrill Co., 1952], p. 161.) How should this have affected the hustler's trade? Since hustlers vend merchandise for direct consumption, the depression ought to have stimulated their business to the extent that they marketed merchandise essential for everyday living. The hustler's con, however, often depends on representing merchandise to be very expensive but available at a low price because it is "hot." Thus while hustlers might have done better business during the depression with mundane items, their con game may not have been amenable to that alteration. Of course, even during the depression there were quite wealthy "marks" available; there were fewer of them, though, than during the periods of prosperity before and after it. In any case, the claim that the hustlers would have fared better had they been able to adapt their sales strategy to less exotic items rests on the observation not that rich people were nonexistent but that the market among the poor and unemployed was far larger.

and I'd give him six or seven dollars a day plus lunch just to drive those hustlers around. Now the young guys had the energy and the old guys had the skill, so I figured that before long I'd have two good hustlers where I only started out with one. Well, I would say that nine out of ten of the young guys I started out that way turned into real good hustlers, even better than the guys I put 'em with. A lot of 'em were men with young families and they saved their money. Some of 'em I got to buy houses. I showed 'em how to save their money.

By 1940 I would say I had thirty hustlers buying from me. I owned three trucks and, I think, six cars which I rented out.

Vincent stocked a number of different products for his hustlers. His main items were furs, perfume, cloth for men's suits, and sweaters. He selected items by his estimation of their "flash" appeal. They were packaged well, bore expensive price tags, and often concealed either the quality or the quantity of the goods they contained.

In 1938 Vincent stopped buying sweaters from a New York distributer when he discovered that the factory making the sweaters was located in East City. He cut out the New York distributor and went directly to the factory.

At first they didn't want to sell me direct. They were making their money through this distributor in New York. Well, I was a cash buyer and I was dealing in volume, so they took a bulk order from me for five hundred dozen. I told the guy I wanted them all one size and he couldn't believe me. "What you gonna do with the small people? The large people? The extra-large people?" he says. I told him I only sell to medium people. He couldn't figure me out.

Now I was buying bulk, which means he didn't put 'em in boxes. I do. The sweaters were matched pairs—one with sleeves that buttons down the front and the other a sleeveless. That one costs almost nothing to make. They were brushed cotton; the hustlers sold 'em as cashmere. I started out with boxes with two golfers on them. Just two outlines on the cover of the box, nothing else. Then I had another with "Imperial Knitwear" in gold on the box. You could just smell the money on a box like that, but you had to keep changing boxes, 'cause the word would get around. Each box had blank labels on it. So the hustlers just wrote the size on the label. Who's gonna try a sweater on in the street any-way?

Well in two years I put that company in real business. I was getting two, sometimes three hundred dozen a week from them. They had to get a bigger factory! And what do you think hap-pened? They started to go legitimate on me. By the end of 1940 they didn't want my business no more. They were making legiti-mate expensive sweaters, real good stuff, and making more off them than off me. Then they started on bathing suits and before I knew it I couldn't buy off 'em any more.

You see now, that's something else it's important to put in the book. Not only about sweaters but about any merchandise you wanna name. So many companies started out dealing in swag and phony stuff that are multimillion-dollar companies today. These guys started out makin' that phony stuff for me and today that company's 100 percent legit. That's true for a lot of places. I know dozens of guys who were swag dealers to start out and today they're the biggest.[2]

Shortly after the war broke out, Vincent was approached by the owner of a small knitting mill. He had heard about Vincent's trade with the big mill and sought some of Vincent's business. As it turned out, this man was a German who was on the verge of bankruptcy because Jewish merchants and buyers refused to deal with him. Vincent, who had lost his contact with the big mill, decided to do business with him and loaned him money for his materials.

I staked Hugo in the beginnin' partly 'cause I felt sorry for him. But he could make anything. He had all the machines and in the beginning only his cousin, his wife, and his daughter were working for him. Well, we started with the same kind of stuff I had before,

2. Hall concurs with Vincent's observation here, although somewhat less enthusiastically. "In brief, the executives in this business of dealing in stolen goods are experienced men, frequently specialists in their chosen fields, able to evaluate merchandise expertly and to compete generally on the basis of their special skills. *Indeed, many criminal receivers reenter legitimate business despite the police phrase 'once a fence—always a fence.'*" (Ibid., p. 157.) (Italics mine.) Vincent often repeated the observation that many legitimate merchants began as dealers in stolen merchandise. Of course, this observation served the purpose for Vincent of diminishing the stigma of his unrespect-ability.

but one day he comes to me and says we might be able to get this
certain kind of material out of New Town for only thirty-five
cents a yard. Now that's one yard but sixty inches wide. The only
trouble is that the stuff is dangerous, it blows up. You see this big
chemical company had tons and tons of gun cotton left over from
World War I. They were supposed to dump it but instead they
sold it. Anyway this company in New Town is makin' material
out of it.

So Hugo and I go up there and at first they don't wanna sell
me. Well, I'm a cash buyer so they finally give me some off colors
at a good price. We put the stuff on Hugo's brushing machine and
what do you know? We're in the Alpaca sweater business!

So we start with the exploding sweaters and sell them until
1945, when Hugo gets this big government contract for real wool
sweaters. So he goes legitimate and I'm out of sweaters again. Only
he doesn't go legitimate. He starts shorting the government on its
sweaters and gets into all kinds of trouble.

Vincent's buying and selling was never limited to sweaters. The
forties were for Vincent a succession of deals, schemes, bargains,
and operations of all varieties. In 1941 he cooperated in the manufacture of phony electric razors. This lasted a bit more than a year
before a Cease and Desist order was issued.[3] Through the war years
he traded large quantities of black-market stamps. The black-
market economy and the hustlers'-market economy are natural
companions. While one can make considerable profits at elevated
black-market prices with genuine goods, selling phony hustlers'
products often doubles or triples the already exorbitant profits.[4]
Vincent explains:

3. The order was issued not because the razors did not work (which was
also true), but because they were sold under a name very close to that of a
legitimate electric razor.
4. The black market and the market in stolen goods are similarly inter-
related. "A major distinction between the black market and the market for
stolen goods is that prices are higher than the official market price in the
former and lower than the regular price in the latter." (Ted Roselius and
Doug Benton, *Marketing Theory and the Fencing of Stolen Goods*, report
prepared for the National Institute of Law Enforcement and Criminal Justice,
Law Enforcement Assistance Administration, United States Department of
Justice [August 1971], p. 21.) This distinction between the two markets makes
their marriage, that is the trade in stolen black-market goods, especially profitable. The fact that the goods are stolen drives the fence's costs down. The

Now during the war I did some business with the black-market guys. They were the most cutthroat bastards you'd ever wanna know. One time I got them with nylon stockings. See, I found this mill in New Town that had their nylon taken away from them when the war started. They had about a thousand dozen of nylons but they had no feet in 'em. I bought every box they had for sixty cents a box, six pairs to a box. The black-market guys bought 'em off my hustlers for twelve dollars. I sold most of 'em that way and hustled the rest of 'em myself. You know that today, every so often somebody will tell a story about how they got stuck with nylons with no feet during the war. Sometimes I tell 'em it was me, other times I just listen and laugh about it.

In 1947 Vincent set up his own sweater factory. He employed six women in the evenings and bought the same explosive cloth from his New Town supplier.

Now the factory I had lasted from 1947 to 1951, just before I was arrested. I got women who worked daytime jobs sewing in factories to work for me. I'd bring in dinner every night at quarter of six and they'd start to work at six-thirty. I paid 'em good and

---

fact that the goods are not otherwise available drives the purchaser's price up. Normally the fence competes against legitimate market prices, but with stolen black-market goods he competes against highly elevated black-market prices. Also, the psychological atmosphere in both markets seems to be similar. In the black market customers buy goods which they could not obtain otherwise even though they pay higher-than-legitimate market prices. In the stolen-goods market the consumer pays less than regular-market prices but could obtain those goods in the regular market if he wished to do so. Clinard reports a Gallup survey in 1945 which showed that one person in five would condone black-market buying on occasion. (Marshall B. Clinard, The Black Market [New York: Rinehart and Co., 1952], p. 93.) I know of no similar survey of attitudes about the purchase of stolen goods, but sometime during the 1920's the Chicago Council Committee on Crime, as part of its investigation, performed a small experiment, as follows (quoted in Charles Edward Merriam, Chicago: A More Intimate View of Urban Politics [New York: Macmillan Co., 1929], p. 65):

> At one time during a crime investigation we undertook to study fences or receivers of stolen goods; and among other devices we set up a shop with various kinds of goods, which we undertook to sell to purchasers who understood the goods had been stolen. The investigators came back with a smile of triumph, showing a long list of prospective purchasers and seeming to think they had clinched the case. I laughed and said, "Boys, you have proved too much." Too many were willing to buy. We encountered something nearly approaching a custom.

gave 'em dinner free and they'd work till nine. It was extra money for them and their families.

In the beginning I had a cutter, but I learned how to do that myself. I'd cut enough on the weekends to keep the women going all week. They'd box and fold, put on labels and price tags, everything.

Now I had twenty-five thousand boxes in that place and they were stacked to the ceiling. In the center of the stack we had a horse parlor. We had more lines coming out of that building than the phone company. And you know how they got in and out? Through a tunnel. The boxes were stacked over a trap door to the basement. The guys would go in on the other side of the street down through the basement and into my stack of boxes. What the hell, they paid my rent and we never got raided once.

I had my factory until about 1951. What happened was Arthur Godfrey got on the radio one morning and told the whole story about the explosive cloth and how people were selling it. And that was it. Within a week we were out of business. The police were after me but they were more interested in my supplier in New Town.

During the forties Vincent also traveled regularly to New Town, where he bought furs for his hustlers. He was able to buy at prices less than those of small department stores, because he bought large orders and paid cash. Vincent is proud of the times he has been offered jobs by large, legitimate stores.

One day I'm in the City and I'm buying furs. Rabbit mostly, but skunk and other stuff too. They were nice coats: I was paying twenty-eight dollars for 'em and we could make a hundred, a hundred and a quarter easy. One day the guy I'm buying from says that this guy, Benny Blummer, wants to meet me. I didn't connect the name right off, so the guy says, "You know, Blummer's Department Store." Well, Blummer's is a big place and this guy's got to be a multimillionaire. So I says, "Sure." Only the guy makes me promise not to tell him what I'm gettin' my coats for. (I found out later Blummer was paying thirty-eight to forty-five dollars for what I was paying twenty-eight dollars.)

Well, he's a little, short Jew and he says to me [here Vincent speaks with a Jewish inflection], "Mr. Swaggi, how come you got no store, no advertisements, no nothin', and you sell twice as many coats as me?" I tell him I work hard, you know, kiddin' him

along. Anyway we talk for a while and he offers me $10,000 a year
to come to work for him. I said, "I'm sorry, Mr. Blummer, but I
make $10,000 in ten weeks." Then I tell him how I work my
business, misrepresenting the furs an' all that. He says OK, but if
I ever want a job as a buyer I should let him know. After that we
got to be friends. I'd see him every so often in East City. We'd
chat, he always liked me. I've had lots of offers like that, people
wanting me to work for them, but I never took any of 'em 'cause I
always did better on my own.

The war years and the war economy helped Vincent's business.
In 1943, with the possibility of being drafted imminent, Vincent
decided to help out his country:

About 1943 I joined the Voluntary Coast Guard. We were
supposed to watch the waterfront, and seeing how I practically
lived down there as a hustler I figured I'd be good at it. I learned
about the Voluntary Coast Guard from a friend of mine who
wanted to get out of the draft.

Anyway, I signed up and they gave us this course at night at
the university. They told us about espionage, sabotage, theft,
everything. Well I went to these classes, but I never took no
paper or pencil. Everybody else did. There were lawyers, bankers,
all sorts of big people in my class and they'd write down everything. One day after class the Warrant Officer asks me how come
I don't take no notes or ask any questions or nothing. I told him,
"What's the use? It's all common sense anyway. And I know
everything that's going on on the waterfront." We talked for a
while, we went out for coffee, and I explained some things to this
guy. After that he didn't bother me.

Now when I started in the Voluntary Coast Guard I'd take my
truck down to the waterfront. I knew all the guys down there. If I
caught somebody taking something, instead of reporting him I'd
just take away what he was stealing and throw it in my truck. That
way he wouldn't get in any trouble. That worked OK for a while,
but my commander got word of it and told me not to bring my
truck to work anymore.

I only lasted about three or four months in the Voluntary
Coast Guard. I started to have internal hemorrhaging and had to
have half my stomach removed.

During the forties Vincent expanded his hustling operation,
broadened his business interests, and learned about many of the

procedures a successful businessman must know: marketing, book-keeping, inventory, taxes, and personnel. He was developing "contacts." Vincent's "contacts" for stolen property included, naturally, those who would sell it and those who would buy it.

I would say that the early forties was when I started my real fencing. I had hot stuff in my store in New Town, but that was just from one place mostly. In East City I started to build up my truck drivers and my waterfront men. In the beginning I met them through hustling. I'd say something like "You interested in some nice sweaters?" and the driver would come back with "No, but could you use some shoes?" or dresses or hair dryers or whatever he had. Right then I knew I had him. I'd buy what he had and tell him that if he had anymore I'd be willing to take it. I'd give him my address or my phone and we'd be in business. Now one driver would tell another and so on, until pretty soon I had dozens of drivers bringing stuff to me.

Your truck drivers are basically honest family men. Many of 'em would never steal anything. But everytime they'd get an overload they'd drop it off to me. I've had some drivers bringin' stuff to me for ten years. They don't even stop, some of 'em. Just throw the carton on the pavement and yell, "See you tomorrow, Vince."

I'd say that 75 percent of my business came from drivers. Now of course some drivers were more regular than others. They had deals with shippers or warehousemen. I'd give them a key to one of the garages I rented. They'd just load in the stuff they had and I'd pay 'em later. Other drivers who didn't have routes near my area would give me a call. I'd meet 'em in my truck and tell 'em to unload right on the sidewalk next to where I parked. I'd leave my truck and have a cup of coffee just to be sure they wasn't being tailed. In a few minutes, out I'd go. I'd load stuff in my truck and I'd be off.

Now it works pretty much the same way on the other end too. I knew plenty of guys in general merchandise: manufacturers, little stores, auctions, and what have you. Talking with them, if they didn't want what you were selling, chances are they knew somebody who did. Or maybe they had a brother or an uncle in a certain business. And don't forget all through the forties I had my hustlers too. So I was pyramiding, you know, getting bigger and better, getting to know more and more people.

For Vincent the business of developing outlets for his stolen property holds neither surprise nor romance. Although he is proud today of the speed with which he can dispose of merchandise of almost any description, he finds my curiosity about how one locates and develops outlets for stolen merchandise rather surprising.

I don't see why you make such a big thing about the people I sold to. Everybody's looking for a bargain. For a couple a years I even had a priest. He was a little Puerto Rican guy. Seventh-Day Adventist or something. He had a church near my store. He comes in one day and he buys some stuff to sell in the neighborhood. I give him a good price so he comes back. I started to school him, telling him to tell his people that the profits would go to the church.

He knew what I was doing, all right. One day he even offered to let me use the basement of his church as a drop. He could really sell merchandise, though. I actually made a hustler out of that guy.

Any hustler can tell you that 9 out of 10 people got larceny. Maybe even 99 out of 100. Now what makes you think that just because a guy owns a business he's any different? If the price is right and a man can use the merchandise, he's gonna buy. No question about it.

Through the forties, Vincent developed contacts with a wide variety of businessmen willing to buy from him. His truck-driver patrons increased, partly through his own contacts, partly through word of mouth, and occasionally through a reference from one of Vincent's hustlers. Although from time to time Vincent bought from full-time thieves, throughout the forties they represented perhaps only twenty percent of his business.

This whole business is word-of-mouth. One driver tells another, one thief tells another, one guy who owns a store tells somebody else who owns one. I had thieves then, but mostly guys who clipped cartons off trucks or out of warehouses—small guys. You see, with drivers you're safe. It's very rare there's a repercussion. But with thieves you know that sooner or later they gotta get caught. When they do you gotta be able to stand up.

I never had no arrest until 1951, so the cops didn't know what I was up to for maybe eight or nine years. They knew I had my hustlers, but they never knew about the swag [stolen goods].

The arrest in 1951 came when Vincent was thirty-seven years

old. Although Vincent always claims that his record was clean until that time, he does not count the arrests he incurred in Mid-City under his half brother's name, nor the suspicious-vendor's-license arrest in East City in 1929.

Vincent explains the events leading up to his first arrest:

In '50 I moved to a better location downtown. I kept my other store but my new place was bigger. I figured I could use the other place as a drop. Anyway one day this guy comes in. He's a real good-looking, colored guy. Speaks beautiful. He's dressed up as a minister. He says, "I understand that you buy merchandise." I say, "Yes." He says, "I have a parish in the city and often people who die will leave their belongings to the church. I wonder if you would be interested in buying some of them?" So I says, "I don't know what you have. It depends." Anyway he asks me to wait a minute and he goes out to his car. He comes back with two or three fur pieces and a handful of jewelry. Now I give him a ridiculous price; I figure we'd bargain. But he takes it! I can't figure what's happening. Either he's stupid, or he don't know what he's got. So I buy it and he's gone.

Two days later he's back again. Same ridiculous price. This time though he's got a projector, a TV, and some other stuff. I buy. Well after a couple of weeks he's been in maybe six or seven times. I know this is hot stuff. It's gotta be; he's gettin' it too fast and he's givin' it up too easy.

So I tell him, "Look, you're not kiddin' anybody. This is hot stuff and you're no more a minister than I am." "Well," he says, "you're right." He had a real smooth racket going. He'd go door-to-door in his minister's outfit. He'd ring the bell and if anybody came to the door he'd tell 'em he was collecting for his parish and give 'em a sob story. If nobody was home, he'd signal to three or four guys following him in a car to hit the house. They'd clean it out. If you had food in the refrigerator, those guys would eat it. You know, I found out when that case came to trial that those guys would crap on the floor or pee on your furniture when they were ready to go.[5] I guess it was their kick. Anyway I done business with 'em.

Pretty soon another guy starts comin' in with merchandise—

5. See Albert B. Friedman, "The Scatological Rites of Burglars," *Western Folklore*, July 1968, pp. 171–79. Friedman claims that it is a ritual of good luck and defiance for some burglars.

"Greenie." Everything he wore was green. Green jacket, pants, socks, even green shoes. He was working with this minister and they're both bringing me loads—at least three or four times a week. Well, one day I get a call and it's a guy who says he's a friend of Greenie's. And he wants to sell me some stuff. But the stuff he starts describing is stuff I already bought. Right away I'm suspicious. So I tell him I'm in general merchandise and don't handle that stuff. Now I know something's up.

That afternoon a detective comes into my store and tells me that some guy on my street's been buying a lot of swag from colored guys. I knew this detective because he was a customer. He didn't know what I was doing because I had a clean record. He tells me though that the name of the guy buying the swag is "Vince," like me. I tell him that there must be a dozen "Vinces" on my street. Anyway he leaves.

Bang! Three hours later three detectives are in my store with a search warrant and one of the colored thieves. Now this guy hasn't seen me but once or twice. The cops have got the thieves but they don't have the minister or Greenie. So I tell the detectives to look around; I got nothing to hide.

They didn't find nothing but they took me down to the station house. First, I talk to the detectives, then I talk to the lieutenant, then the captain. They tell me, just return some of the goods and they'll let me off. They say they got the thieves and they know they put a stop to the burglaries so all they want is some of the goods. Finally I call my brother Tony, who's working for me, and I tell him to go to a drop I got and bring some merchandise down. So he brings down a couple of minks and a projector, and the cops nail him as he walks in with it. They tell me either it's Tony or me. They're gonna lock one of us up. Now I am mad. "What a fucked-up deal this is," I tell the captain. "Look, let Tony go, he don't know nothing."

They let Tony go and they bring me before a magistrate. I got my lawyer and all the colored guys got public defenders. When I come up, one colored guy is waiting to get on the stand and right in the middle of the courtroom this detective who arrested me is telling the guy what to say. Now I had a stupid lawyer, so the magistrate, who I knew, says, "Mr. Ringman (my lawyer), can't you hear that detective prompting that witness? Mr. Swaggi, step forward. What are the charges against this man?" The D.A. says twenty-one counts of burglary, larceny, receiving stolen goods, and conspiracy. The magistrate says, "$500 bail." The D.A. says, "$500 on each?" "No," says the magistrate, "$500 on everything. Next case." Well, I paid up my bail and got released and I still felt OK, because they didn't have Greenie or the minister.

Now the next day I get a call from the minister. He's in New Town. I tell him things are really hot and no matter what happens don't come back in the state. Two days later they pick him up in the city. He's an addict and he needs to get to East City for drugs.

Anyway, all the time the cops are coming in my store with deals. Return the merchandise, I'll get a light sentence; return the jewelry, I get probation; all sorts of crap like that. I threw 'em out. I wasn't going for anything after what they done to me. Their word meant shit.

Well, my case came to court and every one of the thieves turned on me. They had a deal. You know, twenty-one burglaries and that minister never went to jail. My lawyer was a jerk. I fired him right in the courtroom. Anyway I took the stand and denied that I knew they were burglaries. I told them that I believed the minister was really a minister and how I don't judge nobody by race, creed, or color. The judge told me after it was over that I either should get a psychiatrist or an academy award. He said that right in the courtroom and then sentenced me to two years because I wouldn't return any of the goods.

So I went to jail. The way I figure it, it was like a vacation. I needed a rest and the jail wasn't bad. Ya see, in those days it was better in jail than today. The guys in there knew what they were doing. They were wise to it. Today you got a whole different kind of prisoner. They're junkies or punks who just don't know what's goin' on. They make trouble for themselves. They don't listen to the old cons and they make trouble for everybody.

Now I got some good ideas in there. I had my brother, Tony, start buying all the stuff those guys made. You know, the boats, the little chairs, all that stuff. I took everything the guys made. Of course the prisoners knew who was buying their stuff, so they treated me real good. Even the warden knew it was really me buying that stuff. He thanked me for it. For years after I got out I was still selling the stuff those guys made. They'd let me drive my truck right inside the gates to pick it up.

Although Vincent claims to have considered his jail term something of a vacation, his wife suggests that he was terribly depressed during the months he spent there. The two reports may not be entirely contradictory, however. Vincent is not one to let any situation pass without considering the advantage it might bring him. Nor does he let indecision, sadness, or disappointment show lightly.

The judge gave me two years. I was out in four months. How many guys you know have done that?

I had Donna go to this law firm and ask to have a lawyer put in an appeal [for review of sentence]. Only it wasn't no ordinary law firm. The judge's son was a member of this firm. So it cost her three or four hundred bucks and I got up before the judge to get out early. Now I don't think the judge ever saw a penny of my money but he's gotta figure it can't hurt his kid's business if he takes it easy on me.

But when I come up before him he's gotta go through all the bullshit. [Here Vincent sits up in his chair, screws up his face, puts on his legitimate voice, and pretends to look down at imaginary documents as he makes this speech.] "Hmmm, Mr. Swaggi, I see you have maintained an excellent record in prison and the court is aware that this is your first offense. I believe you have paid your debt to society." All bullshit! He knew what he was going to do before he even looked at my record. All he had to see was his son's law partner.

After Vincent had been released from prison he was placed on parole. From his parole records I learned that he was a model parolee. He reported once a month as required, and impressed his probation officer as "an industrious and enterprising man." The probation officer never appeared too clear as to what Vincent did to earn his living. The officer did state that Mr. Swaggi owned a general-merchandise store in which he "bought and sold anything on which he could make a profit." The officer was apparently unaware of the irony of that description.

While Vincent was building his trade in stolen property, he was also settling accounts with those who he felt bore responsibility for his conviction and jail sentence.

All I could think about when I got out was how I could nail those black bastards who set me up. I was a regular one-man army against black thieves. I'd take what they brought me for next to nothin' and then fix 'em up good. They never knew what happened.

Well, I'd say that lasted maybe a year; I figure they paid for what they done to me. See, I've always been good to colored people. Today some of 'em call me their "white father." I used to go in their homes an' everything when I was hustling, but that year, '52, I just had to get even for what they done to me.

Between 1952 and 1958 Vincent made his most dramatic economic advances. His business flourished. He moved his family to a middle-class neighborhood far from the center of the city. He bought property on the boundary between the city's busiest retail district and most active commercial district and transferred his business there. He worked seven days a week starting at six in the morning, and was available for "deals" in the middle of the night when the situation called for it. He was in business.

Chapter 4

RUNNING A FENCING BUSINESS: PRACTICES AND PROCEDURES

WORK PLACE AND ROUTINE

Vincent's store, like a pool hall, gas station, or police station, is a male environment. It is so not by explicit design or decree—indeed, women are frequent customers; rather, it lacks the touches which would advertise it as territory constructed by or for women. The floor is usually dirty. Merchandise is stacked to the ceiling on steel shelving; some of it is displayed in cardboard cartons lined up against the walls. Still more is piled on the glass display counter that runs the length of the store to the left as one enters. The cash register sits about halfway down the counter; it is old and mostly contains change. Vincent keeps the big money in his pocket.

The room is rectangular, actually more like a long corridor than a room. Three or four odd chairs, remnants from never-fashionable kitchen sets, and a high, four-legged stool sit to the right, just past the middle of the store. The chairs belong on a first-come, first-served basis to the regulars of Vincent's working world—the three or four men one always seems to find in the store. But the chairs are often yielded to an old woman with packages or a young one with a baby.

In the back, built into the room, is a shabby little office hardly bigger than a small bathroom. It is dark, but Vincent usually flips on the bare lightbulb when he walks back there to deal or talk on the phone. In the office are a short clothes rack and a desk. The rack is for suits or clothes that special customers have asked Vincent to put aside. On the desk, next to the telephone, is a bottle of scotch and some glasses. A drink is sometimes part of talking business.

Just outside the office there is a long clothes rack. A few suits, coats, or dresses always hang there. Even when Vincent has large quantities of clothing to sell, he regularly places only a few pieces of each item on the long rack. If your size is there you had better buy it before it's gone; if not, Vincent will offer to see if he might have something in the back room that would fit you. Occasionally, a booster will bring in an exceptionally fine suit or coat fresh from a local department store. Vincent will hang it from the nails he has driven in the back wall for that purpose. A customer who buys a suit at half the department-store ticket price, with the store tickets still on it, knows he's getting a real steal.

The store is a comfortable place to be. The bathroom, back behind the office, is clean enough. Every hour or so somebody goes for coffee after asking anyone who happens to be there whether or not they want any. In the summer Vincent keeps beer in the refrigerator in the back room. One always smells cigars.

The merchandise is more or less arranged. On the steel shelving to the right are children's toys, household goods, shoes, and some sweaters, shirts, blouses, and pants. On the floor, in cardboard boxes, there might be more of the same, something that just arrived, or an item (like ballet shoes, linen napkins, or phonograph records) that doesn't seem to fit in any of the shelf departments. On the left, behind the long glass display counter, are small items—transistor radios, electric toothbrushes, film, perfume, and the like—which are best kept beyond easy reach of some of Vincent's less respectable customers. Most of the items have price tags on them, little stick-on tags with handwritten prices that advise the customer what he would pay for the item in a department store. To determine the price on any item marked or unmarked, in the store, one asks Vincent. Because Vincent is the only one who can give real deals and set prices from which no appeal is possible, most customers go to him to be waited on.

Vincent relies on his brother Tony to mark prices, move and stack the stock, and wait on customers when things get busy. Customers or regulars help Vincent and Tony with heavy cartons, knowing that they might pick up a good deal or merely because Vincent asked them to. At Christmas time the store is often so busy that regular customers find themselves pressed into service waiting on other customers or fetching merchandise from the stockroom.

Most days have a pattern to them. Periods of activity can be anticipated and time to relax more or less counted on.

By 6:00 A.M. Vincent is at the store. He is dropped off outside the front door by a friend who has been taking him to work every morning for more than a decade. He looks in the front door, checks the lock, and continues down the street to the restaurant that expects him. He walks in and, after saying good morning to the woman tending the cash register, goes to a corner table, where he meets the same four friends, all of them businessmen on Vincent's street. Vincent orders a cup of coffee and a glass of orange juice, and joins the discussion of whatever matter is up for consideration. All the businessmen except Vincent are Jewish wholesalers. Politics, wives, children, and the stock market are important but tangential subjects; Vincent seems to hang back somewhat in such discussions, although he listens closely and critically to what is being said. Business—deals, opportunities, trends—takes precedence over anything else as a topic of discussion. Offers are made to consign merchandise; promises to send over samples of one item or another are given; advice is requested and tendered on the wisdom of adopting, dropping, or changing a line of merchandise. By a quarter to seven Vincent is at his store.

More often than not a customer with something to sell is waiting for him. The customer might have anything, but Vincent, after twenty years in the business, has a sense of what to expect.

It's logic, what happens. You take your thieves. Let's say they

*pick up something at five or six o'clock the night before. They're
gonna be at my store bright and early. Or take your delivery men.
When do they deliver? In the morning, before the customers start
comin' in. When's a thief gonna take his truck? In the afternoon,
when it's empty? Forget it! How about your hustlers. They gonna
go knockin' on people's doors at seven o'clock? No, they're gonna
be gettin' merchandise from me. How about the other businessmen on the street? They gonna talk deals when they're all gone by
noontime? Never happen, they wanna get there first.*

*In three hours, from seven to ten, I do enough business to
quit for the day. Wheelin' and dealin' you gotta start early and
fast, buddy.*

So Vincent's day begins with everything happening at once.
Thieves have merchandise to sell. Buyers for it are in the store.
Customers stop by on their way to work—perhaps to buy, perhaps
to make note of something and return to consider at noontime.

By ten o'clock Vincent has been up for five hours. He goes
across the street to the diner and has his second breakfast at a
window table, from where he can watch the front door of his store.
Perhaps a friend will join him, perhaps his girlfriend, perhaps a
detective. After coffee, two eggs over easy, toast, orange juice,
maybe a deal, or just some friendly conversation, Vincent walks
back across the street to check with Tony to see if there have been
any calls or visitors in the forty minutes he has spent eating and
talking. Around a quarter to eleven Vince walks down the street
to the office of his best friend, Sam Levin. Sam is near seventy, a
college graduate, easily a millionaire, and the owner of a very large
distributing house. His wife died some years ago, and Vincent says
his children like him only for his money. Sam respects Vincent's
business sense and enjoys his company.

*Every morning I drop by to see Sam Levin. I sit with him and
we talk about deals. He'll ask me what I think about a certain
item, whether I think people will go for it. He listens to me. We
open his mail. He gives me part of the stack, he takes part. Now
I'm the only guy he'll let do that. Anything on his desk I see, I
can pick it up and read it.*

*Sometimes he'll get some fancy high-class salesman in from New
Town who's tryin' to sell him something he ain't sure about. If I'm
not there, he'll call me over to look at it. So I go over and he'll
say to the salesman, "This is Mr. Swaggi, a dear friend of mine,*

I'd like his opinion on this item." If the item is on the desk I'll say, "Sam, I don't even wanna look at it. I don't like the box." Then Sam will say, "Aw, come on Vince, just look at it." "No," I'll say, "How the hell you gonna sell a box like that?" Well, meanwhile the salesman is shittin' his pants. You know, Sam's a big buyer and here I am screwin' up this order for him. Anyway, we go back and forth with that sort of bullshit for a while 'til that salesman begins to hate the box himself. Then I leave, and if I like what the guy's got, I tell Sam, "Shit, Sam. I dunno, if you wanna take a chance on that thing go ahead. It's your business." See, that's a code that I like it. When I go, Sam'll steal it from him.

Sam knows I take hot stuff but he don't wanna hear about it. He's always tellin' me to be careful. Sam Levin is a wonderful man.

By a quarter to twelve Vincent is back in the store. In a few minutes customers on their lunch hours will start coming in. Some will grab a sandwich and eat it in the store. Others will drop in for a minute or two, just to say hello or to find out if Vincent has any new bargains. Still others will come in to check the bargains they spotted on the way to work. Most of the lunch-hour customers work in the three or four office buildings close to Vincent's store. Between a quarter to one and one o'clock the lunch-hour trade reaches its peak, with those who ate elsewhere earlier in the hour wandering in to join those who ate in the store and those who didn't eat at all.

After one o'clock trade drops off almost as quickly as it began. Some offices maintain a twelve-thirty to one-thirty lunch hour, however, so a few customers are always present until half-past one. At one-thirty Tony leaves for lunch, customers or not. Vincent stays around to take care of the last of his buyers, and in the next hour begins trading with a special group of sellers.

Around half-past one the boosters [shoplifters] start comin' in. Most of 'em work just a couple of hours a day. All of 'em work lunch time. That's when everything's so busy, customers shopping their lunch hours want to buy and get in and out. Things get so rushed the security guards don't know what they're doin'. Just like with me, that's the busiest hour of the day. I'll tell ya, if I had a department store I'd keep a skeleton crew all day except for lunch hour. Then I'd flood the store with security.

Some of 'em walk to my store, a few of 'em have their own cars, but that's rare, and most of 'em take taxis.

Vincent wheels and deals with shoplifters, waits on customers, and runs the business until two-thirty. If things slow down he will leave to have a light lunch. If not, he'll send Tony or one of the regulars out to bring him back a sandwich. After three o'clock Vincent often walks down the street to one of the wholesalers who has a deal for him. He may call in advance and bring a sample of some cases he'd like to sell. From three to four-thirty anything can happen, or, except for a half-dozen customers, nothing.

Except for holidays, when he sometimes stays open until eight or nine in the evening, from twenty-past four on Vincent waits for a lull in business so that he can close the store. Sometimes it doesn't come until after five; sometimes everything can be finished and the store empty at twenty-past four. Often he'll have to wait for a worker who has promised to bring a quantity of his employer's goods to him after work. The regulars help him close up: lock and bolt the back doors, put the steel grates on the windows, turn on the burglar-alarm system, and turn on the night lights. Vincent has been robbed three times in the last five years.

Depending upon when he can get away, Vincent rides home with one of the regulars, a neighbor who passes at four-thirty, his daughter, who helps out at the store occasionally, or, once a week for the past year, me. He goes directly to his apartment. Once inside he pours himself a glass of Cutty Sark, which he takes with him into the bedroom; turning on the radio meanwhile to keep him company. He undresses and takes a shower, changes his underclothes and shirt, and leaves his apartment. Since his wife is no longer with him, Vincent eats at home only when his daughter comes by to make dinner. Otherwise he eats alone at a mediocre Italian restaurant a block from his home.

After dinner Vincent walks to a small store that he owns in his own neighborhood. By now it is locked, but he opens the door and walks up and down the aisles to see that it is in order. The woman who runs it for him has known him most of her life. He locks the door and walks back to his apartment, stopping to buy two newspapers.[1]

---

1. I believe most readers would be surprised to find out how much both the police and Vincent rely upon news stories to keep them apprised of

Once in his apartment again, Vincent turns on the TV and reads the paper. Neither his daughter nor his girlfriend likes him to be alone, so one of them tries to be there with him. His daughter is divorced; his girlfriend isn't. Three years ago, when he was younger and healthier, thieves and drivers would come by at all hours with merchandise. Vincent has managed to stop such evening business now, and except for one or two thieves whom he permits to come to his house, he stops business at five o'clock.

I've stopped that bullshit now, but a couple a years ago it was murder. Twelve, one, two, three o'clock in the morning the door-bell would ring. I cut the bell wire and they'd bang on the door and throw pebbles up at my window. That's the business. It never stops.

And truck drivers, comin' up from the South, they'd park at the curb, blow their horn, and yell, "Ho! Mr. Vince, ho, Mr. Vince!" I'm tellin' you it was crazy. I'd go downstairs in my pajamas and take the cartons off the truck with him. Would you believe it! Two o'clock in the morning unloading swag off a truck in my pajamas. I tell you, you gotta be crazy to be in this business.

Now at that time I was living with Rhoda. She couldn't take that kind a thing at all. So while I'm out there pullin' swag outta the back of a truck in my pajamas she's got her head out the window screamin', "Get that stuff the hell outta here. It's all stolen goods, I know it. Don't you idiots know it's the middle of the night?" She'd yell that right out the window at the top of her lungs. The stupid drivers wouldn't know what to do. Ooo! She hated my business, you know. She liked the money I made, even though she'd never say so, but she hated the business.

Vincent spends many of his evenings alone watching television, reading the papers, or listening to the radio. Infrequently, he will go out on a deal or his daughter will take him to dinner, or per-

---

goings-on in the world of crime. For both Vincent and the police, crime stories are not only reports of the activities of people whom they may know, but also indices of public concern about particular crimes. On occasion Vincent will claim that some entirely legitimate goods in his store are the fruits of a particularly public burglary or robbery he has read about. Such a claim, Vincent finds, often increases his customers' interest in buying them from him. Additionally, both Vincent and the police are interested in the public reports of crimes about which they have inside information. Vincent has often advised me to be on the alert for a story about a particular offense. Frequently he has done so a week in advance of its appearance.

haps his former wife, whom he left more than a decade ago, will drop by. Vincent goes to bed by ten.

When I go to bed I lay there and my whole day goes before me. I can see each deal I made, how much I paid, what I got, exactly the number of pieces. It's quiet, not a sound and I can tell you every move I made that day. As soon as I'm through thinkin' about it, then it's gone. If I got somethin' and sold it, I figure it's over an' that's it. It's outta my mind completely.

Then I start thinkin' about the next day. What kind a deals I'm gonna work, who I'm gonna sell to. I piece it all out. That's when I work out my best ideas.

Six days a week Vincent lives by the routine just described. On Sunday morning he doesn't open his store until nine o'clock, and he closes by one in the afternoon. The character of business as well as the hours change on Sunday. Vincent claims that the local businessmen who crowd his store on that morning come to get away from their wives. Usually Vincent has coffee and doughnuts sent to his store. Refreshments seem to add to the more social, less businesslike ambience of Sunday morning. The businessmen review last week's triumphs and discuss this week's opportunities.

More often than not, a friend of Vincent's will bring his wife and children by to say hello and show Vincent how much the children have grown since last he saw them. They will always leave with a toy as a gift from Vincent, regardless of whether their father is a thief, cop, lawyer, or businessman. To add to the Sunday morning mixture, one or two wealthy, widowed women always seem to drop by. They are candidates for expensive minks or jewelry Vincent may have picked up during the week, but if nothing is available, they let Vincent know what they are looking for. He always promises to keep his eyes open. He will call them during the week if he comes across what he thinks may interest them. Vincent's widows, perhaps four or five strong, seem to find his friendly and affectionate graciousness quite attractive. Vincent is Sicilian and never drops his air of masculine gallantry toward women, regardless of their looks, age, wealth, or status. Finally, because Vincent's store is, with the exception of a diner and a drugstore, the only business open in this area of the city on Sunday, one or two customers who by chance have found themselves on Vincent's street may wander in.

There are certain days and events that break the pattern described above: the month before Christmas, an especially big deal, the death of a friend, illness, an arrest or trial, trouble at home. During the time I have known Vincent, though, interruptions of the pattern have been rare. The routine is a refuge from the irregularities of his trade. It reflects the expectations of customers and thieves, to whom Vincent has reciprocal obligations. The effort required to maintain that routine from 5:00 A.M. to 10:00 P.M. is, despite Vincent's complaints, gripes, and observations on its madness, testimony to his enjoyment of it.

THE FRONT

Vincent is a businessman; he buys and sells merchandise in order to make a profit. Some of his merchandise is stolen; some of it is not. There is only one advantage to trading in stolen goods: one can buy them cheaper than legitimate goods and thus make a greater profit.[2]

At any given moment, roughly eighty percent of the retail stock on Vincent's shelves is legitimate. This does not mean that the merchandise costs the same as it would in a department store. Rather, Vincent prides himself in buying dead stock, damaged merchandise, factory close-outs, overruns, and the like at especially low prices. Having traded legally and illegally for more than twenty years, Vincent enjoys a large number of contacts in the business world whom he solicits for such buys. For example, Vincent recently bought three cases of name-brand wigs from a friend in a drug distribution center. In drugstores the wigs normally sold for $7.99, but the drugstores that bought them found them dif-

2. The fence's profit margin may or may not be greater than that of the legitimate businessman; it all depends upon what kind of fence one is. If one is a "secret" dealer selling goods to customers who do not know those goods are stolen, the mark-up is usually higher than in the legitimate market, because the dealer bought the goods below wholesale price and sells them as if they were legitimate. If one is a "public" fence like Vincent, one's profit margin is generally similar to that in the legitimate market. Although goods are purchased at lower than wholesale prices, they are also sold at lower than regular retail prices. Thus the "public" fence's profits tend to come from the volume of his trade and the rapidity with which he can sell merchandise on account of its being offered at lower prices than in the legitimate market.

ficult to sell even when they were marked down to $5.99. Thus the supply house found itself stuck with cases of wigs no one would buy. Vincent bought three cases for $125. At 120 wigs per case, that represents a wholesale cost to Vincent of 35¢ per wig. Although the price tag on them in his store reads $6.00, Vincent is selling them quickly at $4.00.

Vincent has a number of explanations for why he is able to sell legitimate merchandise that a neighborhood drug, clothing, variety, or general merchandise store cannot sell.

First, I buy right. I'm a cash buyer and I know where to buy. That means I got better prices. Nobody can stay with me when it comes to buyin'. And I don't mean hot stuff either. I mean legitimate. When it comes right down to it, some stuff I can buy legitimate cheaper than I can buy it hot.

I told that to a judge once, you know, Judge MacFee. He says to me, "Mr. Swaggi, how many years have you been buying merchandise?" I tell him, "All my life, Your Honor." So he says, "And didn't you suspect something when that man offered to sell you this merchandise for that price?" "No sir, Your Honor," I said, "I can buy merchandise so cheap you wouldn't believe it, Your Honor." Then my lawyer asked me, "Mr. Swaggi, would you tell the court what the big sign which hangs over the door of your store says?" "Sure," I says, "it says, 'Everything less than Wholesale,' and that's true, Your Honor." "Well," the judge says, "I'm going to have to go down to your store one of these days and see some of those bargains."

Take perfume, for instance. When a line don't move for six months, the dealers 'll give it away. Ten cents on the dollar for what was goin' retail for six ninety-five. You gotta know what you're doin' and I been at this business for a lotta years, buddy.

Next, I sell my merchandise. You go to a store today, what happens? You see something you want and you bring it to the cash register yourself. That ain't sellin', that's buyin'. With me, I ask the customer what he wants, show him what I got, have 'em try something on, tell 'em how good it looks on him or how much his wife would like it. That's sellin'. What the hell are you in the store for if it ain't to sell? Hell, if you didn't have to sell, all you'd need is some girl at a cash register to take the money.

Vincent's aggressive but pleasant salesmanship and his lower prices on legitimate merchandise are important factors in keeping his customers coming back. The fact that his customers know he has stolen merchandise to sell at prices lower than at any legitimate outlet also figures importantly in his trade in legitimate goods.

See, most people figure all of the stuff in my store is hot, which you know it ain't. But if they figure it's hot you can't keep 'em away from it. It's just like the old hustler bullshit all over again. People figurin' they're gonna get something for nothing. You think I'm gonna tell 'em it ain't hot? Not on your life. In fact I tell 'em it is hot. I got this guy who comes to my store, you know who he is, only we can't put his name in the book on account of he's so well known. Anyway, he's got a loudspeaker in his car. Sometimes when he drives by he'll say, "Ladies and Gentlemen, I want to call your attention to Mr. Vincent Swaggi's store on the corner of the street. All stolen merchandise, Ladies and Gentlemen, all stolen merchandise." See, that's the kinda bullshit I gotta put up with with the clowns I know. But when you come right down to it, he's helpin' my business by sayin' that.

There was a store in this city some years ago. The guy who owned it took an arrest for being a fence. After that he never bought nothin' hot. But he'd pass the word around to his customers in the neighborhood that on such and such a night he was gettin' a truckload of hot suits. Well, he'd have the truck pull up to the back of his place and unload the suits, maybe ten, eleven o'clock at night. By midnight they'd all be sold, twenty-five bucks apiece and every one legit. So he makes only eight or nine bucks a suit. Five, six hundred suits in an hour ain't bad. Plus his customers would help him unload the truck!

Far more important to Vincent's business than the psychological edge his trade in legitimate goods gives him in dealing with retail customers are the multiple advantages that such a legitimate business identity gives to his trade in stolen merchandise. Collectively, these advantages are commonly referred to as a "front." To explain the interplay between illegal and legal trade which constitutes the front, it is necessary to explicate the legal elements of the offense of receiving stolen goods.[3]

3. Federal law prohibits receipt of stolen goods in ten sections of title 18 of the United States Code: 18 U.S.C., sec. 641 (receipt of property stolen from the United States); 18 U.S.C., sec. 659 (receipt of property stolen from an interstate or foreign carrier or depot); 18 U.S.C., sec. 662 (receipt of

Receiving stolen goods can be legally adjudged a crime if and only if it is proven that (1) the goods in question are in fact stolen goods; (2) the accused did in fact have them in his possession; and (3) he had reasonable cause to know they were stolen. In running his fencing business Vincent constantly employs procedures that render the discovery or proof of one or more of these elements difficult or impossible.

The Goods Are Stolen

In order to establish that particular goods are, in fact, stolen it is necessary that the owner be able to identify them.[4] The extent

---

stolen property within the special maritime or territorial jurisdiction of the United States); 18 U.S.C., sec. 842 (h) (receipt of stolen explosives); 18 U.S.C., sec. 1660 (receipt of property taken by an act of piracy or robbery); 18 U.S.C., sec. 1708 (receipt of property stolen from the U.S. mails); 18 U.S.C., sec. 2113 (c) (receipt of property stolen from a federally insured bank); 18 U.S.C., sec. 2312 (receipt of a stolen vehicle moving in interstate or foreign commerce); U.S.C., sec. 1315 (receipt of stolen goods, securities, moneys or fraudulent State tax stamps which are part of interstate or foreign commerce). Sec. 341 of title 18 prohibits conspiracy to commit any of these offenses and therefore is also a receiver statute. In addition every state has a statute prohibiting the receipt of stolen property: Ala. Code tit. 14 sec. 338; Alaska Stat. sec. 11.20.350; Ariz. Stat. Ann. sec. 13-621; Ark. Stat. Ann. secs. 41-3934, 41-3938; Cal. Pen. Code. sec. 496; Colo. Rev. Stat. sec. 40-5-2; Conn. Sess. Laws, Pub. Act. no. 828 sec. 128 (1969); Del. Code Ann. tit. 11 secs. 791, 792; Fla. Stat. Ann. sec. 811.16; Ga. Code. Ann. sec. 26-1806; Hawaii Rev. Stat. sec. 761-1 to 761-10; Idaho Code sec. 18-1307; Ill. Ann. Stat. ch. 38 sec. 16-1; Ind. Ann. Stat. sec. 10-3030; Iowa Code Ann. sec. 712.1; Ky. Rev. Stat. Ann. sec. 433.290; Kan. Stat. Ann. sec. 21-3701; La. Rev. Stat. sec. 14:69; Me. Rev. Stat. Ann. tit. 17 sec. 3551; Md. Ann. Code art. 27 sec. 466; Mass. Sess. Laws ch. 681 (1971); Mich. Comp. Laws Ann. sec. 750.535; Minn. Stat. Ann. sec. 609.53; Miss. Code Ann. sec. 2249; Mo. Stat. Ann. sec. 560.270; Mont. Rev. Codes Ann. sec. 94-2721; Neb. Rev. Stat. sec. 28-507 to 28-510; Nev. Rev. Stat. sec. 205.275; N.H. Rev. Stat. Ann. sec. 582-10; N.J. Stat. Ann. secs. 2A: 139-1 to 2A: 139-4; N.M. Stat. Ann. sec. 40A-16-11; N.Y. Pen. Law secs. 165.40 to 165.65; N.C. Gen. Stat. secs. 14-71, 14-72; N.D. Cent. Code sec. 12-40-19; Ohio Rev. Code Ann. sec. 2907.30; Okla. Stat. Ann. tit. 21 sec. 1713; Ore. Rev. Stat. sec. 165.045; Pa. Stat. Ann. tit. 18 sec. 4817; R.I. Gen. Laws sec. 11-41-2; S.C. Code of Laws sec. 16-362; S.D. Comp. Laws sec. 22-37-18; Tenn. Code Ann. secs. 39-4217, 39-4218; Tex. Pen. Code art. 1430; Utah Code Ann. sec. 76-38-12; Vt. Stat. Ann. tit. 13:2561 (cf. Vt. Proposed Crim. Code sec. 1957); Va. Code Ann. sec. 18.1-107; Wash. Rev. Code Ann. sec. 9.54.010; W. Va. Code sec. 61-3-18; Wis. Stat. Ann. sec. 943.34; Wyo. Stat. sec. 6-135.

4. This is a practical, common-language statement, not a precise or comprehensive summary of the law on the matter. On some occasions circumstan-

of Vincent's legitimate trade assures that an especially precise identification of stolen property will be necessary.

Look, you got a store, I got a store. Some shine [thief] takes a load of merchandise from you and sells it to me. Even if detectives find out it's me that's got it, how you gonna know it's yours? Say it's suits, Botany suits. How are you gonna know they're yours? I got Botanys, you got Botanys, every store in town's got Botanys. On stuff like that you don't even have to cut the labels out. Somebody brings me suits like that, name brand, I don't even have to touch 'em. Just put 'em right up on the rack.

Now, of course, if you got suits nobody else is supposed to have, say Sears or Macy's, then you just cut the labels off and you own 'em. And there ain't a thing nobody can do once you got those labels off.

Now most of your small stuff, shirts, sweaters, children's toys, women's blouses, all you gotta do is take 'em outta the cartons. The carton's got numbers on it. Get rid of the carton and you're set. Leave the labels in and put 'em on the shelves.

[I ask about items with serial numbers.] Well, take typewriters. If it's from a house burglary, that's no problem. It's almost certain the guy don't know his serial number. Do you know the serial number on your TV set and camera and typewriter? [I answered, "Yes."] Well, you know what you're doin' so you don't count. Anyway, most people don't. Now if it's from a factory or an office and they come in on you, then they're gonna know it's what they're lookin' for so you gotta scheme somethin' else. But I got this guy who I can send typewriters to who owns a typewriter store. All he's gotta do is change a few numbers and put it in the window. When you buy from him, he gives you a two-year service contract so he don't have no back-ups.[5]

---

tial evidence of the theft has been held as sufficient proof. See *James v. State*, 8 Ala. App. 255, 62 So. 897 (1913); *Bell v. State*, 220 Md. 75, 150 A 2d 908 (1959). Generally, the identity of the goods as stolen must be clearly established. Some statutes that contain statements such as "intent to deprive the rightful owner" require that that owner be "strictly" established. See *State v. Bean*, 49 Del. 247, 113 A. 2d 875 (1950); contra, *Williams v. State*, 216 Tenn. 89, 390 S. W. 2d 234 (1965); *State v. McGraw*, 140 W. Va. 547, 85 S. E. 2d 849 (1955).

5. By "back-ups" Vincent means interference by the police or others that could stop the orderly flow of illegitimate merchandise and possibly result in the arrest of the dealer. In the particular instance referred to above, the service

See, with me I got bills, too. Suppose some detectives come in and say somethin' I got ain't legit. Well, first they gotta have a warrant. It's not like the old days, anymore, when they could just walk in and grab what they wanted. Now they gotta have a warrant and it's gotta say exactly what they're lookin' for. Say they find what they want. Chances are I got a bill for it. [I ask how he just happens to have a proper bill.] Look, how many things you think I buy legitimate, with bills, each year? Hundreds! I gotta keep all those bills you know, for Uncle Sam. So two months ago I bought seventy-five suits at auction. You know what that bill says, "One Lot of Suits Sold to Vincent Swaggi, Paid in Full." It don't matter what those detectives have on that warrant then. Those are my suits.

I do that with bills a lot. Like a while ago I had a guy bringin' me electric razors and hot combs. Every day or so he'd bring me a dozen of each. So what did I do? I bought two dozen legitimate from the supplier he was workin' for. Now, if there's a back-up, I'm covered.

It would be laborious to explain in detail all of the ways in which Vincent manages to alter and conceal the identity of stolen merchandise. When necessary, gems can be taken from their settings, minks refashioned, serial numbers changed, labels removed. Suffice it to say that most goods can be sufficiently altered or merged with legitimate stock to avoid identification. There are limits, however, imposed by time and skill, and certain merchandise may be sold only to customers who are willing to assume the risk of possessing identifiable stolen property. Such sales are made without bills or receipts, and as of their conclusion possession of the property is no longer a matter of concern for Vincent. Nevertheless, during the time Vincent possesses such identifiable items he sacrifices the cover that his legitimate business front gives him for this aspect of the offense of receiving.[6]

---

contract ensures that for two years following the sale of the typewriter with altered serial numbers only the illegitimate dealer will be called to repair it. The procedure prevents any serious "back-ups" because in the state in which Vincent does business the time assigned by the statute of limitations for the crime of receiving is eighteen months.

6. It may be helpful to mentally keep separate those advantages (for Vincent's trade in stolen merchandise) accruing simply from his owning a business, from those which he creates by his own acts in order to give the

He Had Possession of the Goods

The law requires, as we have said, that for a criminal prosecution one must also prove *possession* of stolen goods. In order to do so, the police must first find the stolen property and then establish the fence's possession or control of it.[7] To the end of thwarting the discovery of stolen property in his possession, Vincent employs certain devices and requires certain procedures on the part of those who would sell to him. Principal among the devices employed is the drop.

THE DROP. There are two common senses in which "drop" is used in the vocabulary of fences and thieves. In the first, it refers to a place other than the fence's place of business in which the fence stores stolen goods, usually for a short time, in order to keep their location secret from the police, from thieves, or from both.[8]

---

appearance of legitimacy. Simply because he owns a store, (1) Vincent has the right to hold various quantities of diverse merchandise; (2) he has the right to hold bills of purchase; (3) he has the right not to be disturbed in the holding of merchandise unless there is precise knowledge (probable cause to suspect) that some part of it may well be stolen merchandise; and (4) since his particular trade is often with distressed merchandise, his possession of goods that are altered to avoid identification is not especially suspect. By his own acts, Vincent creates the appearance of legitimacy or obliterates the appearance of illegitimacy by (1) changing or destroying identification numbers, (2) removing identifiable characteristics, (3) falsely claiming that particular receipts cover stolen property, (4) forging those receipts, (5) maintaining receipts with vague descriptions of merchandise, and (6) intentionally mixing stolen stock with legitimate stock.

7. Statutes on receiving stolen property are not limited to physical possession. Many include provisions for "effective control," "concealment," "buying," etc. (e.g., Alaska Stat., sec. 11.20.350; Fla. Stat. Ann., sec. 811.16). Vincent does a substantial part of his business with samples of merchandise. In such situations he may not only not physically possess the merchandise he has bought and sold; he may not even see it. Vincent claims that "there is an old saying in the fencing business: 'If you didn't see it, you didn't buy it.'" I am not sure about the antiquity of the saying, but there is no doubt that it accurately reflects the difficulty of proving possession.

8. The definitions given in the two major collections of criminal cant and argot are a rough approximation of this first meaning. See Eric Partridge, *A Dictionary of the Underworld* (New York: Bonanza Books, 1961), pp. 207–08; and Hyman E. Goldin, Frank O'Leary, and Morris Lispus, eds., *Dictionary of American Underworld Lingo* (New York: Twayne Publishers, 1950), p. 62. Neither mentions the technical distinction elaborated on in this section.

It is this sense of "drop" that is meant when a fence says, "I kept the merchandise in a drop." When the word is used in this way, it is normally preceded, in a prepositional phrase, by "in." Another sense of "drop" is meant when a thief says, "The fence told me to leave my swag at a drop." Here the thief means a location other than the fence's place of business at which the fence instructed the thief to leave the merchandise or transfer possession of it to the fence or his agent. In this case the fence might then put the merchandise in a drop of the first sort, or might take it directly to a buyer. When "drop" is used in this sense, it is normally preceded, in a prepositional phrase, by "at."

The two meanings of "drop" correspond to different institutional arrangements. A drop of the first kind is a relatively permanent location, which the fence may own or control. It may be a house, garage, parked trailer, warehouse, or any other location which is stable and secure for storage. The drop of the second definition may be only an impromptu, agreed-upon location at which goods will be taken from the thief by an agent of the fence. It may be an empty warehouse, a street corner, a loading platform, or a rented truck with the engine running. The usage of different prepositions with the two meanings of the word reflects these different arrangements. In the first sense, "in" suggests the control which the fence exercises over his "drop." In the second sense, "at" suggests but a temporary meeting place selected for the purpose of transaction.

Vincent's explanation for the use of hiding-place drops is brief and direct: "You put it in a drop so nobody knows where it is. They can't stick you with it if they can't find it." Drops for the purpose of transaction are a much more complicated matter.

The whole idea of havin' a guy leave his stuff at a drop is so he don't know where you got it. Maybe he's tryin' to set you up or maybe he's got a tail on him. You never want to let him know where you got the swag. So you set up a drop.

There's lots a ways to do it but if I think there's trouble I'll just have 'em leave it on the pavement. Say it's a driver and I think he might have a tail on him. I'll tell him I'll meet him at such and such a corner in my truck. When he gets there I'll tell him to just keep drivin' until I blow my horn. When I do, he stops and puts the cartons on the pavement right there and takes *off. Then I park my truck and watch the load for ten minutes. Maybe I'll go in and have coffee somewhere, I dunno what I'll do. So after ten minutes if nobody stops and I see he ain't bein' tailed, out I go and pick up the stuff.*

Most of the time you don't have to worry about that stuff, but, you know, sometimes you gotta take precautions.

Like one time—oh, this is goin' back maybe ten, twelve years— I had this guy bringin' me small appliances. Waffle irons, toasters, fry pans, you name it. I had him puttin' it in a garage I had somebody rent for me. He'd put the stuff in and I'd take it out the next day. Now this guy was a rubbish truck driver. He was workin' with a guy on the inside. Anyway, in with the rubbish every day was a few appliances. I told him any time you think you're bein' followed go straight to the dump. Don't worry about the stuff, just dump it. One night, sure enough, the company put a tail on him. He spotted them and went right by my garage to the dump. Those security guys arrested him but they couldn't make nothin' stick. On top of that, they sat all night at the dump waitin' for somebody to come pick up the stuff.

Also, you gotta remember that when you're talkin' drops you're talkin' bulk merchandise, loads of stuff. It don't make no sense to talk about drops for jewelry. You just put it in your pocket or in a drawer somewhere.

You wanna know where your fences get their drops, just look in the newspaper some night. Find how many garages are for rent. You send somebody there to give a phony name and for twenty bucks a month you got a drop. Hell, I musta had a hundred different drops in my life. Use one for six months, then get another one.

Although drops are a part of the mechanics of Vincent's illegitimate business, he uses them infrequently. In recent years Vincent claims that he has "quieted down." He therefore prefers to avoid deals in which the possibility of difficulty is substantial. Instead, Vincent protects himself in other ways against possible proof that he possessed particular stolen goods, most importantly by the speed with which he can sell the merchandise he receives.

I'll tell you something. The most important thing in this business is moving the merchandise, how fast you can get rid of what you got. Look at it this way. Take your average detective. He's workin' on a case that happened two months ago. He ain't gonna get to your case for weeks. Well, maybe if he's workin' on one particular guy he's gonna be on his tail. But mostly they are so overworked they ain't gonna get to what you're doin' for weeks.

I would say that most of my stuff is in and out inside of three hours. I get somethin' in the morning and by noon it's all gone. When it comes right down to it chances are I got it sold before the guy who owns it knows it's stolen. See, with speed like that there's no way nobody's gonna nail you.

Another protection in the matter of possession of stolen property is the number of outlets he has for various merchandise.

A good fence is somebody who can get rid of anything. It don't matter what it is, I can handle it. Now, me, I'm known for furs and jewelry and general merchandise mostly, but in my life I would say I've handled just about any item you could name.

If you got the contacts that means you ain't gonna be sittin' on your merchandise no three or four days.

Finally, Vincent demands from the people who sell him stolen merchandise certain behavior patterns in the transfer of goods to him.

Store Demeanor. You see, I school my thieves and drivers. Watch sometime when one of my boosters comes in the store. First thing he does, he puts his bag down by the front door. Then he just looks around at the shelves like he's lookin' for something to buy. When I'm ready I'll give him the OK to come over and tell me what he's got. Remember I still ain't looked at his merchandise. Maybe I'll give him a little bullshit about how I ain't interested in what he's got, but then I'll have him bring it over. See, all that time if somebody's followin' him they're gonna come in. So if I didn't buy nothin' there's nothin' nobody can do.

Use of Samples. Now that's for a booster. With somebody who got some cartons you do it a little different. First he's gonna only show you some samples if he's got a whole load. He ain't gonna carry all the cartons in the store if he don't know you're gonna buy 'em. If the samples are what you're interested in you ask him where he's got the rest of his load. Say he's got it in a truck. Well, then you can have 'em leave it at a drop or whatever. Maybe you'll have 'em bring 'em around to your loading platform. Say you do, and it's somethin' I ain't gonna sell in my store. Well, most of the time I make a call and I can have a buyer by the time he gets his truck around to the loading platform. I'll tell 'em to leave his truck there. Then, say, I make a price with him. I'll tell him to go around the corner and get me some cigars or a cup of coffee. If the guy who I'm sellin' it to is close by, I'll have him have his truck there when the thief gets back. We load it in the other truck and the deal's over, just like that. Twenty minutes everything's finished, an' nothin' hot ever came in my store.

Marks Identifying Goods as Stolen Not Permitted in Store.

I had this guy a couple a years ago who was murder on post office trucks. He'd follow a guy 'till he went in a big office building for a delivery, then, Zap, he'd hit the truck. Now ya see with post office trucks all the packages is wrapped, so you don't know what you're gettin'. So I had to school him: you forget the big boxes right off. They ain't worth shit. What you're lookin' for is the small ones with jewelry. See, you gotta check the wrappings. The heavier the wrapping the more it's worth.

I made him take all the wrappings off before he brought it in my store. And I made him throw 'em away, too. You don't want all those post office numbers around. After he does that he's clear. He can walk in and sell it to you with the FBI standin' right there. There ain't no problem at all.

Store Name on Carton.

Your drivers, of course, are a whole different thing entirely. First of all, I wanna make it clear and you can put this in the book like I told you: most of your drivers are honest, hard-working men with families to support. They'd never steal a thing. I have lots of drivers who bring me stuff like that. They wouldn't take nothin' but if they get an overload it comes right to me. I had that deal with some drivers goin' on fifteen years. Now they know what to do. They take off the label on the carton and just write the name of my store on it. Then they just drop it off. If they're in a rush they just come back later and I'll pay 'em then. You got a bunch of drivers like I do and they're your bread and butter. Never no trouble, no bullshit.

[I ask if it wouldn't be better if they didn't write the store name

on the carton.] What am I? What am I? A businessman, right?
You know any businessmen who get cartons with no labels on
'em? No, right? He puts my name on it and it's just another
delivery. No name and it's swag. Suppose I go out on the sidewalk
to get it and some security's been tailin' him. What am I doin'?
I'm outside my store, pickin' up a package with my name on it.
If it ain't mine, it ain't mine, but I gotta open it up to find out,
don't I?

THE USE OF OTHER FENCES.   I'll tell you somethin' I do which
you never seen me do that's right what you're talkin' about. Say I
got a guy who I ain't too sure about, but I want his merchandise.
All I do is send him down to another fence and tell him to buy it
for me. Like the other day I had this guy who said he knew Leggins [one of Vincent's more dependable thieves]. Now I told
Leggins always, never to send anybody to me unless he checks it
out with me first. So I get suspicious. Well, the guy's got three
cartons of panty hose in his car and I can use it, so instead of me
buyin' it direct, I tell him I can't use it but I'll make a call and
see if I know somebody who can take it off his hands. So I call
Red (a fence in another area of the city) and tell him to buy it
from him at a certain price, and I send him down there. Then I
send Tony down to pick it up. Red made twenty bucks on the
deal and there wasn't no trouble. Sometimes you just get a funny
feelin' about a deal so you do somethin' like that.
      [I ask why Red was willing to do that for only twenty dollars.]
Well, for one thing he don't know what he's doin'. He thinks the
reason I'm sendin' him down there is because we can't come to a
price. See, I told him to buy it for eighty and Tony will be there
with a hundred. So the thief walks in and I told him to try to get
ninety offa Red. Red's only gonna give eighty and he might try to
Jew him down to sixty. If he does, so what? I'm gonna give a
hundred either way. So he's got a sure twenty, maybe more, for
three minutes work. For a little guy like Red that adds up.
      The strategies Vincent uses to avoid proof of possession of
stolen property depend in large part on his legitimate business
identity. That identity covers the comings and goings of vendors
of stolen merchandise, who are otherwise not distinguishable from
customers and legitimate deliverymen. It renders the moving of

merchandise, the discussions of price, the examination of cargoes, and the dealings with samples all entirely normal. It makes the deposit of unattended cartons at the front or back of Vincent's store an everyday practice for Vincent in common with his wholesaler neighbors. Hence it is not only by designing elaborate procedures that Vincent succeeds in frustrating attempts to prove his conduct illegitimate, but also by making his illegitimate conduct indistinguishable from the normal activities of the legitimate business world. Nowhere is this more in evidence than with respect to the requirements of the law in establishing the third element of the offense of receiving stolen property.

He Had Reason To Believe the Goods Were Stolen

Even if one can prove that a fence possesses or has possessed certain property and that that property was indeed stolen, it is still necessary to prove that at the time of purchase the fence had reasonable cause to believe the property was stolen. This is normally determined in court by demonstrating that the price the fence paid was substantially below market levels.[9] The fence's pro-

9. Again I must add that my statements here are rather crude condensations of collections of statutes and rulings that are almost as diverse as the occasions of purchase they are designed to cover. The problem the law has tried to tackle is the "state of mind" implication in this element of receiving. To that end, some states have introduced statutes which imply a rebuttable presumption of guilt when the character of the buyer, seller, or goods seems suspect.

Goods: E.g. Mont. Rev. Codes Ann., sec. 94-2721; N.J. Stat. Ann. sec. 2A:139-1; N.Y. Pen. Law., sec. 165.55.
Buyer: Cal. Pen. Code, sec. 496; Idaho Code, sec. 18-1307; Mich. Comp. Laws Ann., sec. 750.535; N.Y. Pen. Law, sec. 165.55.
Seller: Mont. Rev. Codes Ann., sec. 94-2721; N.J. Stat. Ann., sec. 2A:139.1.

These attempts, however, appear to raise some serious constitutional questions about the shift such statutes effect regarding the presumption of innocence (Christie and Pye, "Presumptions and Assumptions in Criminal Law: Another View," *Duke Law Journal*, 1970, p. 919, quoted in U.S., Congress, Senate, Select Committee on Small Business, *An Analysis of Criminal Redistribution Systems and Their Impact on Small Business*, 92d Cong., 2d sess., pp. 16–17):

One of the few almost universally recognized presumptions in the State courts is the jury instruction that, in a prosecution for the know-

tection against possible proof of this element of receiving rests, therefore, on devices establishing a record of reasonable price and intending to cast doubt on the question of whether a reasonable businessman would have suspected that the goods he purchased were stolen.

[*Question to Vincent: "Let's say you got caught red-handed. They caught the thief an hour after he sold you some stuff, they come in, it's half in the cartons, half on your shelf, the numbers match up and everything. What would you do?"*]

What you need is a bill and a check. You don't even need a real billhead, any piece of paper is OK. You got that and you're home free.

[*I ask how he gets the thief to write him a bill.*] He don't write the bill, I do. I take a piece of paper and—say I buy three cartons of MacGregor sweaters, #2605—I write that on the paper. I put down the numbers and all. Then I write "Sold to Vincent Swaggi" for say, $200, Paid in Full, check number so and so. Then I make up some phony name and tell Tony to sign it.

[*Here I ask in disbelief how the thief they just caught ends up with check number so and so?*] He don't. Just listen to me for a

---

ing possession of stolen goods, knowledge that the goods are stolen may be inferred from the unexplained possession of recently stolen goods. Typically, this so-called presumption is not the result of any legislative action but merely the result of a State supreme court's approval of a jury instruction of this effect or affirmance of a conviction in which the only evidence of knowledge was the unexplained possession of recently stolen goods. The only important issue involved here is whether a sufficient rational connection exists between the unexplained possession of such stolen goods. For, whether or not the jury is instructed on the point, it is very likely to make this inference even if no specific reference is made to a presumption. Accordingly, even if all "presumptions" were struck down—[a] position that Justice Black advocated in *Turner*—because they place the burden of coming forward on the defendant and because they deny the defendant the right to have the evidence on which he may be convicted presented to the jury, the defendant is still confronted with the same dilemma. If the jury is likely to convict him on the basis of the evidence of recent possession that has been presented by the prosecution, he will have to come forward with evidence, regardless of his constitutional right to remain silent. The situation is not like that in a narcotics prosecution, where the jury is told, from unexplained possession it may infer that the narcotics were distributed in a package not bearing tax stamps or were illegally imported—something that would not ordinarily occur to the jury.

minute, will you Carl? Then I take the check outta my book and write it up for two hundred to the phony name and Tony signs it again on the back. Then I take it down to my bank and deposit it with the rest of my stuff for that day.

[Still lost, I ask, "So what does that do?"] It gives me a legitimate deal, that's what it does. See, so when you get in court now you got proof you paid the right price. [Vincent looked at me and explained what he thought I should have seen instantly.] Look, I say this man came in and said his brother-in-law is going out of business and he wants to get rid of these few cases of sweaters. He knows I'm in general merchandise so he comes in to ask if I want to buy. I say yes and I make up a bill 'cause he don't have any and he signs it. Then I give him a check. He takes the check and then asks me if I'll cash it for him. I say OK and that's it. See now? I got a bill and a check which just goes in and out of my bank and I get a cancelled check, date and everything, for my receipt.

This anecdote describes a procedure which in its general form (phony bill, check to fictitious name, deposit as record of transaction, and appropriate description of the transaction in court) is a very strong defense against conviction for receiving stolen goods. Since it occupies a central place in the operations of Vincent's illegitimate dealings it is important to analyze both its limitations and its implications.

The false bill—cancelled check procedure is not applicable to all varieties and quantities of goods. For example, one would not be able to claim that a relative going out of business was interested in selling a truckload of general merchandise represented to be the remainder of his store's inventory, if the merchandise still bore price tags of a known department store. Nor could one construct an adequate explanation of this kind for possession of a truckload of liquor or other commodity that requires a special license for one to trade in it. Further, cashing a check at Vincent's store of an amount adequate to establish a reasonable purchase price on a very large quantity of merchandise would appear to be exceedingly suspect. Nevertheless, for the vast majority of general-merchandise goods in the medium quantities in which a store like Vincent's would normally trade, the false bill—cancelled check procedure creates a believable image of normal business practice.

The scheme does have a technical fault. It is the matter of two fictitious signatures, one appearing on the check, the other on the bill. There is little likelihood that they would match the handwriting of the thief. This does not seem to trouble Vincent, who claims that with just two signatures to work with, "Handwriting analysis is a bunch of baloney." Actually Vincent has produced this evidence only at preliminary hearings and at the police station, where such analysis, reliable or not, did not occur.

The fence must also have the capacity to "stand-up" under police interrogation and in court in order to carry off his story and, eventually, convince a jury that he is telling the truth.

A fence has to be tough, somebody who can take it without falling apart, if you know what I mean. Let's face it, the cops know you bought hot stuff and they think they got a good case. So you pull some bullshit which they know is gonna get you off, they're gonna get pissed off.

Then if it goes that far and you gotta go to court, the D.A. is gonna be after you. You just gotta stick by your story, that's all, and not let it bother you.

Vincent considers his courtroom abilities one of his strongest assets and so is not troubled by the necessity for this additional skill required to work the scheme described in his anecdote.

The availability of the phony bill–cancelled check procedure may explain the rather casual way in which Vincent regards the various artifices and manipulations by which he protects his trade in stolen goods. On more than one occasion thieves have entered the store with stolen merchandise without following the procedures for store demeanor that Vincent requires. When that happens Vincent seems neither upset nor worried and more often than not he will assume the thief is in a hurry and not mention it to him. On one occasion Tony, whose job it usually is to remove stolen merchandise from cartons and then dispose of them, insisted it was one-thirty, his lunch time, and the cartons would have to wait until after he had eaten. Vincent was not pleased by this behavior on Tony's part, and although he complained about how stupid his brother was, he did not remove the cartons himself. It may credit the phony bill–cancelled check scheme with too much effect to say that it is responsible for the casual way in which Vincent occasionally takes his serious business; he also knows that less than one purchase of stolen goods in a hundred will involve any police investigation that reaches him.

But infrequent police investigation does not adequately explain Vincent's infrequent use of storage-type drops for stolen merchandise. Secret locations under fictitious names are simply not normal business procedures; if trouble developed, explaining a hidden storage area might prove to pose more problems than the advantages such an area offered. Vincent has often described to me how he sees his dealing in stolen property as having developed a certain sophistication and elegance during the years he has been working at it.

Carl, the way I look at it, when I started out I was a ward leader; then after a while I was a politician; now I'm like a statesman. I don't have to worry about that little stuff anymore. I'm past that already.

INFORMANTS

Were it not for informants—people who for favors, money, or spite give information to the police—the fence's life would be less complicated and the detective's task almost impossible. Consider the realities of their respective worlds without the informant.

The fence would know that each buyer would never divulge the source of his stolen property were he caught with it. He could buy goods freely from anyone who walked into his store, knowing that the thief would never tip the police on account of his feeling that the fence had given him a bad bargain. He would be confident that a thief who brought him merchandise before had not made a deal to set him up this time because he owed a detective a favor. He would know that inquiries from other fences about what merchandise he had were idle curiosity, conversation, or genuine requests to buy. He would rest easy with the knowledge that even if the police promised probation for three or four counts of grand larceny, the thief he just bought from would not give him up.

Likewise, I have never known a burglary–theft squad detective who did not consider informants essential to his work, and this judgment is supported by every study I know of on police informants.[10]

10. Criminological research has generally demonstrated the abuses possible with paid informants: Jerome Skolnick, *Justice Without Trial* (New York: John Wiley and Sons, 1969), pp. 112–38; William A. Westley, *Violence and*

For Vincent, there are two kinds of people who give information to the police. One is an informant who in exchange for information "gets a license to steal." The other is the thief who when caught offers to "give up" his fence in exchange for police promises of probation. The latter situation Vincent accepts reluctantly. The former, on occasion, makes him angry. Both affect the way he does business.

A few years ago Johnny Rocco opened a store two blocks from me. I heard he was buyin' stuff but it didn't bother me. I figure, what the hell, there's enough business in this city to go 'round.

Well, one day he comes into my store. He's wearin' a trench coat and dark glasses. He leans over the counter and outta the side of his mouth he says, "I'm interested in some TVs, what can you do for me?" You know, real old-time gangster bullshit. Right away I figure he's some kind of a nut. Nobody acts like that except in the movies. Anyway I tell him I can get him some, only they'll cost him sixty apiece. Meanwhile, a salesman just came in the day before who said I could have all I wanted for forty apiece, totally legitimate. Anyway, Rocco says to me, "Are they hot, Vince?" So I play along with him and I look to each side like I'm checkin' for cops in my own store and say, "Red hot!" So he says, "How many can you get me?" "Fifty," I say. "OK," he says, "I'll take 'em, give me a call." And he walks out.

Now I know what that rat bastard's up to. He's tryin' to set me up. He never even asked what kind of TVs they were. He didn't know if they were color, black and white, nine-inch, twenty-inch, nothin'. He had to be tryin' to set me up.

So I get the TVs and give him a call. I tell him I got 'em in a drop only he don't get 'em 'till he pays me first at the store. So

the Police: A Sociological Study of Law, Custom, and Morality (Cambridge: M.I.T. Press, 1970), pp. 40–43. Police publications argue strongly in favor of the system: Malachi L. Harney and John C. Cross, The Informer in Law Enforcement (Springfield: Charles C. Thomas, 1960); Carroll S. Price, "Sources of Information," Police, March–April 1960, pp. 47–51. The long and complicated history of the status of the informer before the courts seems to involve not only matters of abuse and the necessity for police information, but also the protection of the informer from harm and the right of the accused of confrontation under the Sixth Amendment. Needless to say, with so many issues at hand, legal articles, decisions, and opinions have ranged widely. For a concise review, see "The Informer Privilege: What's In A Name," Journal of Criminal Law and Criminology 64 (1973): 56–66.

in half an hour he comes by with a truck and gives me $3,000. Then he says, "OK, where's the TVs?" I say, "In the back room, take your truck around and pick 'em up." "I thought you had 'em in a drop," he says. "Yeh," I tell him, "my back room is my drop." Then he loads all of the TVs himself because he don't bring nobody to help him.

A couple of days later he comes in again. He says, "Hey Vincent, I thought you told me those TVs was hot. They ain't hot at all." Then I let him have it. "Who told you that, you rat bastard, your FBI friends?" "Oh no," he said, "I found out another way." "The hell you did," I said, "If you ever try to set me up again I'll kill you." Then he gives me all this bullshit about how this guy he knows can find out if stuff's hot and all sorts of crap, but I knew better.

While it is probably true that Johnny Rocco's particularly inept performance betrayed his real intention, other characteristics of the situation would have made Vincent suspicious and unwilling to sell to him even without his gangster-movie performance.[11] Vincent prefers to sell to "legitimate" businesses, which would be unlikely to be in league with the police. Other fences, because of their own illegitimate dealings, may well be trying to pay a debt to the police by setting Vincent up. In Johnny Rocco's case, he had been in business only a short time and, importantly, had neither arrests nor convictions to testify to his trustworthy character.

You see, I know who the informants are. All you gotta do to find out who your informants are is make 'em think they can set you up. Tell 'em you got somethin' hot with numbers all over it just sittin' around in your store. If the cops show up, you got your informant.

The guys you gotta watch are the ones with no arrests. The cops gotta know what they're doin' and if they don't take no arrests they got a license.

Surprisingly, though, Vincent may deal with people he knows

---

11. On other occasions Vincent has remarked to me that he thought film characters strongly influenced the styles if not the techniques of thieves. He claimed that in the early days of his career one could easily find George Raft poseurs flipping coins under lampposts. Today he claims that imitations of black screen stars abound.

or suspects to be informants. One such suspected informant is "Willie."

I've been doin' business with Willie for years. He is one of the best truck thieves in the city. Now there's somebody who's gotta be givin' information. I know personally that the police got him twice this year and he got out of it both times. See, when that happens you gotta figure he's givin' information.

[I ask, "Why doesn't he try to set you up?"] He's too smart to try that with me. He's gonna give up nothin' thieves and junkies. I told him years ago, I said, "Look, Willie, you got friends, I got friends. If you get any ideas about talkin' about me you better forget it 'cause if you do you ain't never gonna make it to the trial to say anything about it." He don't have no reason to set me up anyway. I'm the one takin' what he's got and I been very good to him over the years.

Vincent's threats and his reputation as a man with important contacts deter some potential informants. Others are not deterred, and in anticipation of them Vincent employs other procedures. Before discussing them it is important to stress the distinction between a "set up" and a "tip."

A "tip" is simply information supplied to the police that Vincent is going to buy or has bought particular merchandise. The tipster may be a thief, a friend of the thief, or someone who happened to see the transaction in the store. Against the tip Vincent uses all the defenses against receiving that we have listed above. A "set up" is a different matter. It is planned entrapment of the fence, in which the police are participants. Unlike the tip, a "set up" is illegal. If all else fails and Vincent finds himself on trial, he is aware of the opportunities offered by playing the role of the legitimate businessman entrapped by overzealous police and a disreputable informant.

Vincent has played it when it was true, when it was partially true, and when it was entirely false.

Almost a Set Up

About four years ago I'm at my store one morning and somebody starts bangin' on my back door. I go back and there is this little colored guy standin' there with a couple of cartons. He says,

"Mr. Vincent, I got some sweaters here for you." Well I ain't never seen the guy before so I says, "You must have the wrong store, my friend. I didn't order no sweaters." So he starts pushin' his cartons up on my loading platform. Well, right away I figure somethin' ain't right so I start kickin' 'em off. Just then a detective comes around the corner of my building and says, "OK, Swaggi, that's it. I got you." "The hell you do," I told him, and I shut the door and walked back into my store. So he starts bangin' on the door yellin', "Open in the name of the police. Open in the name of the police." I don't do nothin'. I just go about my business.

So in a couple of minutes he comes around the front door and says I'm under arrest for receiving stolen goods. Then he starts yellin' at me, tellin' me how he's goin' to beat the crap out of me for lockin' him out like that. All sorts of foul language. I tell him that he don't have no case. I got five witnesses in the store who know the goods never came in and who will also tell how he used foul language on me. Meanwhile he don't know what to do 'cause he's holdin' on to the thief while he's talkin' to me. He's got him by the belt and the little guy is yellin' how he can't breathe because the detective is pullin' so hard on his belt. Now this little guy is callin' the detective by name! That's all I needed to hear. "Oh! You two know each other?" I say. "Ain't that interesting." See, right then he knew I knew everything. The whole thing was a larry [an old carnival term meaning "a mess," "a mix-up"], but he figures he's gonna threaten me before he leaves. So he calls me a few more names and says how he's gonna really get me. I just stand there and I ask him what division he's in. He tells me and I say, "OK, that's all I want to know." Well, eventually he left.

I called his Captain. Now it just so happens that his Captain is an Italian. He belongs to the same American Legion post as me. Anyway, I told him the whole story and I said, "Look, I can understand as how there can be mix-ups, but there just ain't no excuse for an officer of the law callin' a man a 'dago son of a bitch.' I had customers in the store at the time," I told him, "and that kind of slur on Italians is just uncalled for." Well, the Captain said he'd take care of it. The next day that detective was at my store apologizing to me and my brother. He asked me to see if I could stop them from transferring him out to the edge of the city. You

see, that's what they do to you if they wanna get you in the police
department. So I did. I called the Captain back and he didn't get
transferred. See, I got a good reputation with the police.

A Tip Becomes a Set Up

You remember Johnny Rocco? He got me my arrest in 1966.
This was about two months after he tried to set me up the first
time. He started coming around my store again. I didn't want anything to do with him but he used to come by and just hang
around. Well one day he comes in and I had four big cases of
blouses I just bought sittin' in the back. Now he didn't stay long,
maybe a minute or two. Not ten minutes later two FBI agents
come walkin' in. They ask if they can look around so I tell 'em OK
They walk right to the blouses. All the boxes got numbers on
them. They take a couple of boxes and give me a receipt for them.
That afternoon the same two guys are back with a warrant—receiving stolen goods, interstate shipment. What could I do? If I
said they couldn't look around they would'a got a warrant anyway.
So I put up my bail and then I started to think about it. How the
hell did those guys know I had those blouses? They musta gotta
tip. Then it hit me. That rat bastard Rocco. He called 'em after
he left my store.

Well, now I figured we're just gonna have to teach Mr. John
Rocco a little lesson. So when we come to trial I let the prosecutor
do all the talking. He didn't have nothin' to say. The blouses came
outta an interstate truck, the numbers matched, they were in my
store. Then they put an FBI agent on the stand. My lawyer asks
him how he knew the goods were in my store. He says an informant told him. Then he asks him if he knows a Mr. John Rocco.
He don't say nothin'. He just stands there lookin' at my lawyer.
He asks him again. Nothin'. Now the judge tells him to answer
the question. The prosecutor then stands up and asks if he can
have a conference at the bench.

Then my lawyer put me on the stand. He asked me to explain
what happened and where I got the blouses from. So I say, "That
morning my friend, Mr. John Rocco, came by in his truck. He said
he had some cases on the back, but he didn't have the key to his
store with him and wondered if I'd do him a favor and let him

drop 'em off for a couple of hours at my store. He told me he had to go pick up some other merchandise and he wouldn't have room for all of it on the truck. I figured it wouldn't be no trouble for me to hold it for him for a few hours, Your Honor. I mean, I believe in helpin' out my fellow man when I can." Then I said to the judge, "Your Honor, I would like to say somethin' else too if you will let me." He said, "Certainly, Mr. Swaggi, if it bears on the matter at hand." Then I went on, "I have known Mr. Rocco for some time now and I am sure that he would never have asked me to hold those blouses for him if he thought they were stolen. I mean that just wouldn't be right and I am sure he wouldn't have done it, Your Honor."

You see, now I had them. My lawyer then insisted that the case could not go on unless Rocco were forced to testify. But how could the Feds do that? They had been doin' business with him and they wasn't about to let my lawyer get to him on the stand. He would'a split Rocco and the Feds wide open. So then they had another conference with the judge. When they were through he let me off an' bawled out the FBI agents in his chambers.

See, now that's my rule in court; you can put it in the book. Say, "Swaggi's rule is always go after the informant. He's probably a rat bastard and the cops ain't gonna take no chances puttin' him on the stand."[12]

Generally, then, the strategy Vincent employs in court is to structure the case as an entrapment when he has been caught with the merchandise. However, Vincent has also been called into court on a receiving charge when a thief has been caught and his testi-

---

12. There are some structural characteristics of Vincent's manipulation here of the informant system which ought not to go unmentioned. Rocco did nothing illegal, but Vincent knew he was a valuable informant. He also knew that the police had an obligation to protect his identity. Thus, even if Rocco were not guilty of entrapping Vincent, the assertion that he was would not permit the police to respond by putting him on the stand. The story Vincent told made the testimony of Rocco necessary. Even though the right to non-disclosure of an informant's identity is a privilege of the state, the state may not exercise it when the informant is alleged to be a participant in the crime: Rovario v. United States, 353 U.S. 53 (1957); Smith v. Illinois, 390 U.S. 131 (1968). Although it is often alleged that the informant system is necessary for the detection and prosecution of professional or quasi-professional criminals, Vincent here used the knowledge of informants that he has acquired only because of his criminal experience. Whether or not this strategy against the "tip" is used by other fences, I do not know.

mony is the only case the prosecutor has to go on. Vincent's strategy in such a case is to show that the thief has an interest in claiming that Vincent was the receiver. The claim is, of course, that the police have promised to give him a lighter sentence if he will implicate someone as his fence. With only the thief's testimony it is difficult to prove the fence's participation if the latter can not be apprehended with the goods in his possession to corroborate the thief's testimony.

The reader will recognize that there is a time factor involved in the choice of defense when an informant is involved. If Vincent is arrested immediately after the transaction in possession of the stolen goods, he is likely to claim entrapment. If he is arrested a day or so later (and consequently without identifiable goods in his possession) on the testimony of a thief who implicated him in exchange for a lighter sentence, he will claim that the thief's testimony is not credible because (1) he is a thief, and (2) he has been bribed by the police to testify against him. The matter then becomes one, of course, of whom the judge or jury believes.

Although Vincent does not suffer from the stigma of a court appearance as a nonprofessional without a record might, he still prefers to stay out of court if at all possible. It is a truism that one is never convicted unless one goes to court. Thus, Vincent prefers to offer his defense at the station house or preliminary hearing, where he trys to prove that no case exists against him. For reasons that include the complications introduced by the defenses described above, the police are aware of the problems they will have in trying to make an arrest stick on Vincent. This respect for Vincent's particular skill and resourcefulness is one way of accounting for his "piece-buy" arrangement:

You see, it's very rare I buy a complete load any more. Somebody comes to me with thirty cases of cigars, I buy ten. Oh, I'll send him on to somebody else an' maybe make a piece off of that deal too, but me, I only take a part of the load.

Let's suppose there's a back-up. Now, you know the thief is gonna bargain and the first thing the police are gonna ask him is who he sold it to. If you take the whole thing all the pressure's gonna fall on you. The Captain's gonna want to know why you wasn't picked up an' so's the judge. Now you see if you only bought a piece of the load the detective can say, "Who else did

*you sell it to?" If he gets another name the pressure's off you. He
can go after him, make an arrest, clear things up. You see, if you
got a thief for a big hijacking or something, it just don't look
right if you don't go after the fence.*

There are, of course, other explanations, explanations with some
historical precedent. They are, however, better left for systematic
examination after we have drawn a more complete portrait of the
day-to-day operations of Vincent's business.

To this point the descriptions of Vincent's operating procedures
suggest that legal proof of the crime of receiving is quite difficult
to attain. In part this is due to Vincent's resourcefulness and skill
at his occupation and at the performances it occasionally demands.
But the difficulty in convicting any fence is also inseparable from
the character of the business he conducts. The fence is a businessman and in most cases trades both legitimately and illegitimately.
In his illegitimate trade he models his operations after the normal
procedures and practices of the business world. In his legitimate
trade he buys and sells with an eye toward covering his illegitimate
activities. This managed similarity is designed to frustrate the
epistemology of law and render it incapable of discriminating between the fence's legal and illegal activities.

The skillful employment of a front and the tailoring of one's
illegal trade to fit it are only a part of the business of being a
fence. For if fencing is a business, then customers—buyers and
sellers—are at the core of it. Vincent's relationships with them
will be considered in the following chapter.

Chapter 5

RUNNING A FENCING BUSINESS: WHEELIN' AND DEALIN'

In the preceding chapter I attempted to describe some of the ways in which Vincent manipulated his legitimate-businessman identity. In this chapter I attempt to describe some of Vincent's business skills as they are colored and shaped by his illegitimate trade. Buying and selling have been Vincent's life. He enjoys business and is extraordinarily good at it.

CUSTOMERS—UP FRONT

I got the greatest customers in the world. From the biggest to the littlest, they come to me.

Vincent's up-front, walk-in customers have found him in any number of different ways. Secretaries always seem to have found out about Vincent from other secretaries; they bring girlfriends to his store before and after work and on Saturday. The bank tellers down the street know Vincent because he banks there. The waitresses at the diner occasionally suggest to their customers that they try Vincent's store, as does the barber, the counterman at the walk-up luncheonette, and the store owners on the street who handle merchandise that Vincent does not. Executives working in the nearby office building walk by his store twice a day to and from the subway stop.

Policemen, detectives, lawyers, tipstaffs, and an occasional judge learn about Vincent's bargains in their official and unofficial contacts with drivers, boosters, and thieves. Customs officials, waterfront workers and inspectors, an insurance adjuster or two, private detectives, and crime reporters seem to be plugged into similar information channels. Probably the largest single group of Vincent's retail customers is in some way connected with law enforcement. Certainly the second largest group of retail customers is connected with law violation. Both groups are cautious of one another and often Vincent is obliged to manage the comings and goings of the latter when the former are present.

I suspect that, if one were to control for race, thieves and detectives would have similar tastes in clothes, cologne, housewares, and many other items that compose the fare of general merchandise. Perhaps the single most distinguishing difference between the two groups as customers is that the law enforcers all wear jackets and ties. Vincent is comfortable with both groups but appears to be slightly deferential to the law enforcers and perhaps a bit patronizing to the thieves. Generally a friendly, joking atmosphere prevails, with "What's hot today, Vince?" as a standard opening from Vincent's law-enforcement customers. Although Vincent has heard that question a thousand times he always answers, "Everything," and laughs.

It should not be surprising that shopping at Vincent's has secondary advantages for both groups. Although I have never seen an informative conversation between Vincent and a detective, I know they do occur. Vincent would give advice on how he would go about cracking a difficult case as readily as he does on how to beat a rap.

Similarly, I know that he discusses the security problems on the waterfront with customs agents and how to stop insurance fraud with his insurance-adjuster friends. On the other hand, I have seen him advise drivers, shoplifters, and thieves about the very same problems from their point of view. Giving both types of advice satisfies his taste for working out schemes, and each, naturally, has its own rewards.

An important group of special customers rounds out the catalogue of Vincent's up-front retail trade. They are special because they are either high-status people or have known Vincent for many years. They come by, quite infrequently, to visit Vincent. When they do it prompts a minor celebration. One such customer was a former hustler who now owns a big car dealership and knew Vincent when they were both working the streets. He brought his wife along and showed off pictures of his grandchildren. Another was a former local customs agent who had since made it to a high administrative post in Washington. Still others were nightclub entertainers, one of whom left Vincent an autographed copy of his latest hit record and a rough description of the kind of jewelry he would be interested in on his next visit to the city. Vincent talked for days about a June Taylor dancer who asked him if he'd like to show her the town while she was performing at a local nightclub.[1]

In important respects Vincent's retail customers serve both as an audience and as actors in scenarios in which Vincent plays a number of roles. The old ladies let him be kind; the young ones, a bit dashing and romantic. The law enforcers test his ability at their profession. The thieves often need stories or advice. The celebrities testify to his reputation, and his high-status customers, like doctors and dentists and judges, to his respectability. Some of his more trusting customers even give him the chance to be their doctor.[2] Vincent entertains or performs for customers as much as he sells

1. Vincent turned her down. Later he confided to me, "You know what those kind of girls want? Gifts, drinks, expensive nightclubs. You gotta take 'em to four or five different places in one night. It'd cost a fortune. What do I need that kind of stuff for anyway?"

2. Vincent has a small supply of medical books, a large quantity of pills (drug salesmen's samples which find their way to Vincent via a friend who owns a drugstore supply house), a box of tongue depressors, and a stethoscope, all of which have earned him the occasional nickname of "Doc."

to them. The luxury of using a retail store as a vehicle of self-expressiôn is permitted Vincent only because he earns his real money in trading that his walk-in customers never see.

THE WHOLESALE TRADE

As a fence, Vincent is a generalist. This means he is able to sell at a profit, and hence will buy, virtually anything that is offered to him. Unlike the specialist fence, who may be involved in trading only a single variety of merchandise such as jewelry, clothing, or office equipment, Vincent must have a number of buyers in different businesses willing to take what he has to sell. Vincent dislikes discussing just how many wholesale buyers he has and who they are, but I would estimate that at any one time the number doing regular business with him (once a month or more) is less than thirty and the number doing very regular business with him (once a week or more) is less than fifteen. (For Vincent there is never enough to go around to all his buyers.)

The frequency of a given buyer's business with Vincent fluctuates according to the market situation generally and with respect to the type of good involved, the opportunities for theft, which are related to the market situation, and the type of thief patronizing Vincent at the moment. For example, for some months Vincent bought adding machines and typewriters from a thief who stole nothing else. Vincent's buyer, a purchasing agent for a large corporation, traded with him every day. (Vincent suspects that after he bought all his company could use he became an intermediate fence for a typewriter repair and sales shop and a peddler of the machines to the employees of his company.) The thief who supplied Vincent would steal at least one machine a day and often two or three. The purchasing agent would come by at 4:30 P.M. five days a week and at 10:00 A.M. on Sunday (after church). When the thief was finally convicted (Vincent posted his bail and kept the machines coming for two months after his arrest), the typewriter-and-adding-machine trade slowed to a trickle. The purchasing agent now comes by only once a week and then often only to chat because nothing is available.

Sometimes Vincent may slow a thief down rather than have the authorities do so. I met a warehouse worker whom Vincent told not to bring any more electric razors because at the ten-a-day rate he was taking them it would not be long before the management would grow suspicious. The worker complained that he needed the money, so Vincent suggested hot combs, then electric frying pans, and then steam irons. Of course, when Vincent is obliged to suggest such a shift in the flow of items to a thief it naturally affects the availability of certain goods to would-be buyers. Vincent can suggest items to fill the needs of his own or his customers' inventories, but this has its limitations. For example, a shipper in a clothing warehouse simply cannot take cameras.

Because of the work and time involved in setting up deals with buyers, Vincent prefers the rather stable arrangements possible with shippers, drivers, and warehouse-worker thieves to the more irregular flow of merchandise that comes from store and truck thieves. When one has a regular arrangement it is possible to agree on a fixed price with both the buyer and seller as well as on delivery and storage routines.

About six blocks from me there was this big plumbing supply company. I mean they had a half a city block which was just plumbing supplies. I got to know the guy who was the shipper. He used to come into my store. He knew what I had was hot stuff, so one day I asked him where he worked. He told me, Howard Plumbing, the big warehouse. So I kept talkin' to him and we made a little arrangement: when I put in an order for like a dozen toilets I'd get four dozen. I mean I'd pay for the one dozen but I'd get the three dozen free. He'd get the order in the warehouse and just load the extra on the truck. The driver didn't know nothin' about it.

After we made that arrangement I started to look around for people I could sell plumbing supplies to. Well, before you know it I had half a dozen contractors givin' me orders for sinks, toilets, pipe, solder, everything to do with plumbing. Well, that deal lasted close to a year. They did an inventory and fired everybody in the warehouse. What did the shipper care? I'd say he made easy ten thousand off of me, and who knows how much off of everybody else he was doin' business with.

[I ask, "How much did you pay the shipper on each load?"] He got twenty percent on three for one. It's like this: I order one thing, he sends me four. I pay the company full price on the one and I give him twenty percent on the other three. Say he gives me

four items which cost a dollar each. I give the company a dollar
and him sixty [cents]. Each piece, averaged out, runs me forty
cents. I sell it for eighty [cents] and give my buyer twenty percent
off dealer wholesale.[3]

Although Vincent prefers such stable deals, they are never available in the numbers he would be willing to participate in. It is
unusual, for one thing, to find a shipper who is willing to trade in
the volume described in the above anecdote. Instead, Vincent has
perhaps half a dozen arrangements with shippers who will supply
him with three or four cartons of goods every few months. Vincent is happy with such arrangements because they almost never
involve complications with the law. In the incident above, for example, Vincent enjoyed the possession of a legitimate bill for
every item he possessed (although not in the quantity he possessed it), as well as a plausible story were he caught red-handed
(shipper error which he was about to correct).

Because of the irregular character of his inflow of merchandise,
Vincent's wholesale and retail customers are forever making known
to Vincent the kind of merchandise they would be interested in.
These requests may be regarded as standing orders. However, Vincent's promise to "keep my eyes open" for what they are looking
for is no obligation on his part to fill them. Needless to say, such
standing orders are important in affecting Vincent's decisions to
buy when opportunities become available.[4]

I suspect that Vincent does most of his trading with only a
dozen or so customers. He can do so because a dozen different

3. According to this arrangement, if the shipper made $10,000 from Vin-
cent the company lost $50,000 in merchandise.
4. Some sources have considered the practice of telling a fence what one
wants as the equivalent of an order to a legitimate dealer. See Bruce Jackson,
A Thief's Primer (London: Macmillan and Co., 1969), pp. 86–87. I believe
this to be a distortion encouraged by the use of thieves' testimony to find out
about fences. From the thieves' point of view the fence may often be seen as
making suggestions or expressing interest in one kind of goods or another.
From this the impression arises that the fence is filling direct orders. It is an
impression that is accurate but incomplete. Actually, Vincent receives dozens
of requests each week. They fall less in the "order" category than in the "let
me know if you run across . . ." category. Requests to thieves involve not
only customer demand but also an estimation of the thief's skills, the profit
to be made on the items customers request, the seriousness of the customer's
request, and the complications that might arise in attempting to fill a request.
Vincent can accept the majority of thieves' offers of stolen property not be-

businesses, if chosen properly, can cover almost the full range of merchandise that is ordinarily brought to him. Indeed, five willing contacts—a small retail store (clothing), a drug store (cosmetics), a medium-size contractor (tools, building supplies), a market or restaurant (food, groceries, dishes, liquor, cigarettes), and an auction (almost anything)—in addition to his own store could satisfy the need for markets for the merchandise that ordinarily becomes available to Vincent. Having a dozen willing customers in different businesses not only covers the usual flow of merchandise but gives Vincent the option to choose whom he will sell to, an option Vincent exercises to "spread the merchandise around" and keep the price level up. In dealing in stolen merchandise as well as in legitimate merchandise one can make higher profits on small amounts than on large ones.

Say I got sweaters, ten dozen, which sell for nine ninety-nine in the department stores. If I sell 'em in my store for five dollars I can make say three dollars apiece easy, if I bought 'em for two. But I got 'em layin' around for a week maybe. So I take three dozen and sell the rest for forty dollars a dozen. In half an hour I make what? Sixteen dollars a dozen times seven dozen, a hundred and twelve dollars. Plus I got three dozen left to sell myself. With them I make thirty-six-a-dozen profit, that's another hundred and eight, which on top of the one twelve gives me two twenty clear.[5]

cause he has instructed his thieves to steal but because he has a kind of standing catalogue of requests.

It also bears mention that the fence sacrifices some bargaining advantage when he places an order with a thief. This is so because he creates an obligation to buy, may be obliged to offer an advance price, and divulges his need for the goods.

5. I should note here that Vincent spoke this paragraph at only a slightly slower rate than normal speech. He works with numbers very rapidly, a skill he often employs to his advantage in trading. The accounting works this way:

BOUGHT		10 dozen sweaters @ $24/dozen ($2.00 each)	
SOLD,	wholesale	7 dozen sweaters @ $40/dozen ($3.33 each)	
SOLD,	retail	3 dozen sweaters @ $60/dozen ($5.00 each)	

DEBIT	CREDIT
$240.00	
	$280.00
	180.00
− $240.00	+ $460.00

$220.00 Profit

The unwritten catalogue of standing orders is supplemented by information about Vincent's retail customers that may be called upon when quite special merchandise comes along.

One day this truck thief walks in with two small cartons. He didn't know what they were even, so I got 'em real cheap. I dunno, maybe thirty-five for both. Well, each carton had two dozen dentist drills in it. So I wonder, where am I gonna get rid of this? I remember one a my customers told me his brother owns a dental supply. So I called him and he called his brother. Then his brother come over to see me. You should'a seen him! Was he excited! He gave me a hundred and a half for each case. Oh, I done lots a business with him since then. One time I got teeth, maybe five thousand teeth in one carton. You know, the kind they use for making false teeth. I stole it off the thief and he [the dental-supply-house owner] couldn't buy it fast enough.

You see, you never know what a thief's gonna come up with. I mean the thief don't even know most of the time. So you gotta be ready for anything. You see, I got a buyer for almost anything. I mean we maybe do business once or twice in a year but I know where to go.

Thus, a by-product of Vincent's reputation among his retail customers as a dealer in stolen merchandise is the network of normally quite-removed contacts which he becomes aware of for special items such as those above. More often than not, these contacts follow kinship lines. For example, one of Vincent's customers who noticed a carton of children's ballet slippers on the floor of the store suggested that her cousin might be interested in them because she ran a ballet school. In this case the customer offered to check with her cousin and to report back to Vincent if her cousin were interested. In such a case, the customer is not only selling the merchandise for Vincent but is motivated as well by the possibility of doing a relative a "favor."

An additional advantage of Vincent's reputation as a receiver, and of his friendly associations with retail customers, is his tacit working assumption that they will be willing to act as intermediaries in the sale of stolen goods. Were they not willing to buy stolen merchandise, they probably would not be in his store to begin with. Thus, if he asks about a relative's willingness to buy (as in the dental-supply deal), the possibility that the customer will be offended is extremely remote. More likely the customer will react with enthusiasm at the opportunity to help both Vincent and his relative.

The primary advantage in dealing with Vincent is, of course, his price. Depending on the kind of merchandise and how cheaply Vincent was able to buy it, the wholesale buyer may get anywhere from twenty to eighty percent off the normal wholesale price. The largest discounts are probably given for exotic items (like dentist's drills) and goods that have a very low profit margin (like foods, especially meat). In both these cases, the greater discounts available are more a result of Vincent's bargaining strategy with thieves than of market demands.

There are other advantages to dealing with Vincent. One is that one may obtain a bill for what one buys. Because Vincent is a licensed merchant, such a bill serves as a ticket to legitimize the purchase. Even if one doesn't obtain a bill, buying through Vincent places a step between the purchaser and the thief, thus rendering the buyer relatively safe from detection should the thief be captured. Many of the buyers who do not hesitate to deal with Vincent would have absolutely nothing to do with a thief vending the same merchandise.

Paradoxically, another advantage in dealing with Vincent is that no bill and no record of the sale is ever recorded, if the buyer so desires. This means that profits on the subsequent sale of the merchandise will not be declared for business taxation. With business profit tax in the neighborhood of fifty percent this can represent a substantial savings.

Another type of arrangement involves those buyers whose companies never see the substantial discount Vincent is able to offer.

I have a couple of buyers for big department stores I do business with sometimes. I mean they're not interested in no three or four cases. You're talkin' fifteen, twenty cases now. Anyway, say I got somethin' I'm willin' to let go at two hundred a case. And say the normal wholesale is two sixty. I get in touch with one of these guys and we write up an order through a friend of mine for say two forty a case. Well, the company pays off just like it was a regular sale, forty-eight hundred, and I kick back eight hundred to the buyer. The company don't know the difference. In fact they're happy 'cause the buyer's doin' a good job gettin' the stuff twenty dollars less a case.

Years ago I had a buyer who did regular business with me like *that. I was payin' for his girlfriend. See, he had her apartment, the whole deal. So he couldn't hardly take it out of his paycheck 'cause his wife would'a spotted it. Three, four years that went on. Then he had a heart attack. I think the whole thing was just too much for him.*

The above example is important because it demonstrates the unwitting cooperation of a large corporation in the traffic of stolen property. It is necessary only that a single buyer of a legitimate and respectable department store be willing to deal with a fence in order that stolen property find its way to the store's shelves. Vincent alleges that the department store, while perhaps not condoning the buyer's purchase of stolen merchandise, is not especially zealous in checking to see that everything is fully legitimate.

You think those department stores don't know what their buyers are doing? Well, maybe they ain't got no proof, but as long as that guy's makin' a profit in his department they ain't gonna do no lookin' around. What do they care, anyway? He's still givin' it to them cheaper if he buys from me than if he got it from the factory.

[I ask, "If that's so, why do you bother working the deal under somebody else's name?"] Well, it just looks better. I took a few pinches for hot stuff and there ain't no need of askin' for trouble. So you run it through somebody else, like an auction, and it just looks better, that's all.

It is entirely possible that upper-level management may suspect that buyers are trafficking in stolen property and adopt a no-questions-asked attitude. However, it is also possible that buyers who work a kickback system with either stolen or legitimate property cover their footsteps carefully enough so as not to arouse suspicion. There is not sufficient evidence to settle the question.

It is important to emphasize the advantage which the location of Vincent's store, straddling the boundary between the city's wholesale and retail districts, offers to his wholesale dealing. It places him in daily contact with other wholesale dealers and owners as well as with a sizable number of traders who come to that area to buy and sell. Were Vincent located in a strictly retail area he would be less likely to meet the buyers and sellers that constitute such a huge proportion of his trade. Certainly the speed with which trading takes place would be slowed if for no other reason than the additional time needed to contact buyers and deliver merchandise. Furthermore, there is some doubt about whether or not he would be able to sustain the rather friendly relationships that encourage the no-bill deals and the borrowing of another store owner's business identity. Vincent's location is conducive to the growth of the kind of trust encouraged by proximity and day-to-day contact. Vincent once told me as he stood in the doorway of his store:

The way I look at it, this is actually my street. I mean I am the mayor. I walk down the street an' people come out the doors to say hello. They got a problem, they come to me. You know that store down the street—Katz Furniture? Harry Katz put me in charge of his will when he died. He didn't trust his wife or his kids. And he didn't let none of these Jews around here get their fingers in it either. I took care of everything for him. You know, I saw to it nobody pulled any bullshit or anything. That's the way it is, people just take to me. The mayor of Edge Street, yeh, that's me all right.

BUYING RIGHT: VINCENT'S TRADE WITH THIEVES

Those to whom Vincent sells are, for the most part, businessmen who are aware of the intricacies of merchandising and know the market for the goods they buy. Those from whom Vincent buys are frequently inept and usually ignorant of the market for what they have to sell. They have often expended a small amount of energy for what they have, and frequently need money. Furthermore, they may want to get back to work or make a connection for drugs and are aware that they are in some danger so long as they have stolen property in their possession. Consequently, although the trade Vincent enjoys with those he sells to bears some resemblance to conventional market descriptions, the trade with those he buys from is likely to be unintelligible according to standard economic theory.

I do not mean to suggest, however, that trading between fence and thief is random. Rather, certain assumptions made in the

analysis of normal economic dealing simply do not fit the fence–
thief situation. For example, a norm that has governed the asking
price of thieves for centuries says simply, "When you take something to a fence you should try to get a third of the value of the
goods."[6]

Why should this norm exist? Why does it survive? What relationship does it bear to the economics of fencing? Let us first
look at the simple economic implications of this norm. If the
fence buys wholesale merchandise at one-third of its retail value he
is quite likely to go broke. A $100 retail item purchased at $33
from a thief is likely to sell for $50 to $60 wholesale in the legitimate market. In order to be competitive the fence must sell below
wholesale. Thus, if he sells at 30 percent below wholesale ($35 for
a wholesale cost of $50), he will make only $2 on each item. At
that rate he would be far better off economically in legitimate
business. Consequently, the one-third norm must apply, if at all,
only to those items which the fence will himself sell at retail cost.

But why does this norm exist at all? Why does the presumably
arbitrary figure of one-third govern? Vincent remarks:

You see, it's your small thieves who come in expectin' to get a
third of the ticket. Boosters, snitches, guys like that. They know
they can't get a half so they ask for a third.

[I ask, "Why can't they get a half?"]

I can get it wholesale for half. Why should I bother with them
if I can do just as good legitimate. So they ask a third.

For centuries thieves have been asking for a third of the ticket
price because they couldn't get half of it. I suggest that this is the
only tenable argument in support of a norm that has existed for

6. I do not mean that the fence in fact pays one-third of the retail value
of merchandise, but rather that the thief begins his bargaining with this
amount. Certain types of goods, certain fences, and certain thieves have stood
as exceptions to this "one-third norm," but the literature available on fences'
prices supports my assertion. Cf. Danny Ahern, How to Commit a Murder
(New York: Ives Washburn, 1930), p. 62; [P. Colquhoun], A Treatise on
the Police of The Metropolis (London: H. Fry for C. Dilly, 1796), p. 188;
Edward Crapsey, The Nether Side of New York (New York: Sheldon and
Co., 1872), p. 90; Frank E. Emerson, "They Can Get It For You Better
Than Wholesale," New York Magazine, 22 November 1971, p. 39; Hans Von
Hentig, The Criminal and His Victim (New Haven: Yale University Press,
1948), p. 401; Leon Radzinowicz, A History of English Criminal Law and
Its Administration from 1750, vol. 2 (New York: Macmillan Co., 1957), p.
322.

centuries in the trade between fences and thieves. The thief asks for one-third because it is the next simple fraction after one-half. What else would he ask for—two-fifths, three-sevenths, four-ninths? For many small thieves these fractions do not exist! Even if they knew about them they would be unable to calculate the proportion of the price they represented. The assumption that there are fractions between one-half and one-third can be made only for sellers more sophisticated than the class of petty thieves who have operated without them for at least two hundred years.

The implication for Vincent is that bargaining need only begin at a third. Any fence can buy at a third; Vincent claims, perhaps more from pride than from calculation, "I never paid a third in my life."

The thief differs from the legitimate consumer of goods in a number of ways that bear importantly on his transactions with a fence. Unlike the legitimate consumer, he may have no real knowledge about the product he has in his possession. If the item is not labeled he may have no idea of its price. Even if it is labeled, he probably will not know if the price marked is competitive. Judgments about quality, market demand, and wholesale mark-up are difficult for the most sophisticated consumer; for the thief they may well be impossible. Finally, with high-cost items marketed to a social class different from his own, or items specific to a particular industry, he may have not only no notion of their price but also no idea of their purpose or use. Vincent is aware of such deficiencies in those who would sell to him and utilizes them to his advantage. In each of the following trading situations, Vincent exploits the thief's ignorance about the item he has stolen or the market for it.

Claim: Item Is Incomplete

This mornin' a guy came in with a camera. He's a booster, high-class though, jacket and tie, real respectable-lookin' colored guy. He's got a newspaper in his hand an' in the newspaper he's got this camera. Now he musta just got it 'cause it still had the store tags on it. I think they said five sixty-five, five eighty, somethin' like that. Anyway, he said he wanted two hundred for it.

"Two hundred?" I says to him. "Sure it's worth two hundred if you had the whole thing, but you only got part of it there."

"What do you mean?" he said, "this is the way they had it right on the counter."

"Look," I tell him. "See these holes?" I show him all the holes and places where you put the lights and all that kind of stuff. "This thing don't work unless you got all the parts an' everything goes with it. You want two hundred from me, buddy, you gotta go back and get the rest of that stuff." Now I know he ain't goin' back to that store.

"Aw, come on Vince," he says. "You gotta give me somethin' for it. How 'bout seventy-five dollars?"

Now I know I got 'em. Once they mention a price they gotta come down. They can't go up. "I'll tell you," I said, "I know you, you're a hard-workin' fella and you can use the dough, so I'm gonna give you forty for it." Meanwhile, I take out my small roll⁷ and start layin' out fives on the counter. They was new ones. I just got 'em from the bank. "Aw, come on Vince," he says, "forty ain't very much for a nice camera like this." So when I come to forty I stop. Then I look at him an' put another five down. "Okay," I says, "forty-five. You know I shouldn't even be takin' somethin' like this with all this stuff missin'. Now take it or forget it." "Awright," he says, and he takes the money. So he starts to go out. "Wait a minute," I said to him. "Did you have break-fast?" "No." "Well, come here," I said, and I gave him two bucks. "Here, take this an' go get somethin' to eat. Maybe you'll work better." So he took the money and he left.

You see it's very important to show the thief the money. I mean even a hundred bucks looks like a lot if it's fives and tens. Once they start lookin' at the money you know you got 'em.

Claim: Item Is Useless or Mundane

1. OUT OF SEASON. One of the things your truck thieves don't know is when things get shipped. Now your drivers know, but the guys who take cartons never catch on. Like for example: in March and April I always got guys bringin' me summer stuff—tennis rackets, bathin' suits, summer dresses—all that kind of stuff. It's

7. Vincent keeps two large rolls of bills in his front pants pockets. In his left pocket is a roll of twenties and fifties, and in his right is one of ones, fives, and tens.

what's on the trucks. See, your wholesalers are always working two, three months ahead. Somebody brings me somethin' like that, I tell 'em, "Yeh, that's very nice stuff, but come back in two months when I can sell it." They fuss, but I tell 'em I can't have hot stuff layin' around two, three months 'till somebody's interested in buyin' it. Sometimes I'll even tell 'em, try some store that might be willin' to take a chance holdin' it that long. The thief knows they ain't gonna buy from him. He's gotta give it to me.

Now, of course, for me it's the best merchandise. Brand-new styles for the season comin' up. The little stores don't even know what it's gonna be yet.

2. **UNFINISHED.** I don't know how many times I bought the best pants for next to nothin' 'cause they didn't have the cuffs on 'em. Do you know that most of your black thieves don't know about any kind of pants but ready-made? I tell 'em, "Look, they didn't even finish makin' these yet—they ain't got no cuffs on 'em. I gotta find some tailor to put cuffs on 'em at two dollars a pair. It just ain't worth my trouble." I'll tell you, to be honest I get good pants cheaper than ready-made.

3. **IMPRACTICAL.** You see, most of your black thieves just don't know what they got a lot a times. Like a couple a months ago this guy came in with a stack a rugs. They were Swedish or Danish, I forget which, but they were all small, you know, maybe two or three, the kind you hang on your wall. The guy who had 'em thought they were for bathrooms. I got 'em for nothin' 'cause I told him I could get a whole room rug, 9' × 12' for thirty dollars. See, he just didn't know what they was. The same thing goes for the dishes I had. You saw 'em—the ones by those artists [Picasso and Wyeth]. Thieves come in askin' fifty a case, 'cause they don't know what they got. Hell, the department stores are sellin' 'em for fifty apiece. Thieves figure they're just dishes to eat on.

Claim: Item Is of Poor Quality

1. **JAPANESE IMPORT.** Today most of your cameras, radios, tape recorders, are made in Japan. Years ago it used to be cheap stuff, but no more. Sony, Panasonic, Norelco [sic]—they're all Jap

stuff. Now your thieves don't know merchandise. Well, some of 'em do, but most of 'em don't. With guys like that, right off I tell 'em they got a piece of Jap junk on their hands. See, they just don't know merchandise.

2. MINKS AND FURS. Even your good thieves don't know much about furs. Once in a while you run across a real professional who knows what he's doin', but that's very rare. Of course with me furs are like second nature. I know a good fur ten feet away, whether it's a let-out, whether it's backs or belly fur. There's not one thief in fifty who can really tell you what he's got. For Christ sakes, I bought Chinchilla when the jerk who had it thought he was sellin' me rabbit. He started out tellin' me the coat was mink when it was Chinch. He was dead. I had him right there.

3. JEWELRY. The same goes for jewelry. I got my loop [a ten-power magnification eyepiece] right here. [He shows it to me.] A lot a times a thief won't know if it's glass or diamond. The important thing you have to look for is if the ring or bracelet, or whatever he's got, is real clean. See, if a thief don't know what he's got, sometimes he's gonna go to a jeweler to get it appraised. Whenever they do that, the jeweler drops it in a pot which cleans it up by electricity. If it's second-hand stuff an' it's real clean, you gotta figure he took it to a jeweler already.

Tricks with Prices

See, Carl, what you gotta remember is that the fence is a businessman. He knows all about business. The thief don't know nothin' about it. Oh, now that don't go for a lot of your drivers and hijackers. Nowadays they take all the bills of lading, too. Some of 'em can tell you wholesale, retail, even manufacturer's cost. But your average thief don't know nothin' from wholesale and retail. Every week I get some shine in here who comes in askin' for a third on some carton he stole off a truck. He shows me the bill. I give him some bullshit if I feel like it but sometimes I'll pay him right off what he asks. The only thing is, he's askin' a third of wholesale.

1. CATALOGUES. Take my catalogues, for instance. Almost anything you bring me I can tell you the price. You can put this in
the book if you want. The Sears catalogue is the fence's Bible.
Plus of course I got a lot of wholesale catalogues too. Now you
show a thief a catalogue with a price in it, even if it's a cheaper
item, you can get him to believe it's the price. [How would you
do that?] Let's say a thief thinks somethin' is worth such and such.
I'd say to him, "Look here, son, I ain't cheatin' you. If it was
worth what you said I'd take it in a minute, but I can't be in
business for charity, you know." So I show 'em the catalogue. Depends on the situation. If you figure the guy can read, that's one
thing. If he can't, then you show him a wholesale catalogue with
no pictures. "Look here," I tell 'em, "RCA model such and such—
thirty-four ninety-five." Now that could be the wholesale price on
a seventy-nine dollar radio. You know, even if they can't read they
try not to let on. I say, "You can read, can't you?" and he'll say,
"Sure I's can read" [in a black accent], an' across the top of the
page it says, "Wholesale Catalogue."

2. RETAIL PROFITS. Thieves are gettin' smarter about wholesale
an' retail, so you gotta play it smart with some of 'em. Say I got a
thief who's wise to wholesale-retail, who brings me somethin' from
a real nice store. With somebody like that you can tell 'em what
he don't know about wholesale. I say, "There ain't no way you are
ever gonna get a third of the ticket that store puts on." He'll ask
me why, an' I'll tell 'em. "That store marks up three to one,
sometimes four to one. Why should I take somethin' hot from you
I can get cheaper legitimate?" If he don't believe me I can even
show 'em some of my bills. Legitimate stuff I bought at ten,
twenty cents on the dollar. See, if you got a smart thief, you deal
with him smart.

3. PRICES AND STOCK CODES. I'll tell you somethin', though,
about buyin' an' prices which I have done with a lot of thieves.
Say they get a tray of rings, brand-new, right out of a jewelry
store. Now today most jewelers have a separate tag on each ring.
It's plastic, with a little snap on it. An' the price is marked on each
one. Say you got twenty rings in the tray, average price a hundred
dollars. Would you believe I bought trays like that for less than a

hundred? Well, I have. See, when they put the prices on those tags they don't put no dollar signs, just numbers. So when the thief tells you that the numbers are prices you just laugh at him. I say, "You stupid sonofa bitch, what did you take this shit for? Those ain't prices—those are stock numbers." Then I pick up a plain ring an' I ask him, "Does this piece of junk look like it's worth a hundred twenty-nine dollars? For Christ sake, it ain't even gold. Here," I say, an' I hand it to him, "feel the weight of that— it ain't nothin'. If that was gold you could feel it." Sometimes I take the ring off my hand, which is very big an' heavy, an' let him compare the weight. "Now this is what gold feels like. You get the weight of mine compared to this stuff?"

See, that kind of bullshit really works when the guy ain't too bright. Hell, of course my ring is gonna weigh more. It's a big-man's ring. Besides, you can't even tell nothin' by weighin' rings in your hands anyway.

In addition to the thief's disadvantage in not knowing the quality, price, or market for the goods, he has to sell, he is not provided with those devices the legitimate vendor has for account-ing for what he has sold.

Tricks with Numbers: Quantity and Computations

You know how good I am with numbers. There's very few guys who can keep up with me when it comes to figurin'. I'm just too fast for 'em.

You know, sometimes when I'm figurin' I write in the air like this [Vincent makes numbers in the air in front of his face]. I can really see the numbers in front of me. Guys see me doin' that an' they ask Tony what's the matter with me. He says I'm crazy but I really can do it.

1. COUNTING QUANTITY. First of all, most of your fences count everythin' before they buy it. Not me. See, I can just about tell what's in a carton by lookin' at it. Say a driver brings in a carton. See, what I do, I just open up half the top an' run my hand down the side. You know a lot a cartons ain't all the same merchandise, you know. Sometimes there's one thing on the top an' other stuff on the bottom. Now a lot a times the driver knows what's in the

carton but he don't know exactly how many pieces. Take panty hose, for instance. I bought a carton a while ago. It was a pretty big carton. The driver knew it was panty hose but not how much. He figures maybe a hundred pieces. So I give 'em twenty-five dollars, a quarter a pair, 'cause I know there's gotta be more than that. Well it turned out to be twenty-four dozen, two forty-four, not a hundred pair like he thought.

2. MIXED CARTONS. Also you gotta check what kind a store the stuff is goin' to. You figure, if it's a department store, nine times outta ten it's gonna be all the same thing in the carton. A small store, chances are they're gonna buy less, so you got more of a possibility it's a mixed carton. So say you reach down an' there's somethin' else there. Sometimes you can look; push the other stuff aside an' just get a quick look at it. Me, I can tell right off if I'm gonna make out dealin' better if it was a mixed case or a straight one. But I'll tell you, even if you got a mixed case with somethin' better on the bottom, you got the element of surprise workin' for you if you pull it out. I'll say, "Ha Ha, you bastard, you thought you were gonna stick me with this shit on the bottom, huh?" "What? What?" he says. Then I pull it out. "You thought you were gonna pull a fast one on me this time. Well you can just take this whole box of horseshit outta here an' throw it in the trash. That's the last time we're doin' business, buddy." Then he gets all upset. "Aw honest, Mr. Swaggi, I didn't know that was down there. I wouldn't try to cheat you." See, I do that kind a thing, chances are he ain't even gonna look at what I pulled out. Now I got the edge on 'em an' I can take the carton off him for half of what I would'a given him before, which you know wasn't gonna be very much anyway.

3. QUANTITY AND COMPUTATIONS. These two guys drive up to the store. They got a new Caddy, maybe a year old. Well, you wanna see it. Cartons everywhere. At least three in the back seat, the trunk's tied down with a rope 'cause they can't close it 'cause there's too many cartons in it, and the guy on the front seat's got one on his lap. He comes in an' asks if I'm interested, so I tell him to pull around back an' let me see what he's got. They musta just run across an open truck, 'cause they had seven cartons, five big plus two little ones—all clothes. Shirts, sweaters, socks, gloves, oh

yeh, an' some little-kids jackets. All good stuff. So I put all the cartons in a line in my back room. Now here's somethin' to remember. You got this much stuff an' the guys bring it inside your store, they ain't gonna carry it all out. Just too much carryin'.

Anyway, we start to go right down the line, just like an auction. First carton, shirts, Van Heusen. They're nice; in fact, I like 'em myself. "Whaddaya got? About three dozen? Thirty-five for this." Second carton, sweater sets—one button-down sweater and matching knit shirt, retail approximately eighteen dollars. "Hmmm, sweaters. Three—no, I'll make it three fifty. Let's see, that's about fifty, hell, make it sixty." Next carton, three three-dozen boxes of men's socks. "Oh oh, socks. Can't give you more than a quarter a pair. Let's see, a quarter a pair times three dozen." I ask the thief, "A quarter a pair times three dozen, how much does that come to?" He just looks at me. "Fifteen dollars, right?" He nods. "Wait a minute," I say, "not fifteen dollars, twelve. Twelve pair, twenty-five cents a pair, that's four a dozen times three is twelve dollars." By this time I got him so confused he don't remember there's nine dozen in the carton. Next carton, more socks. "Same deal on these, OK?" Then we come to the two little cartons—men's gloves. "OK ten apiece for these two little ones." Then I stand up without sayin' nothin' about the next carton [more sweaters]. I just opened the top an' sort'a hummed a little. "OK, what does all that come to? Thirty-five and a hundred for all the sweaters, that's a hundred thirty-five, plus ten apiece for the gloves, that's about a hundred fifty, plus fifteen each for the socks. Wait a minute, didn't I say twelve for the socks? Oh, make it twenty-five for both. Let's see, that's a hundred seventy-five." "Hey, wait a minute," they say, "you forgot the children's clothes here." "Oh yeh," I says, "see, I got grandchildren I was thinkin' of them for. How about you give me four for my personal use an' I'll give you two hundred for the lot. Take it or leave it." Then I start countin' out twenties. "OK now, here's a hundred for you an' another hundred for you." They took it.[8]

8. This anecdote was, I think understandably, rather difficult to remember. I have notes on each of the cartons traded, but the dialogue is more or less guessed at. (I should add that this incident made quite an impression on me, and Vincent and I discussed it in considerable length after he told me about it.) While my rendering is not an exact reproduction of what Vincent reported to me, it is, I think, reasonably accurate.

Let us go over the above transaction step-by-step:

1. There were four dozen Van Heusen shirts in the first carton, not three dozen as he had suggested to the thieves. Such shirts normally sell at $7.50 apiece in the legitimate retail market, but it is normal for Vincent to pay $1.00 apiece for them from thieves. Here he offers $35.00 for merchandise worth $350.00 at legitimate retail prices.

2. The second transaction involved sweater sets that Vincent estimates sell at $18.00 apiece in the legitimate retail market. There were three dozen in this carton. Vincent first offered to pay $3.00 apiece, but then raised the offer to $3.50 because he knew the thieves could not multiply by that number even if they actually knew how many sweater sets were in the carton. In this transaction Vincent offers $60.00 for merchandise he estimates to have a legitimate retail value of $348 (36 sweaters @ $18.00).

3. The third transaction involved two cartons of calf-height, name-brand support stockings which sell at $1.50 per pair in the legitimate retail market. To appreciate what finally happened in this transaction, one must keep in mind Vincent's original offer of twenty-five cents per pair. First, the intentional mistake with the $15.00 a dozen was to throw the count off on the total number of socks. There were three three-dozen boxes in each carton, a total of eighteen dozen, not six. Furthermore, Vincent added another mistake, which the thieves (not to mention the reader) may or may not have caught. Three dozen times twenty-five cents is $9.00, not $12.00. Vincent finally paid $25.00 for both cartons, two hundred sixteen pairs of socks with a legitimate retail value of $324.00. The cost per pair to Vincent was about eight and one-half cents.

4. The next transaction involved two very small cartons of men's leather gloves, two dozen pairs in each box. Both because the cartons were small and because the thieves were still confused, Vincent got away with his offer of $10.00 per carton. Vincent estimates that the gloves would cost $8.00 or $9.00 per pair at legitimate retail prices. I find the thieves' acceptance of Vincent's offer of $10.00 per carton extraordinary, but it is possible that they never

even saw what they sold Vincent. In this transaction Vincent manages to get away with paying $20.00 for merchandise with a legitimate retail value of some $400.00.

5. The carton which Vincent "hums" over contains another three dozen sweater sets. He figures them into his total by revising his earlier offer of $60.00 for an identical carton to $50.00 for each carton. The understanding on which this adjustment is conceded is that price ought to go down with quantity. This brings the total cost to Vincent for sweater sets with a retail value he estimates at $696.00 to an even hundred.

6. Vincent ignores the children's snow suits. When questioned about them he implies with his "personal use" statement that he was hoping the thieves would throw them in gratis. There were a dozen assorted snow suits whose total retail value Vincent estimates at $150.00. Vincent paid $25.00.

In sum, Vincent managed to pay only $200.00 for merchandise with a legitimate retail value of approximately $1,800.00.

Not all of Vincent's transactions are as complicated or as devious as the ones described above. Many of his purchases are rather quiet agreements, with Vincent offering a take-it-or-leave-it price. One must remember, too, that many of those who sell to Vincent have worked out "standard" arrangements on the prices they will be paid. These are subject to renegotiation only when the merchandise turns out to be something different from what Vincent had bargained for. For example, Vincent's office-machine thief would ordinarily be paid forty dollars for a used IBM Selectric or Executive typewriter in good condition. When he turned up with another brand, however, Vincent would cut back his price to thirty-five dollars. In such cases, though, Vincent might well buy him breakfast or offer him a drink.

Such "bonus" practices are standard operating procedure for Vincent. I have seen him pay a thief's cab fare, buy him breakfast, give him a sweater for his wife or girlfriend, and hand him toys for his children at Christmas time. Such practices are surely devices for "cooling the mark" after a sharp deal. They reflect Vincent's desire to maintain a good reputation among thieves and also to keep the particular thief coming back with merchandise. A thief who works regularly at his trade and steals quality merchandise is a valuable asset to Vincent. Such a person is as important to Vincent as a dependable employee would be to a legitimate businessman.

Vincent treats his truck driver patrons equally as well. He knows that they will almost never get caught if they exercise reasonable restraint; he tries to coach them if he thinks it is necessary.

See, I school my drivers. I mean, if they got an overload, that's a free thing, a gift. They can bring it to me just like it's legitimate. But stealin', I tell 'em, they just gotta use their heads. You pick a day when it's rainy an' cold an' the shipper's rushed. That's when you wanna throw on an extra carton. Or the same goes when you're deliverin'. If the guy's got five trucks waitin' he ain't gonna count what you got. It don't make sense to steal from your own truck either, if you can just as easy pick up a couple a cartons where somebody else unloaded 'em. Oh, I school my drivers; show 'em how to go about doin' things, you know.

Much the same is true with Vincent's waterfront, railway, and airport patrons, too. He is well aware of the reputation he has with union drivers and workers as a generous and receptive fellow. Vincent has told me a dozen times about how drivers will leave cartons on his doorstep or loading platform, to return for their payment at a time when they are not so busy. He is proud of the trust which such behavior signifies.

It is the case that some who bring merchandise to Vincent suffer more than others from his bargaining tricks. Drivers are a stable group, valuable, unlikely to bring on police investigation, and fairly knowledgeable about the value of what they have to sell. Warehouse workers and shippers are, as a group, equally stable; they tend to work out regular price arrangements of some duration. Shoplifters are safe but supply fairly small quantities; their expectation for a third almost always meets with argument. Occasional snatch-and-grab junkie thieves are undependable and quite likely to bring at least inconvenience, if not trouble, when they are arrested. Vincent deals especially hard with them, for the loss of their trade would be unimportant. Professional or semiprofessional thieves are valuable, at least a notch above the snatch-and-grab thief in their knowledge of merchandise, and worth maintaining not only with less moderate harassment, but also, when it is needed, with bail, attorney's fees, and maybe even a good word in the right place when possible.

No one escapes entirely unscathed, however, no matter how professional or how valuable. Vincent is a professional, too. Thieves expect some degree of hassling with their fence; if they don't get it, they think something is wrong.

I don't always argue with thieves, you know. The other day this thief came in with some stuff an' he said, "Mr. Vincent, I want forty dollars for this stuff. It is very good an' I don't want you to start tellin' me it's rubbish 'cause I know it ain't." I said, "OK here you go—forty dollars." Well, he looked at me an' he couldn't believe it. "You feel awright, Mr. Vincent?" "Whaddaya mean?" I said. "You always tells me how I got junk an' you ain't payin' me half a what I asked." "Well," I told him, "when you bring me good stuff, I buy right." That kind a bullshit's good for business once in a while.

While "buying right" is Vincent's goal, there are times when he fails to meet it. Such shortcomings are rare at this stage of his career. In twenty years of fencing he has developed not only a knowledge of merchandise but a sense for the suspicious situation as well. Nevertheless, errors do occur. Although not thoroughly examining the contents of cartons has its advantages for his trading, it can sometimes result in errors. On one occasion I know of, Vincent bought a carton of shoes which were manufacturer's samples; they were all left foots. In this case, as it happened, he sold them to a hustler whose greed for the good deal Vincent offered him caused him not to inspect his purchase.

A somewhat more serious error caused Vincent on another occasion to lose a large sum of money:

This guy says he's got a load of radios. He brings me in a sample an' they're real nice AM–FM, Magnavox, I think they was. They wholesale around thirty-five, so I made a deal for ten apiece. Now the guy says he's got fifty of 'em back in his apartment. His buddy's watchin' 'em. We take my truck an' drive to this apartment house in the black belt. One a them high-rise projects. Well, the guy goes in an' after about five minutes he's back out again. Says his buddy is fightin' with his girl an' he ain't takin' any radios out 'til he sees half the money. I figure I ain't goin' in that buildin' with all the dough I'm carryin', so I give him two hun-

dred. In those days I used to carry nine, ten thousand on me. Well, you know the rest. The guy never came back. I sat in my truck for an hour before I left. I was pretty mad about it at the time, but now I figure it taught me a lesson an' for two hundred it ain't that bad.

Apparently, Vincent did indeed learn from this incident. For what prompted his telling me about it and about the left-footed shoes and some other failures in his doing business was a similar attempt to sell him nonexistent merchandise. It happened one evening at his home when we were working at one of our regular interview sessions. The doorbell rang and Vincent responded by going to the window to see who was there. His apartment is on the second floor, so the entire conversation took place in something between loud talking and yelling. I stood behind Vincent, out of the thief's view, but could hear everything:

V. "Who's there?"

S. "It's me, Vince."

V. "Whaddaya want, Shakey?"

S. "Can I come up, Vince? I got somethin' for you."

V. "No! I got company. Whaddaya want?"

S. "I got some stuff for you over in that truck there."

V. "What truck? I don't see no truck."

S. "That green one right over there." [He indicates a small green panel truck parked about two hundred yards down the street.]

V. "Whaddaya got? Bring it over here. What's it doin' way over there?"

S. "I got sheets. Three big cartons a sheets. But it's my buddy, Vince. He says you cheated him once before an' he ain't comin' over here 'til he gets his money."

V. "You tell him I'll pay you both when I see what you got. Not until. You drive the truck here."

S. "I can't, it's his truck. Come on Vince, give me twenty-five to bring him an' maybe he'll come over."

V. "See me tomorrow, Shakey. I ain't got time for this bullshit. If you wanna do business get that truck the hell over here now, that's it."

S. "Please Vince, I need the money. He's not gonna come over 'cause he's scared a you."

V. "See you tomorrow, Shakey. Why don't you take it over to Larry's?" [the name of a local small-time fence].
S. "Aw come on, Vince."
V. "See you tomorrow if you wanna do business. I got company now."

Vincent closed the window. He told me, "He ain't got nothin'. He's just tryin' to get a few bucks outta me." Then he thought for a moment and started looking through a list of telephone numbers. "I'll bet that little rat bastard is gonna go try the same crap on Larry."[9] Vincent kept looking for the telephone number but couldn't find it, explaining that he had it at the store but not in the apartment. Vincent finally gave up looking for Larry's phone number, and we resumed our discussion on a new subject. I learned later that Shakey came to Vincent's store the following day and confessed that the incident the night before was indeed a ruse. I suspect that the confession was made not out of guilt, but rather on the assumption that Vincent had seen through it anyway. Shakey explained that his need for drugs prompted his disloyalty.[10]

There is one other, recurring situation that bears upon Vincent's buying techniques. We mention it here because of its potential use as a device to trick the fence into buying something that doesn't exist. Briefly, it is a kickback arrangement similar to that which Vincent uses with buyers whose companies do not condone their purchases of stolen property. Two thieves have merchandise to sell. One calls Vincent in advance of the transaction and explains that he is willing to sell their merchandise at a low price over the protestations of his partner if Vincent will slip him some money without his partner's knowledge. Usually this is done after the trade, but on rare occasions it may be done in ad-

9. This is not a hypocritical statement on Vincent's part, even though he suggested that the thief see Larry. Rather, Vincent suggested Larry because he probably would have called Larry and given him instructions to buy the merchandise for him. Only after he thought about the incident a bit did he realize that it was a phony scheme.

10. I suspect that had Shakey been successful in swindling Vincent out of twenty or thirty dollars, he still would have shown up at the store the following morning. Then Vincent might have acted angry or might possibly have joked about it; either way, the amount would have gone on Shakey's account until he brought Vincent more merchandise.

vance. Clearly, it offers the thief the option of never returning to
the fence if he can get his kickback before the deal takes place.
Attempts to swindle Vincent in this fashion are infrequent, because to secure Vincent's cooperation the thief would have to have
some substantial relationship with him already, which he would
risk losing if he incurred his wrath.

THE COMPETITION

Vincent's ability to "buy right" and to maintain the patronage
of those who sell to him is related to what the competition has to
offer. Vincent has, in general, a rather low regard for the character
and skills of his competitors, a view that is inseparable from his
own professional identity. Whatever their talents, there are some
features of Vincent's operation that give him a competitive edge.

First, his location is convenient to drivers who deliver and to
thieves who steal in the retail district of the city. Vincent is
simply more accessible than most of his competitors.

Second, he always has money to pay for what is offered to him.
The thief never has to wait for it.

*I used to carry a lot of money on me all the time—nine, ten
thousand was nothin'. But I got to thinkin', no need temptin' anybody to shoot me, so I don't carry that anymore. Why should I?
My bank's a block away. I just walk down there. In two minutes I
got more than I need.*

*[I ask, "How much do you carry with you now?"] Cash, I al-
ways got a thousand, fifteen hundred minimum. An' I also got a
couple of cashier's checks. I figure if the banks is closed I can always find somebody on the street who'll take 'em. [Vincent opens
his wallet and finds the cashier's checks. He hands a couple to me.]
Now whaddathey say? [He didn't have his glasses on.] One of
'em's a thousand an' the other's three thousand, right?" ["Right,"
I answered.]*

*See, I figure sooner or later if a thief is really takin' a lot of stuff
he's gotta get to me. I mean he's gonna burn out these little guys.
They just can't handle the merchandise that fast.*

Vincent's last statement suggests a third reason for his superior
competitive position with regard to other fences. Vincent finds

himself at a competitive advantage not only because he can pay immediately but also because he can handle large amounts of merchandise on a regular basis. Additionally, Vincent offers those who would sell to him the attraction of being able to buy whatever they have to sell. This convenience is not so important for the very specialized professional thief, but it is extremely attractive to the regular package or carton thief, the shoplifter, the waterfront, airport, or warehouse worker, and the truck driver.

Finally, all of Vincent's attempts to maintain a positive reputation among those who sell to him serve to make trading with him more attractive than with his less charming counterparts. The "bonus" deals, phony explanations, and occasional bail and legal assistance, as well as his attractive personality and advice, all sustain the opinion that one is better off doing business with Vincent. And his pointing out to his thieves how a particular thief ran into trouble shortly after dealing with one of his competitors encourages the impression that, he, unlike his competitors, has a certain integrity.

I have often asked Vincent about some of the other fairly well-known fences in the city. He usually finds them to be tolerable as competitors, although he always accompanies such concessions with remarks about his superiority. There are limits, however, to the extent to which he will tolerate their competition.

[*I asked, "Do you know Manny Levin?"*]

Yeh, I've known him for years. You might say I taught him how to be a fence. About ten years ago he used to be a bookie. He still is, but not like before. He had a horse parlor in my upstairs room for more than six months. Well, he owned a store out in Carter Heights and bought hot stuff now an' then but a lot of junk, second-hand stuff. Hangin' around my store he picked up a lot—you know, I'd talk to him, tell 'em how to do stuff.

After he moved the horse parlor outta here he really started dealin' big in swag. I didn't mind that, but pretty soon my men start tellin' me that Manny's tellin' them that I'm an informer, he's payin' better prices than me, all that kind a crap. Well one day, this guy I do business with regular says to me that some lady just gave him a business card an' that if he's got anything to sell, this guy gives better prices than me. I look at the card. It's Manny's card, phone number, store address, an' everything. That was it! Now I really got mad. After all I done for that Jew bastard, he pulls this kind a crap on me. I asked the shine where the woman was an' he said sittin' in a car on the corner of my street. Well, I went out there like a bull. She seen me comin' an' took off, but if I would'a got to her I would'a strangled her right there. So I figured I'd arrange a little trouble for Mr. Manny Levin. I'll tell you, Carl, when I get mad I can be treacherous.

First I got this guy I know to sell him a hot load an' then steal it back off him the same night. See, you get him double that way. First you take his money, then you get your merchandise back. It was a simple set up. He dropped the load to him at four an' took it back around eleven, and brought it to me. After that, Manny came by my store sayin' he heard I was out to get him. I said, "No, Manny, I just don't wanna see your miserable face around here no more." He got all upset. Said he never done nothin' to hurt me. I threw him outta my store. Told him never to come back.

Oh, every so often he comes by now, but I just don't wanna have nothin' to do with him. He's very sick now, you know. They say it's cancer.

Price Fixing

An occasional practice of price fixing increases Vincent's ability to buy right still further. I have never seen a completed instance of a fixed price arrangement, but Vincent explains its operation as follows:

Suppose I can't buy at a price I like an' I want the merchandise. Say whoever's got it wants a full third an' I don't wanna give no more than a fifth. So he walks out on me. With most guys I know where they're gonna go. I mean you know from where they live or who they hang around with, or who they done business with before. If I know the guy, I'll call 'em up. Tell him so an' so is probably comin' by with such and such. I'll tell 'em it's mine, an' don't pay no more than a certain amount. So when the guy gets there he'll get the same price or less than I gave him. He [the other fence] makes money for doin' nothin' an' I send Tony down to pick it up in an hour or so.

Such a practice probably has some hidden aspects that Vincent is not aware of. He assumes that the fence to whom the thief goes after seeing him will most likely buy at even less than instructed, but he is probably not aware that the greed of the second fence will serve to support his own claims to thieves that he pays more then other fences would. In addition, as price fixing always limits competition, it will also reinforce the fence's claims to thieves that the amounts offered are fair by prevailing fence-market standards.

Competition Reconsidered

Although we have referred to other fences as Vincent's competitors, the price-fixing practice suggests that Vincent's relationship with other fences is occasionally cooperative in character. In addition, for economic competition to occur it must be assumed that those who sell to Vincent have the alternative of selling to others and are able to weigh the advantages of doing so. Considering the evidence for the ignorance of many thieves regarding their merchandise and the markets for it, I have some doubt about their ability to judge the relative monetary advantages of doing business with one fence as opposed to another. The illegitimate market is relatively insensitive to differences in price. In addition, the channels of information about fences, and their prices and practices, are informal and rather unreliable. Thus, were another fence paying substantially higher prices than Vincent, many of Vincent's thieves and drivers would have no information network through which they would learn about it. Furthermore, the existence of price-fixing practices means that on at least some occasions the alternative of doing better business with other fences is blocked for the thief.

Consequently, the term "competition" can be only precariously employed to describe the economic relationships among fences and their impact on the way Vincent does business. Only in the very broadest sense can competition be said to affect the prices offered and paid. In a psychological sense it may give rise to Vincent's bonus deals, phony explanations, and solicitous manner of doing business. Such practices are effective in reducing or eliminating the threat of competitive selling among his thieves.

Vincent's location, his ability to pay immediately and to buy in large quantities, and his willingness to buy almost anything account far more for the thief's choice to do business with him than the prices the thief will be paid for merchandise. Such competitive advantages should not be considered less significant merely because they do not directly determine prices. In running a fencing business it is most important that one gets the first opportunity to buy merchandise. Location, ready money, and reputation get the thief to come to Vincent first, giving him the chance to apply those techniques of bargaining I have described above. One can always pass up an offer. One can never buy that which has already been sold to someone else.

Chapter 6

THE FENCE AND SOCIETY: VINCENT'S APOLOGIA PRO VITA SUA

> The more weakened the groups to which [an individual]
> belongs, the less he depends on them, the more he con-
> sequently depends only on himself and recognizes no other
> rules of conduct than what are founded on his private in-
> terests.
>
> Emile Durkheim, *Suicide*

It is my purpose in this chapter to report and analyze Vincent's
apologia pro vita sua.[1] It is not my contention that all fences see or
justify their behavior as Vincent does, any more than I maintain
that they all do business exactly as he does. I do contend, however,
that Vincent's explanations are something more than the rationalizations of one particular man with a particular life history. Vincent is neither neurotic nor psychotic. His apologia is persuasive,
successfuly mitigating the seriousness of his criminality not only to
himself but to some others as well. To discard his explanations as
simply fragments of illogic, defense mechanisms, or rationalizations

1. Chapter 26 of John Landesco's *Organized Crime in Chicago,* Part III:
Illinois Crime Survey (Chicago: Illinois Association for Criminal Justice,
1929), pp. 1043–57, is entitled "The Gangster's *Apologia Pro Vita Sua.*" The
Latin expression is, however, traceable to John Henry Cardinal Newman's
literary masterpiece (1864).

would seem at minimum a wasteful use of rather precious testimony.

Vincent is an especially good source for an elaborate apologia. On the one hand he loves his work, knows no other business, and has worked at criminal receiving for more than thirty years. He also has a substantial stake in his identity in this document. On the other hand, he is getting old, has seen a number of his peers die, and is wealthy enough to pack in the business immediately and never want for anything. He is still an Italian Catholic who once took the good sisters' warnings seriously. He has been extraordinarily successful all through his life in persuading people to do what they ought not to do.

One of the problems involved in securing a professional criminal's account for his life is that the only time he need offer it is when he comes into contact with curious or critical members of legitimate society who know he is a criminal. Consequently, one can probably not credit the apologetics of most professional criminals as authentic "working philosophies." But I think the situation with Vincent is different. He is a *public*, professional criminal; almost everyone he knows is aware that he is a fence. His friends and acquaintances include both upperworld and underworld types. In addition, part of his business includes giving off the impression that what he is doing is not "really bad" even though everybody knows it is illegal. The "public" fence always straddles the boundary between the insiders and outsiders in society. His success depends upon getting insiders to cooperate with outsiders through him. I do not believe that the apologia I present in this chapter was constructed just for me. I know that Vincent has explained his mode of life to many others in the same way, and I am further convinced that this is in fact the way he sees what he does.

Although there are no hard data on the subject, it is clear that there is a substantial trade in stolen property.[2] This trade requires, at least in part, the knowing participation of otherwise law-abiding

2. There is no way to make a reliable estimate of the total value of goods passing through the hands of fences like Vincent each year. Since 99% of Vincent's merchandise is new, it is certain that most of it comes from wholesale and retail businesses, including manufacturers, distributors, shippers, and warehouses. Business losses are uniformly entered under the category of "shrinkage," which includes employee theft, shoplifting, bookkeeping errors,

citizens. I venture to suggest that a good many of those who would buy stolen property would be outraged at the thought of committing robbery, burglary, or larceny themselves. Vincent's apologia inevitably plays on themes which support trade in stolen property in the society at large. His explanations are thus cultural artifacts, configurations of sentiment, reason, and perspective which are frequently effective in the rhetoric of our culture in defining the buying of stolen property as acceptable or excusable behavior. This view of Vincent's testimony suggests that the criminologist seeking to understand the role of the fence in society and the sociology of the trade in stolen goods may begin to do so by considering not only the truth of Vincent's apologia (that is, the extent to which it approximates his actual behavior and its effects), but also its capacity to assuage the norms which prohibit buying stolen property (and thus free men to do so if the situation presents itself).[3]

VINCENT SWAGGI: *APOLOGIA PRO VITA SUA*, PART I—"I DON'T DO NOTHING WRONG."

Legally, Vincent's acts constitute criminal receiving of stolen property. In the state in which Vincent works, a conviction carries

---

and some forms of embezzlement. In 1963 the "shrinkage" total for retail stores, estimated at retail prices, was $1,757,000,000. Of this figure, it was further estimated that $1,318,000,000 was due to some form of dishonesty. There is no way of estimating what percentage of this figure represents merchandise that was eventually fenced. One must remember also that this figure applies only to retail businesses and does not include burglary, hijacking, or theft from the cargo industry, including trucking, shipping, or air freight. President's Commission on Law Enforcement and the Administration of Justice, Task Force on Assessment, *Crime and Its Impact—An Assessment* (Washington, D.C.: Government Printing Office, 1967), pp. 48–49.

3. Essays in the theoretical tradition that this chapter follows include the following: C. Wright Mills, "Situated Actions and Vocabularies of Motive," *American Sociological Review* 5 (1940): 904–13; Marvin B. Scott and Stanford M. Lyman, "Accounts," *American Sociological Review* 33 (1968): 46–62; Gresham Sykes and David Matza, "Techniques of Neutralization," *American Sociological Review* 22 (1957): 667–69; and especially David Matza, *Delinquency and Drift* (New York: John Wiley and Sons, 1964). The full theoretical grounds of this perspective on the social order as I understand it are best set forth by Kenneth Burke in *A Grammar of Motives* (New York: Prentice-Hall, 1945) and *Permanence and Change* (New York: Bobbs-Merrill Co., 1965).

the penalty of imprisonment for up to five years plus a fine of as much as $1,000. With the state's indeterminate-sentence law operating so as to perfunctorily reduce all sentences to one-half the maximum penalty, the maximum time Vincent would serve would be two and one-half years. Vincent correctly considers his conviction exceedingly unlikely and his serving a maximum sentence impossible. In more than thirty years of criminal receiving, Vincent has spent only eight months in jail; his only conviction for receiving was more than twenty years ago. The judgment of the law, except insofar as it codifies certain normative evaluations, is irrelevant to Vincent.

Only Vincent's buying and selling of stolen property threatens his respectability. At first glance, such a statement seems a truism; certainly the reason Vincent is of interest to criminology is that he is a fence. Yet, the context in which otherwise deviant or criminal behavior occurs enormously affects society's evaluation of that behavior. Consider the words with which our language reflects a social evaluation of those who violate an identical law in the case of prostitution. Is a "kept woman" a "slut"? Is an "escort" a "whore"? Is a "lady of the evening" a "hooker"? Certainly no poet, specialist in meaning and impression, would use such words interchangeably. Homosexuality, generally regarded as deviant, seems infinitely more acceptable to society when it is packaged in respectable speech and attire than when it appears in lisping drag. Likewise, it seems easier for society to regard the addiction of the physician or the alcoholism of the housewife as a "disease" than to accept the same affliction in the street addict or skid-row bum. Although other factors are also effective in shielding the white-collar criminal from the social and legal definition of his acts as crime rather than as civil or administrative violations, it would seem that his face of respectability saps our enthusiasm to class and house him with "real" convicts.[4]

The apparatus and behavior of the fence are not especially dif-

4. Cf.: "Legislators admire and respect businessmen and cannot conceive of them as criminals; that is, businessmen do not conform to the popular stereotype of 'the criminal.' " Edwin H. Sutherland, "Is White Collar Crime Crime?" in *White Collar Criminal*, ed. Gilbert Geis (New York: Atherton Press, 1968), p. 360. See also Richard Austin Smith, "The Incredible Electrical Conspiracy," *Fortune* (April 1961), pp. 132–80, for an application of Sutherland's observation.

ferent from that of the legitimate businessman. They exist as synecdochical evidence of respectability and affirm that, with the exception of the fact that the fence buys and sells property which is stolen, he is no different from his legitimate-businessman counterparts. For Vincent, his store, his customers, and his legitimate associates simplify his apologia pro vita sua. He need not contend with offensive side effects of his deviance on his presentation of self for they are absent or minor. Instead, he can get right on to the business of showing why his buying and selling stolen goods ain't really that bad after all.

DENIAL OF RESPONSIBILITY

The way I look at it, I'm a businessman. Sure I buy hot stuff, but I never stole nothin' in my life. Some driver brings me a couple a cartons, though, I ain't gonna turn him away. If I don't buy it, somebody else will. So what's the difference? I might as well make money with him instead of somebody else.

In the above statement Vincent (1) denies that he ever stole anything in his life. He then asserts either directly or by implication (2) that there is an important distinction between stealing and receiving stolen goods; (3) that the criminal act of receiving would take place even if he were not the one to do it; and (4) that he does not cause the goods to be stolen. Let us consider each of these defenses separately.

He Never Stole Anything in His Life

In two rigorous senses Vincent has stolen. First, in a number of anecdotes about his childhood (see Chapter Two), Vincent has described his juvenile industry at theft. He dismisses those events as irrelevant to the above statement, explaining that although he says "never in my life," his childhood does not count. This is illogical in a strict sense of the words used. However, biographical claims are often intended more as moral advertisements than historical descriptions. When such is the intention, it is quite acceptable social form to exclude from public reflections on "true character" those moments of one's life when one was not in full control of one's self. Consider such statements as, "All my life I've followed the Golden Rule." (From age 2? 7? 19? 21?) Or, "He really is a gentle man, but watch out when he's drunk."

Second, according to a strict legal interpretation of his adult behavior, Vincent does steal. He does, as the common-law definition of theft provides, "take the goods of another, without permission, with the intent to permanently deprive that person of his rightful property." However, the law makes distinctions between theft and receiving (often attaching a lower penalty to receiving), and I suspect that few readers are troubled by Vincent's simultaneous claim both that he has never stolen anything and that he does buy stolen property. It is, for most of us, an understandable social distinction. What Vincent means is that he is not a thief.

There Is an Important Distinction Between Stealing and Receiving

Vincent claims not to be a thief, and we understand what he means. For Vincent himself, there are differences not only between thieves and receivers, but also between thieves and drivers.

See, Carl, what you gotta understand is when I say "driver" I don't mean "thief." I don't consider a driver a thief. To me, a thief is somebody who goes into a house an' takes a TV set and the wife's jewelry an' maybe ends up killin' somebody before he's through. An' for what? So some nothin' fence will steal the second-hand shit he takes? To me that kind a guy is the scum of the earth.

Now a driver, he's different. A driver's a workin' man. He gets an overload now an' then or maybe he clips a carton or two. He brings it to me. He makes a few bucks so he can go out on a Friday night or maybe buy his wife a new coat. To me, a thief an' a driver is two entirely different things.

Those things which distinguish the driver and the thief in Vincent's estimation may point to distinctions that the larger society makes between receiving stolen goods and actually stealing them. The fence, like the driver, does not enter homes or stores to remove property; there is no danger of violence in his presence. A thief, on the other hand, could do anything: he may well be a drug addict, rapist, robber, burglar, or assaulter, or, if the situation arose, a murderer. Society has no clear expectations about the limits of criminality involved.

On the other hand, a fence, Vincent claims, is a businessman who buys and sells stolen property. Like the driver, the fence commits his crime in the course of behavior which differs only minutely from that of legitimate members of his trade. And like the driver, the fence has a relatively stable social identity: the driver will presumably be at work again tomorrow; Vincent is in his store every day of the week. Vincent buys and sells things, waits on customers, and walks public streets openly. Truck drivers perform public tasks as well. Thieves are shadowy figures, sneaking around behind the scenes and even hiding their right names behind aliases.[5]

In sum, when Vincent begins his apologia by saying "I never stole nothin' in my life," he magnifies a common distinction between a receiver and a thief. He means, first, that he does not actually take merchandise from its owners. But second, and more importantly, he means that the fear, disgust, and distaste which "thief" connotes to some people should not and do not properly apply to him. The law, his customers, his friends, and his neighbors know there are differences between thieves and receivers, and so does Vincent.

Receiving Would Take Place Even Without Him

By saying "If I don't buy it, somebody else will," Vincent attempts to minimize his responsibility by pointing to the presumed consequences of his private refusal to buy. They are, he asserts, nil; therefore his responsibility is nil. This is a patently attractive moral position, and one which is echoed frequently. Let us first

5. The matter of "potential for deviance," by which I mean people's estimations of the probability that one type of deviance implies the capacity for other types, merits systematic criminological examination. As an example, our treatment of the insane by incarceration seems to presume that relatively mild violations of social propriety suggests a capacity for more serious and perhaps violent deviance. Similarly, before the time when long hair was co-opted by an economic establishment willing to capitalize on it, long hair seemed to be regarded by many as a certain sign of the willingness of the wearer to engage in other, non-tonsorial, forms of deviance. Likewise, society may well assume that, all other things being equal, a thief has a greater "potential for deviance" than a fence.

examine the accuracy of the assertion before evaluating the moral position which Vincent derives from it.

Would someone else buy the merchandise if Vincent refused? I think they probably would. Although Vincent is able to dispose of some merchandise which other fences might have great difficulty selling (e.g. dental supplies), the vast majority of merchandise in which Vincent trades could be handled by many other fences. The related question, of course, is whether or not the particular thief or driver who approached Vincent with stolen property would be able to locate another fence to sell to if Vincent refused. This is problematic. In my estimation, many would find another outlet almost immediately, some would find one after a bit of looking and asking, and a very few might not be able to find another buyer. Depending on the character both of the merchandise and of his friends and neighbors, the thief or driver might well be able to sell stolen merchandise to them at a better price than he could get from Vincent.

If the accuracy of Vincent's statement is conceded, its moral implications remain to be considered. Certainly one can find examples of the same form of rationalization being offered in quite disparate social situations. The physician on trial for performing a criminal abortion claims that he performed the requested operation rather than have the woman find another, possibly less competent, conspirator. The arms manufacturer claims that he cannot be held responsible for a war because if he had not sold weapons to the participants they would have bought them elsewhere. Likewise, the conscripted soldier who opposes war but fights anyway may take comfort in the knowledge that his participation will not affect the waging of a given war or its outcome.

The moral position upon which such arguments rest is that a person's culpability for participation in an immoral or illegal act disappears or is mitigated if the act is likely to occur even if he does not participate in it. Such a position can be extended to cover situations even less pleasant that those listed above. For example, it removes responsibility in almost all incidents of mob violence. Is no one in a lynch mob responsible because others are also willing to string the victim up? Is looting at a riot scene excusable because others are looting too? Is vandalism blameless when it is a group affair? To push the position harder still, one could envision a small team of paid professional killers who always shoot their victims simultaneously so that no one gunman feels guilty. Even firing squads, so legend has it, reject such nonsense by actually loading one gun with blanks.

Responsibility for action is responsibility for action. Whether or not an act is likely to occur without one is simply irrelevant to the evaluation of one's own conduct. To surrender that elementary premise of simple moral philosophy is to abandon the responsibility to refuse to participate when one believes that others are doing wrong. Middle-class mothers everywhere, sensitive always to the seductions of the world, have correctly admonished their children who "went along with the crowd": "Just because everybody else jumps off a cliff doesn't mean you have to." It is an admonition of considerable rhetorical sophistication which has absolutely nothing to do with jumping off of cliffs, but gets instantly to the heart of patently attractive denials of responsibility like "If I don't buy it somebody else will."

He Does Not Cause the Goods To Be Stolen

With this statement Vincent suggests his relationship to drivers (and, by extension, thieves) who supply him with stolen merchandise. In Vincent's consideration he is merely a commercial respondent to theft whereas it is thieves and drivers who must bear responsibility for it.

For Vincent, the etiology of theft is a considerably less difficult problem than it is for criminologists: people steal because they want money. Why else should anyone steal? In general, why they want money is their own business, but Vincent, like most small businessmen, is close enough to those he works with to reflect on their motives. For most thieves, Vincent finds that drugs, gambling, and "high living" (Cadillacs for blacks is Vincent's most frequent example) are the main incentives for illegal earnings. Drivers, on the other hand, often use the proceeds from what they sell to add "a little extra" to the family income. To Vincent, it is preposterous to suggest that it is he, rather than the factors which thieves and drivers themselves cite, that is responsible for theft.

Some recent criminology, at least, claims otherwise:

> This coaching (in methods of theft) by the fence in rational
> criminal techniques may lead to a reevaluation of the risks

involved in criminal activity, which can be an important
escalating career contingency. . . . Additionally, this same
effect is achieved merely by meeting the fence and conclud-
ing a successful transaction with him.

If we can argue . . . that we will always "produce" deviants
so long as we have an established machinery for processing
them, then it might also be legitimate to suggest that the
same can be said about the impact of supporting elements.
Thus the continued existence of fences, tipsters, and similar
types will tend to assure that we will always produce new
deviants.[6]

Thus, Shover contends that fences encourage thieves and drivers
by approving of their stealing and advising them how to steal
successfully. In addition, fences may, simply by their continued
existence and availability as fences, tend to assure the continuing
existence of a population of drivers and thieves.

Shover's argument is compelling, and with a few technical
reservations (see pages 164–166 in this book) Vincent is inclined
to agree with this sophisticated sociological rendition of the old
adage "If there were no receivers, there would be no thieves."
However, Vincent's sense of his own personal responsibility for
the stealing by thieves and drivers is quite a different matter. It is
at this individual level that the norms of Vincent's world and
Shover's sociology part company.

In the same way that Shover's argument suggests that the continued existence of public bars assures the continued existence of
a population of alcoholics, or the manufacture of high-powered
cars "produces" highway speeders, or the existence of gambling
casinos "escalates the career contingencies" of compulsive or in-
temperate gamblers, Vincent conceeds that fences are a part of the
machinery that sustains and encourages theft. But with a logic
that I suspect is familiar to, at least, bartenders, high-powered-car
manufacturers, and casino owners, he argues that "I don't force
anybody to do business with me who doesn't want to." Vincent
further insists that adults are adults and "should know what they
are doing."

6. Neal Shover, "Structures and Careers in Burglary," Journal of Criminal
Law, Criminology, and Police Science 63 (1972), pp. 545–549.

Vincent views his own life history with a similar sense of individual responsibility. He can see how some of his early experiences—street hustling, his orphanage term, his association with his Uncle Hoppo—may have encouraged his becoming a fence. ("I guess I picked up a lot of my ideas from hangin' around with Hoppo and those guys.") But there is no sense in which Vincent would blame anyone else for where he is and what he does today. To do so would strike Vincent as unmasculine, the mark of a weak person or cry baby.[7]

In denying his responsibility for theft in this way, Vincent takes the question of his responsibility to an area with which he is most familiar—one in which moral and legal grounds for establishing responsibility are constantly shifting. Consider the case of the vendor of alcoholic beverages. One can state categorically that if there were no alcohol there would be no abuse of alcohol, no alcoholics, no drunken driving, no public drunkenness. Nevertheless, it is generally conceded that vendors of alcohol ought not to be held responsible for their customers' abuse of it. Normally, the consumer bears the total responsibility for his use or misuse of what he buys. However, in particular circumstances, the vendor may acquire both legal and moral responsibilities for his customers. He cannot, for example, sell liquor to minors, nor, according to the law in many states, can he sell it to an obviously intoxicated person. In still other states, the law requires that he provide transportation home for a patron who is unfit to drive. In each of these special cases the loss or absence of the consumer's adult capacities may legally if not morally oblige the vendor to assume them. There is some point beyond which legal responsibility cannot be extended for practical reasons, but how far ought one to

---

7. Or, occasionally, the ploy of criminals hustling those with social-worker mentalities (Robert Earl Barnes, "The Fence: Crime's Real Profiteer," *Reader's Digest* [September, 1973], p. 155):

> My criminal career began when I was ten years old and I stole a bundle of comic books from a drugstore doorstep. When I tried to trade them to the local barber for some in his shop I hadn't read, he wouldn't barter—but he did offer to buy all the comics I could provide for two cents each. He never asked, but I'm sure he knew they were stolen. From that first transaction, I learned what every professional thief must know: there's no use stealing unless you know someone willing to pay for the goods you steal. . . .

extend moral responsibility? Should a bartender serve a customer who has cirrhosis? Or, are even the above laws too morally and legally paternalistic, denying one's right to get drunk in public if he wants to?[8] There are no certain grounds, legal or moral, upon which to settle such questions.

Similar problems, both moral and legal, are involved in many transactions between buyers and sellers. The question is always "Who is responsible?" and, ultimately, it must be resolved in favor of one party or the other. The bartender must know if he is obliged to serve the intoxicated person who demands another drink or if he is obliged to refuse him and call a taxi to take him home. When Vincent argues that it is the thief or driver and not he who is responsible for theft he employs a notion of responsibility which is derived from and is peculiar to business transactions. For Vincent, responsibility is an either/or proposition, as it must be in relations between buyers and sellers. It works on the principle of subtraction: if the thief is responsible for his stealing then Vincent is not.

The highly peculiar quality of Vincent's subtractive sense of responsibility becomes apparent when one takes it out of the context of business transactions. Elsewhere, the notion of responsibility is governed not by a principle of subtraction but by a principle of addition. It is perfectly normal to refer to two, three, ten, or even hundreds of, people as being responsible for a given act or event. And it is, of course, with this additive concept of responsibility that the law prohibiting criminal receiving is justified and the moral responsibility of the criminal receiver established. Simply stated, the thief is responsible for his stealing and the criminal receiver is responsible for encouraging that theft.

8. A case in point: an article in the London *Times*, for Friday, March 8, 1974, entitled "Publican Criticized over Death of Customer."

A publican served two double measures of Chartreuse and five double Pernods to a customer who had already drunk 11 or 12 pints of beer, an inquest heard today. The customer fell off his bar stool and died. . . . The coroner said both Mr. Moseley [the publican] and Mr. Lewis [the man with whom the customer was engaged in a drinking competition] were both stupid and irresponsible in their actions. Mr. Ross's [the dead customer's] drinking was incredible and abnormal and Mr. Moseley in particular ought to have realized it was reaching the danger level. Irresponsibility did not amount to manslaughter.

DENIAL OF VICTIMS

The first line of defense in Vincent's apologia is his denial of responsibility for theft and his argument that for him to refrain from buying stolen goods would be inconsequential. His second line of argument is to deny that his activities have any meaningful victims or inflict any significant injury. To appreciate Vincent's second defense one must consider some of the experiences from which he reasons.

More than most people, Vincent witnesses extensive violations of the law against receiving. He sees respectable society, including police and judicial officials, coming to him for bargains that they know are suspect. Because of his reputation, he is often solicited by otherwise legitimate businessmen interested in buying something that they deal in should he come across it. He also encounters respectable types who find something romantic about his being a fence. For example:

I got to know my doctor real good when I was in for my last operation. Somebody told him about me, I guess. Well, I started tellin' him about stuff, you know, buyin', sellin', thieves, boosters. He just couldn't get over it He wanted me to get him some hot suits. You know, have him pick out the suits and send some boosters in to get 'em. He really wanted to do it. You shoulda seen how excited he was talkin' about swag. Imagine a guy like that, a big doctor an' all, gettin' so excited about hot stuff.

This widespread trafficking with him, and occasional fascination for his work, have consequences for the way Vincent sees his own behavior. First of all, he is conscious of a certain hypocrisy in society's attitude toward dealing in stolen property. He is aware of the legal prohibition against receiving, yet sees frequent evidence of willful, guilt-free violation of it by those who ought to know better. Vincent's recall of occasions when highly respectable citizens bought stolen goods or what they thought were stolen goods is extremely acute. Legitimate citizens of high status are truly "significant others" for Vincent.

Indeed, Vincent sees the patronage of such legitimate citizens as a reflection of his own worth. Their buying from him and maintaining friendly relations with him are considered by Vincent to constitute an important vindication of the possibly shady character of what he does. It is true that Vincent is an attractive and enjoyable person; but even if his friendly acquantances seek him out only for this social aspect of his personality, Vincent finds it easy to perceive that they are not sufficiently offended by his receiving to limit their association with him.[9]

Given the highly supportive character of Vincent's immediate environment, he is able to think of his victim and the injury he receives as someone or something "out there," removed from him physically and normatively, and separated by the intervening actions and responsibility of the thief or driver. Only very rarely does Vincent ever confront the victim of a theft. The latter is likely to direct his rage at the thief, his employee's carelessness, or his faulty security system rather than at the fence who eventually buys what was stolen from him.

From this detached perspective, Vincent contemplates the extent of his victims' losses:

Did you see the paper yesterday? You figure it out. Last year I musta had $25,000 worth a merchandise from Sears. In this city last year they could'a called it Sears, Roebuck, and Swaggi. Just yesterday in the paper I read where Sears just had the biggest year in history, made more money than ever before. Now if I had that much of Sears's stuff can you imagine how much they musta lost all told? Millions, must be millions. And they still had their biggest year ever.

Vincent reads Sears's declaration of success as evidence of the inconsequential character of his receiving their stolen merchandise. Hence he considers any possible claim on their part that he or hundreds of others like him are substantially harming business as at least greedy if not absurd. The logic of such an analysis is the same, on a larger scale, as the "Ma Bell can afford it" reasoning

9. The idea of innocence by association raises important questions for researchers in the sociology of deviance. Simply by associating with deviants the field researcher gives tacit reinforcement to them. My association with Vincent was interpreted by him as quite complimentary, and the vast majority of thieves I have interviewed have felt similarly flattered. My generally nonjudgmental attitude was uniformly construed as approval. Likewise, I find that a text like my own is easy to interpret as being supportive of deviant careers in spite of my protestations that it is primarily descriptive and analytical, in the way sociology must be. A similar case can be made regarding the degree of attention paid to militant blacks in the liberal press. (See Nathan Glazer and Daniel P. Moynihan, *Beyond the Melting Pot*, 2d ed., rev. [Cambridge: M.I.T. Press, 1970], p. lxxxvii).

invoked by the pay-phone patron who receives a windfall from a malfunctioning unit. Vincent does not stop there in his consideration of Sears's success, however.

You think they end up losing when they get clipped? Don't you believe it. They're no different from anybody else. If they don't get it back by takin' it off their taxes, they get it back from insurance. Who knows, maybe they do both.

Carl, if I told you how many businessmen I know have a robbery every now an' then to cover expenses you wouldn't believe it. What does it take? You get some trusted employee, and you send him out with an empty truck. He parks it somewhere an' calls in an' says he was robbed. That's it. The insurance company's gotta pay up. The driver makes a couple a hundred bucks and it's an open-an'-shut case. You can't do it every year but once in a while it's a sure thing.

Oh, there's millions a ways to do it. You come in in the mornin' an break your window. Call the cops, mess some stuff up. Bang! You got a few thousand from the insurance company. I'm tellin' ya, it happens all the time.

Thus Vincent denies significant injury to Sears not only because of their net profits but because they can be seen as recovering most of their loss from insurance payments or through tax write-offs.[10] The reality for Vincent, in sum, is the comparatively trivial effect of theft on the insured victim. Inconvenient, perhaps; devastating, no! Hence: no real injury, no real victim.

The problem remaining is the general effect on pricing that theft produces. As a businessman, Vincent is in agreement with his counterparts that theft and shrinkage result in higher mark-ups and higher prices. But Vincent again falls back on the question of

10. Months after Vincent told me about his views on Sears's profits in spite of their losses from theft, I ran across the following obscure news item (John Manning, ed., "No Money Down" [Philadelphia: Publication of the Model Cities Consumer Protection Program, vol. 1, no. 3], p. 3). It is rather perverse to print it here but I cannot resist the irony.

SEARS FASTBUCK: Second Income News relates how Richard W. Sears, founder of Sears, Roebuck, got started in business. Sears was a railroad telegrapher with a sideline business of selling watches. His gimmick was to buy watches at $2 apiece, affix $20 price-tags, and mail them to fictitious locations across the country. When the packages came back "undeliverable," Sears would open them in presence of fellow employees and palm the watches off as "bargains"—at $10 apiece.

the ultimate consequences of his particular refusal to buy. Assuming his thieves and drivers could not find anyone else to sell to, the entire result of Vincent's private refusal to buy might amount to a penny a person for the entire year, if it were distributed over the total population of the city. And on the other side of the ledger, Vincent reckons that some of his other services to the general welfare of the community more than balance what he takes out.

The questions of the moral responsibility involved in buying stolen goods, and of the consequences of such an act for any putative victims, would be even less problematic for Vincent's customers than for Vincent were they to confront them. Given that a particular item is on Vincent's shelf and is known to be stolen, a particular purchase will not affect Vincent's survival as a fence. I do not believe that a rational economic argument can be made against an individual decision to buy stolen goods. The claim that theft costs everyone as reflected in higher costs and insurance rates is inadequate. It costs everyone surely, but those who buy stolen goods manage to offset these higher costs and rates. In fact, were it simply a question of a personal economic strategy, one might argue that the only way to beat the consequences of the thieves' market is to patronize it. The only argument left seems to be to appeal to a responsibility to the general welfare of others.

To legalize receiving stolen goods would legitimize an institution which is intolerable. It would encourage theft and have a pernicious effect on society. Clearly it is an absurd suggestion. But the conflict is still real. The department-store sweater costs $15.99. Vincent is selling it for $10.00. In this particular case it is a question of saving $5.99 or making an economic gesture to the general welfare. All day long Vincent sees the general welfare lose out to bargains.

VINCENT SWAGGI: *APOLOGIA PRO VITA SUA,* PART II—"I THINK I'M A PRETTY DECENT GUY."

To this point Vincent's apologia has focused on what he considers to be the particularly benign features of his occupation. He finds no victims and no real injury. He denies responsibility for theft and its encouragement. He maintains that his private refusal to buy stolen property would be inconsequential. Vincent reaches these conclusions about the character of what he does by interpreting his day-to-day behavior in the most favorable possible way. I have been able to point to these errors in Vincent's analysis because this portion of his apologia was an analysis of concrete events. In short, I could compare Vincent's evaluation of what he does and has done with descriptions of the events themselves.

In this second portion of his apologia Vincent changes the character of his account from a professional, offense-specific defense of his criminal career to a more general evaluation of his character. The assertion Vincent made in Part I of his *Apologia Pro Vita Sua* was that he didn't do anything wrong; the assertion he makes in Part II is that he is, all things considered, a nice guy.

Because the terms of Vincent's argument change in this second portion of his apologia, it is difficult to criticize what he says. Specific acts, their consequences and interpretation, are not at issue. Hence the critic of Vincent is disarmed, because no particular act of Vincent's will disprove his claims. Contrariwise, the nature of the way Vincent makes his argument ensures that a complete display of evidence in favor of his claim (viz., in spite of everything he has done, he is a decent fellow) need not—indeed can not—be made. I have called the sensibility within which Vincent comprehends his good character "the metaphor of the ledger."

THE METAPHOR OF THE LEDGER

Sure I've done some bad things in my life. Who hasn't? Everybody's got a skeleton in his closet somewhere. But you gotta take into account all the good things I done too. You take all the things I done in my life and put 'em together, no doubt about it, I gotta come out on the good side.

As a businessman, Vincent is familiar with the use of a ledger for evaluating the success or failure of enterprise. He knows that there are different ways of setting up and managing accounts. Some entries are puffed a bit more than they deserve; other profits don't show up in the counting. Occasionally, one shows a loss so as to make things look normal or to prevent having to pay too much in the end. Business accounts, properly managed by able accountants, set things in order for the businessman and those who are interested in judging what he has accomplished. When all is said and done, the ledger tells whether or not one comes up in the red or in the black.

A metaphorical ledger is equally useful in evaluating life histories: good in the credit column is balanced against evil in the debit column. Thus, acts of charity and benevolence offset entries of greed or selfishness. It is an attractive metaphor. From the scales of justice to the Great Book of St. Peter, the notion of a balancing between good and evil has proven to be a persuasive one for the common comprehension and consideration of penance, indulgence, grace, judgment, atonement, salvation, and contrition.[11]

To Vincent, a businessman all his life, the metaphor of the ledger comes easily. In accounting for his conduct, Vincent considers his criminality and his exemplary behavior on the same balance sheet.

When it comes to fences I consider myself in a class by myself. I don't consider your street-corner fences, buyin' an' sellin' second-hand stuff, to be anything like me at all. For one thing they're all no good. They're all cheap, greedy bastards who'd sell their mother if they had a chance. I figure I have a certain class, ya know, a certain way of doin' things. To me them guys are nothin'. They're stupid, ignorant people. I can't even stand bein' around 'em.

Thieves and Drivers

In reckoning credits for his self-evaluation, Vincent points to those good things he has done for people which his role did not require him to do. For example:

Take what I done for Artie, for instance. Now there's a guy,

---

11. Reference to a Book of Life wherein all of man's deeds are recorded is found throughout Scripture. For example, Rev. 20: 11–15 states:

[11] Then I saw a great white throne and him who sat upon it; from his presence earth and sky fled away, and no place was found for them. [12] And I saw the dead, great and small, standing before the throne, and books were opened. Also another book was opened, which is the book of life. And the dead were judged by what was written in the books, by what they had done. [13] And the sea gave up the dead in it, Death and Hades gave up the dead in them, and all were judged by what they had done. [14] Then Death and Hades were thrown into the fire; [15] And if any one's name was not found written in the book of life, he was thrown into the lake of fire.

he's been a thief for years, an' nothin' to show for it. That year alone I musta given him $25,000. One day I'd give 'em a hundred bucks, the next day he'd be back askin' for a loan. So I had a talk with him. I told him, "Look, you're makin' good money. Why don't you put it toward a house?" So we set up a little deal where I'd keep a little each time we had a deal; then when he had enough we'd put it toward a house.

Well it took about three months an' he had about $1,500 with me. So I got a real-estate agent I knew to get him a place, nothin' fancy but a pretty good neighborhood. It was colored but clean. Well, you know what happened? His wife came down with his kids an' she couldn't thank me enough. They had been livin' in one of those welfare high rises and she hated it. Every now an' then she comes by to tell me how things are goin'.

Don't get me wrong. I made a lot of money off of Artie, but I set him straight too.

What places Vincent's efforts in Artie's behalf on the credit side of the ledger is the fact that Artie and his wife appreciated Vincent's assistance and that Vincent did not have to give it. Vincent has repeated similar anecdotes to me frequently.

I am good to children. You know "Eyeball," right? All the trouble I had with him? His wife came in at Christmastime last year. When she left she had at least a hundred dollars worth of clothes and toys for her kids. I knew Eyeball was in jail an' she didn't have nothin'. Carl, if you knew how much stuff I gave to people, outright gifts, you wouldn't believe it.

Would you believe it if I told you that I got a thief who calls me "his white father"? It's true. I been good to him. Posted bail for him a couple of times. He tells everybody, "Vincent Swaggi, he's my white father."

The matter of the posted bail in the second anecdote raises a number of complications in the matter of crediting Vincent's generosity. One could interpret Vincent's bailing out the thief as self-serving, since Vincent knew that once back on the street, the thief would resume bringing him merchandise. The extent to which such actions should be seen as impelled by generosity becomes even more problematic in those cases where Vincent benefits more than does the recipient. Many people turn to Vincent for "help" when they are in a jam and don't know what to do. Providing alibis, referrals to persuasive lawyers, loans at high interest, and the kind of encouragement a man occasionally needs to get back to his work are all well appreciated. Just a little bit of help sometimes pays off handsomely.

I had this guy bringin' me radios. Nice little clock radios, sold for $34.95. He worked in the warehouse. Two a day he'd bring me, an' I'd give him fifteen for the both of 'em. Well, after a while he told me his boss was gettin' suspicious 'cause inventory showed a big shortage. So I asked him how he was gettin' the radios out. He says he puts 'em in his locker at lunch an' takes 'em to me after work. So I ask him if anybody else is takin' much stuff. He says a couple of guys do. I tell him to lay off for a while an' the next time he sees one of the other guys take somethin' to tip off the boss. They'll fire the guy an' clear up the shortage. Well he did it an' you know what happened? They made my man assistant shipper. Now once a month I get a carton delivered right to my store with my name on it. Clock radios, percolators, waffle irons, anything I want, fifty off wholesale.

Though Vincent is reluctant to place such profitable assistance in his credit column, one must consider the matter from the perspective of the newly appointed shipper: Vincent advised him well. He saved him from his suspicious boss, cleared his reputation, got him promoted, probably with a raise, and made it possible for him not only to increase his earnings from theft but to steal with greater security as well. For Vincent, on the other hand, such an incident cancels itself out; it was good advice which paid off. Yet, although such events cannot, because they paid off so well, be offered individually as evidences of virtue, in the aggregate they enhance Vincent's professional self-conception. However, they leave a residual magnanimity which surfaces in statements such as the following:

I treat the people I deal with right. If they're in a jam an' I can help 'em out, I'll do it. And I don't mean just your high-class types either. I mean thieves, drivers, police, customers, anybody. I'm known for helpin' people out when I can.

You don't have to be a bastard to be in this business, you know. You can treat people decent. Some guys, like my brother, never learn that. They think a black man comes into the store, you can push 'm around, call him "colored" or "boy"; you just can't do that no more. Times have changed.

*I am liked by the people I do business with. No doubt about it.
They know I treat 'em right. Look at my window. You see any
grate over it? How long have you known me? More than a year
now, right? Did you ever see that window broken? With all the
characters I do business with, how long do you think it would be
before somebody threw a brick through it if they didn't like me?
I am known for bein' good to people. That window's been there
ever since I had this store. Nobody ever touched it.*

Vincent is sensitive to the opinions people have of him, even if
those people are only thieves and drivers. When his daughter's
home was robbed, he explained, "You know, Carl, if it's somebody
I know, I'm hurt. If not, God bless 'em." This remark, although a
bit more sentimental than usual for Vincent, is interesting. It
reveals both an expectation of occupational loyalty and a kind of
professional respect. "God bless 'em" ought not to be interpreted
as implying a passive response, however. Vincent worked very
hard at locating the culprits.

The difficulty in finding unambiguously creditable behavior for
the positive side of the ledger is that in relations with thieves and
drivers the roles of "good fence" and "decent guy" are in part
congruent. Self-interest becomes visible in generosity, and profits
make altruism suspect. Such an opinion is possible, though, only
to those permitted a full account of the fence's operations. While
Vincent is aware of the payoffs for him in acts of apparent
generosity and assistance, his thieves are not. His manipulation of
them with such impressions has been documented in earlier chapters. If Vincent is liked, appreciated, and thanked, he does not advertise his altruism; in fact, he is likely to minimize the importance
of his own acts. ("It was the least I could do. Don't get me wrong,
I made a lot of money off of him.") By doing so he is thus freed
to accept the gratitude and appreciation of those he helped. These
responses Vincent remembers, reminds me of, and credits to the
good side of the ledger.

Customers

Vincent's customers provide him with frequent opportunities
for creditable behavior, but just as with thieves and drivers, questions of self-interest plague Vincent's accounting. "Bargains," "Just-
for you" prices, and doing people "favors" by selling them mer-

chandise at 30% below wholesale evoke favorable attitudes, but just don't qualify as hard evidence of goodness, because they are too much a part of what is required in a fence's business. The following incident is clearly creditable to the good side of the ledger, but it also suggests how difficult it is to be good when self-interest is suspected.

The other day this old lady comes in my store. She's Irish, got a brogue so thick you could cut it with a knife. I can tell she ain't got much. I mean her clothes were cheap an' she's got this real thin cloth coat on. You remember how cold it was last Wednesday? Well, she's real old-country, kerchief on the back of her head an' all.

She says she's lookin' for a sweater 'cause it's so cold out. I tell her she don't need a sweater, what she really needs is a good heavy coat. She says she ain't got enough money for a coat now. So I ask her how much she got an' she says six dollars. "Six dollars," I say. "Are you in luck, Mother. I have a special sale on coats today, but you can only get one if you're Irish."

"I'm Irish," she says. "No," I say, "really?" I'm givin' her the whole bullshit, you know.

Anyway, I show her three coats I got in the back. They were samples, retail maybe $45 or $50. "Are you selling these for only six dollars?" she says. "Ya," I say, "but only today and only if you're Irish. Are you sure you're Irish?" "Aye," she says, "I sure am." Then you know what she says to me? She says, "What's wrong with these coats?" Fifty-dollar coats for six dollars and she asks me what's wrong. "The buttons are the wrong color. They're black an' they should be brown." I gotta tell her somethin' or she wouldn't buy it. So I take her six bucks so she won't think it's charity.

You know, she comes back to shop every so often. Do you know she still doesn't understand I gave her that coat. She thinks I had to sell that coat for six bucks 'cause the buttons were black instead of brown.

It is important to remember that within a few minutes after this incident of generosity Vincent was probably back at his characteristically very sharp trading. There is no illogic in bargaining extremely hard at one moment and virtually giving away goods at the next. The former confirms a professional, businesslike self-conception; the latter demonstrates that one is a good man.

Generosity and creditable behavior are possible only when the motives of Vincent's customers are innocent. To be generous when the recipient of your generosity is an able and aggressive economic foe not only is unprofessional but also leaves one open for being seen as a sucker.

I got this guy who comes in every so often, he's an insurance agent. He walks all over my store—behind the counter, in the back room, everywhere. He's a real tight bastard, a Jew. I can't stand him, you know. One day I got a store full of customers. I'm sellin' like mad. He's pullin' stuff off my shelves an' he comes over with a couple of sweaters. "How much for me, Vince?" he says. I say, "Whaddaya mean, 'how much for me?' " So he says, "You know, what's my price on this stuff?" So I really let him have it. I start yellin', "What the hell makes you think you get a special price? What makes you think you're better than anybody else? Take this old lady here. You think you're better than her? She's the one who really deserves a special price." Well, the whole store gets upset. The guy don't know what to do. "OK, OK, Vince," he says. "Take it easy. I didn't mean nothin'. Take it easy. Tell me what the price is, I'll pay it." "No," I says. "To you it's not for sale; you ain't buyin' nothin' in here today." I told him that. Threw him right outta the store. I'll tell you, sometimes I just can't stand that kind a guy.

With those who by definition do not act out of self-interest, on the other hand, charity and generosity are easy to establish.

You know how much I do for children, right? The other day this nun comes in from the House of the Good Shepherd. Oh, I known her for years. If you knew the stuff I gave her—shoes, clothes, toys, everything. Well, she comes in and my brother and Kelly, Happy, an' another hood are all in the store too. Well, I give her a pile of girls' dresses I was savin' up. Then I says, "Wait a minute, Sister, I think we can do a little more for you." So then I turn to everybody in the store an' I say, "When was the last time you gangsters did anything for the little children of this world?" I said, "I'm gonna give Sister here twenty dollars an' I'm gonna put four tens out on the counter. Each one of you guys puts up a ten, the Sister here gets another ten too." Well, my brother, he runs in the back room, and that fatso, Happy, runs out the door. Both of 'em have more money than they know what to do with, but they're just cheap bastards. So Kelly and the other hood are stuck.

*They gotta put up the dough or they look bad. Well, I gave the
Sister the other twenty, too. On the way out, she says to me, "Are
those men really gangsters?" I said, "Ya, they been in rackets all
their lives." Then she says to me, "Hmmm, they did look a little
shady."*

The Police

Sometimes Vincent claims credit for his actions for reasons more
subtle than outright charitableness or benevolence. This is particularly so with respect to his acts of cooperation with the police.

*I had a computer once, you know. [I respond, "A computer?"]
Ya, a computer. Two guys drove up to my store in a truck. They
said they had a machine in the truck they wanted me to look at. It
was a computer right out of the University. I don't know how
they got it out, but it was about as big as that chair [a large re-
cliner]. I said, "Look, there ain't nobody nowhere gonna touch
that. It must have a million numbers on it." Well, we talked
about it for a while an' they took my advice. I gave 'em fifty bucks
an' told 'em to unload it on my platform. Then I called this In-
spector I know an' told him what I had. Do you know he got the
report it was missin' right while I was talkin' to him on the phone?
That machine was worth twenty or thirty thousand dollars. If I
didn't take it off those shines, they would'a dumped it in the river.
See, the police department knows that I'll help 'em out when I
can. An' I never took no reward for doin' that, either.*[12]

Vincent's assistance here qualifies as creditable behavior not so
much because it was virtuous in itself (the computer was returned
rather than destroyed), but because no special claim for its goodness was made (no reward was taken).

And sometimes Vincent's motives for what would be considered

---

12. Maurer notes that pickpockets occasionally return wallets containing
valuable papers to their owners after the money has been removed. Usually
this is done by disposing of the empty wallet in a post office box. "This is
not done," says Maurer, "for reasons of sentiment, or fair play, or consideration for the sucker. It is done for reasons of public relations. . . ." David
W. Maurer, *Whiz Mob* (Gainsville, Fla.: Publication of the American Dialect
Society, 1955), p. 119. "Public relations" are far more essential to the fence
than to the pickpocket, and the similarity in public relations technique is
notable.

creditable behavior are more subtle than those of either simple benevolence or simple self-interest or a mixture of both:

I had two guys, black guys, drive up one day. They had rifles. I could tell just by lookin' at 'em they were Army rifles. So I told 'em I'd take all they could get, an' they said they had thousands of 'em. They left, and right away I got on the phone to a guy I knew from the FBI. I told him I didn't want the guys arrested, but I didn't want all these guns gettin' into the hands of Black Power, either. So I got the OK to buy. They found out they were comin' out of a boxcar an' stopped it. I figure I done a good thing there, don't you?

I agreed, as Vincent knew I would. And so did the FBI. Vincent demonstrated not only civic responsibility but also self-sacrifice: he could have made a great deal of money. He also evidenced certain limits on what he will do, apparently owing in this case to his harboring certain fears and attitudes regarding potential recipients of the weapons. But self-interest is always in dogged pursuit of Vincent. The reader is invited to consider the above anecdotes in light of Simmel's classic understanding of gratitude:

> This irredeemable nature of gratitude shows it as a bond between men which is as subtle as it is firm. Every human relationship of any duration produces a thousand occasions for it, and even the most ephemeral ones do not allow their increment to the reciprocal obligation to be lost. In fortunate cases, but sometimes even in cases abundantly provided with counter-instances, the sum of these increments produces an atmosphere of generalized obligation (the saying that one is "obliged" ["verbunden"] to somebody who has earned our thanks is quite apt), which can be redeemed by no accomplishments whatever. This atmosphere of obligation belongs among those "microscopic," but infinitely tough, threads which tie one element of society to another, and thus eventually all of them together in a stable collective life.[13]

13. George Simmel, "Faithfulness and Gratitude," in *The Sociology of George Simmel*, ed. and trans. Kurt Wolff (New York: The Free Press, 1964), p. 395.

DEVIANT BEHAVIOR AND THE METAPHOR
OF THE LEDGER

No one has ever seen a real "ledger" for life. Yet it is an old
theme, and one which has caused no small amount of controversy.
The theological grounds of the debate between Luther and the
Roman Catholic Church were not simply the abuses of the
Roman Church in selling indulgences, but whether or not good
works (like giving money to the church) could, in the heavenly
ledger, balance out sins.[14] However, in no way does the metaphor
of the ledger disappear with the Reformation. One finds it equally
reflected in the *values weighed* and *balanced* under the *calculus
of price* in *utilitarian* ethics.[15]

But Vincent's sense of the metaphor of the ledger is neither
careful Catholic theology nor a neo-Benthamite utilitarianism. It
is, rather a common-sense perception of the vague standard by
which most of us evaluate men—one that is metaphorically
embedded in our language almost everywhere we speak of evaluation. Consider "pay off," "dividend," "cost," "value," "price,"
"good" and "goods," "waste," "profit," and "debt." The words of
business come easily to us in our reflections on morality. The
judge declaring that the prisoner has "paid his debt to society"
speaks in the moral metaphor society is willing to hear. Vincent—
a businessman, Catholic, and self-made man—takes to the metaphor of the ledger naturally. It does not emerge as his instrument
for moral evaluation in concrete references to a real book of life
or a real ledger kept in heaven. Vincent does not believe in such
a real book in any way. Rather, the mechanism of the metaphor

---

14. In 1517 Luther posted his Ninety-Five Theses on the side door of
the Castle Church at Wittenberg. Theses no. 40 and no. 44 (quoted in John
Dillenberger, ed., *Martin Luther* [New York: Doubleday and Co., 1961], p.
494) are particularly relevant:

>   no. 40 A truly contrite sinner seeks out, and loves to pay, the penalty
>   of his sins; whereas the very multitude of indulgences dulls men's
>   consciences, and tends to make them hate the penalties.
>   no. 44 Because, by works of love, love grows and a man becomes a
>   better man; whereas, by indulgences, he does not become a
>   better man, but only escapes certain penalties.

15. See "Secular Mysticism in Bentham" in Burke, op. cit., pp. 188–94,
for Burke's study of the metaphors which seduced Bentham.

of the ledger is hidden in the way he organizes his apologia and the impression he intends from offering his positive anecdotes.

When Vincent says, "You gotta take into consideration all the good things I done, too," the question in response might well be "Why?" To ask it would be to challenge the metaphor of the ledger hidden within it. But Vincent would not understand the question, any more than most of us would think to ask it. The metaphor of the ledger is driven deeply enough in our consciousness that the question would be dismissed as annoying "philosophical meddling" with what everybody knows is "just common sense."

But, as we have seen, Vincent's eye for the loophole works as well with the metaphor of the ledger as it does with the morality (and law) of criminal receiving. His sense for the balance between good acts and bad, for the credit he earns for his charity, and for the existence of a debit column in every man's ledger allows him to make a favorable accounting of his life. In so doing, he manages to preserve his faith in a moral order not notably different from that which most of us accept. However, his sense of the metaphor of the ledger allows him to loosen the restraints of that moral order just enough to emerge from a thirty-year criminal career with a positive, moral, decent self-image.

Chapter 7

THE SOCIOLOGY OF VINCENT'S PLACE

There are many paths which stolen property takes from thieves to eventual consumers. Some are relatively uncomplicated and involve only the thief or his agent selling to friends, neighbors, and acquaintances under the cover of friendly or neighborly privacy. Other paths lead through sheltered markets like bars, luncheonettes, and beauty parlors with the encouragement if not participation of their proprietors. Still other paths, like that characteristic of the trade in stolen securities, are at once more specific and technical and require skilled and sophisticated conduct of the successful dealer. With notable exceptions, descriptions of these and other paths are lacking in the criminological literature, and no reliable information is available on the relative contribution of different patterns of sale and distribution to the overall flow of stolen property from thieves to eventual consumers.

This poverty of criminological information taxes the analysis in this chapter in three different but not unrelated ways. A primary difficulty is the absence of a satisfactory conceptual vocabulary for talking about the trade in stolen property and Vincent's place in it. It is obvious that Vincent is but one type of dealer in stolen property, but it is unclear exactly how one ought to draw lines which link him to others like him and distinguish him from other, unlike types. Similarly, the spotty and uneven character of descriptive information that is available makes comparison of Vincent's ways of doing business with those of his contemporaries, on the one hand, and those of his predecessors, on the other, highly unreliable. Virtually all such information is secondhand, and most of it is informed by romantic or correctional attitudes toward the fence which introduce understandable, but nevertheless impedimentary, distortions. Finally, as against the limp and distant portraits of most other fences, the detailed portrait of Vincent assumes an authority which may be unwarranted. That is, the model of Vincent may appear bigger, more important, and more representative than it ought to be. Thus, while considering the sociology of Vincent's place some cautions, corrections, reservations, and distinctions are necessary.

THE RECEIVER'S RELATIONSHIP TO THEFT

A history of attentions to criminal receiving and the trade in stolen property could be written about the saying "If there were no receivers there would be no thieves." It has served as a rallying cry for reformers at least since Patrick Colquhoun's pioneering studies of receivers in late eighteenth-century London.[1] Even then Colquhoun was obliged to acknowledge its antiquity: "Nothing can be more just than the old observation, 'that if there were no receivers there would be no thieves.' "[2] Since Colquhoun, many other students of the fence have repeated the phrase exactly as

1. Colquhoun wrote two books which dealt extensively with the trade in stolen property: A Treatise on the Police of the Metropolis (Printed by H. Fry for C. Dilly in the Poultry, 1796) and A Treatise on the Commerce and Police of the River Thames (London: Printed for Joseph Mawman, 1800). The latter volume contains a list of twelve different types of receivers to be found along the Thames at the turn of the century.
2. Colquhoun, Treatise on the Police of the Metropolis, p. 184.

he quoted it, while others have said the same thing in more colorful language. In 1872 a military metaphor captured the imagination of the crime-fighter Edward Crapsey, who observed that without the receiver "the rogues would be an army without arms."[3] In 1887 Matthew Davenport Hill suggested that the thief without the receiver would "resemble a merchant in the desert, who could not exchange his goods for the necessaries of life."[4] It is likely that Hill's observation was intended to counter George Mainwaring's too-true contention that the phrase was actually misleading. Mainwaring maintained that it was actually the case that if there were no thieves there would be no receivers.[5] Most recently Robert Earl Barnes, a thief, added some badly needed insider's precision to the axiom: "Without the receiver of stolen property, none of the burglars—cat burglar, monkey man, or business specialist—could survive."[6]

Although the interests and enthusiasm of the above authors are most manifest in their poetic decorations of "if there were no receivers there would be no thieves," the observation itself is better understood as an hyperbolic plea for attention to the criminal receiver than as an accurate statement of his relationship to theft. Many thieves work without the aid of a receiver and others without the aid of a criminal receiver. The thief who steals money, credit cards, or checks which he passes himself, or goods for his own consumption, has no need of a receiver. Such thieves include petty pilferers, nonprofessional shoplifters, pickpockets, confidence men of many varieties, and those who take money by force or threat of force from institutions and individuals. Furthermore, there are thieves who manage to sell stolen property to unknowing and unsuspecting (and therefore noncriminal) receivers. Even the most scrupulous pawnbrokers, secondhand merchants, auctioneers, and junk dealers buy stolen property on occasion. It is also reasonable to suppose that in the hypothetical eventuality

3. Edward Crapsey, *The Nether Side of New York* (New York: Sheldon and Co., 1872), p. 83.

4. Matthew Davenport Hill, *Suggestions for the Repression of Crime* (London: John W. Parker and Sons, 1837), p. 67.

5. George Mainwaring, (*Observations on the Present State of the Police* [London 1822], pp. 213–14). Mainwaring was of the opinion that receivers ought to be considered a "mere commercial body."

6. Robert Earl Barnes, *Are You Safe From Burglars?* (Garden City, N.Y.: Doubleday and Co., 1971), p. 142.

that all receivers, criminal and noncriminal, were to disappear, many thieves would continue to exist by shifting their stealing to non-receiver-dependent lines. In brief, if there were no receivers, there would still be all sorts of thieves, and possibly more thieves of sorts we don't like than we have now. In either case, reflection on the consequences of the utter disappearance of receivers, criminal or not, is academic even when it is not hyperbolic.

PROBLEMS IN THE CONCEPT OF "RECEIVER"

An historical impediment to thinking clearly about the trade in stolen property that is even more serious than the axiomatic imprecision of "If there were no receivers there would be no thieves" is the concept of "receiver" itself. Born of legal convenience and developed in the naive infancy and awkward adolescence of the industrial revolution, it has never been a satisfactory vehicle for describing the trade in stolen property.[7] Consider the difficulty in applying it to the simple case of Otis that follows.

Otis, a drug addict, steals mostly meat. He steals from the meat counters of supermarkets in cold weather by loading eight flat cuts beneath his long coat: two under each arm, two in his trousers, two beneath his shirt. In hot weather, when his long, heavy coat would raise suspicion, he steals meat only on rainy days, when his raincoat covers his haul. On warm, sunny days Otis shoplifts small domestic items which fit easily into his pants pockets or beneath his light jacket.

All that Otis steals he sells at half the store-marked price to people on his "route." Otis's route consists of some two dozen families in his neighborhood. Otis visits each family once or twice a week. On the average he is able to steal thirty packages of meat per day, which brings him from forty to sixty dollars. All sales are cash; no one gets credit. Otis has no trouble finding customers.[8]

7. The most thorough study of the growth and development of the law against criminal receiving is in Jerome Hall's *Theft, Law, and Society*, 2d ed. (Indianapolis: Bobbs-Merrill Co., 1952), especially pp. 52–62, 70–79, 155–232.

8. The case of Otis is based on an account by Sonny, Otis's brother and a drug pusher, whom I interviewed while he was in prison. See Chapter 8, p. 206 ff.

If one looks at the case of Otis with the concept of receiver as given by law, the only receivers visible are Otis's customers, the families along his route. Their crime is buying stolen property while knowing that it is stolen. Otis himself, the distributor of stolen property, is by law a thief and cannot, therefore, be his own receiver. Legally, this exception is quite reasonable. To fail to exclude the thief from prosecution as his own receiver would make every thief guilty of receiving. Thus, the first difficulty with "receiver" is that it is incapable of comprehending the thief who is his own distributor.

In order to side step that first problem with the concept of receiver and to proceed to more fundamental difficulties, another figure may be added to Otis' case: his wife, Nora. Frequently, Nora sells what Otis steals. She knows other women in her neighborhood who do the same, and she realizes that the arrangement takes advantage of a natural division of labor. Her husband can continue to steal while she peddles what he steals in the course of her normal, neighborly contacts. By adding Nora to the distribution path, a receiver appears where there was none before. But what is interesting about Nora's appearance as a receiver is that she becomes one not for doing what Otis had done (selling stolen property), but for accepting stolen goods from her husband knowing that they were stolen.[9] Nora's selling of stolen property is irrelevant to the question of whether or not she is receiving it.

Jerome Hall has observed that this total emphasis which the law, in the concept of "receiver," places on one small part of the traffic in stolen property distorts a proper portrait of the traffic in two ways.[10] First, it ignores many relevant activities in the distribution of stolen property: organization, interests, intent, skills, and the receiver's relationship to thieves and customers. This defect is especially apparent in the case of Nora. Although she sells Otis's spoils along a regular route and earns a profit which sustains her husband's thievery, she is a receiver, by law, only insofar as she is

9. At common law the situation would have been even more complicated. A husband could be convicted of receiving from his wife, if he knew what he was receiving was stolen and if he had not forced her to steal it. A wife, however, could not be guilty of receiving from her husband; nor because she was unable to commit larceny of her husband's goods, could anyone who received his goods from her be guilty of receiving.

10. Hall, op. cit., pp. 155–56.

a knowing taker of stolen property like her customers, and for no other reason. Secondly, says Hall, "receiver" is a defective concept because "*the ultimate consumer is lumped in the same category as the professional buyer.*"[11] That is, the law not only recognizes no difference between Nora and the families on her route, but also fails to distinguish between the families on her route and Vincent. How Hall chose to revise the concept of receiver, and whether or not that revision is suitable as a way of approaching the sociology of Vincent's place, must be examined here.

HALL'S TYPOLOGY OF RECEIVERS

In the fifth chapter ("Receiving Stolen Property") of *Theft, Law, and Society*, Hall presents this typology of receivers of stolen goods: *The Lay Receiver*—"one who knowingly buys stolen property for his own consumption"; *The Occasional Receiver*—"one who buys stolen property for resale but very infrequently"; and *The Professional Receiver*—"the dealer in stolen goods." Hall admits that the "difference between the occasional receiver and professional receiver is partly one of degree," but adds that "the professional, however, maintains an organization."[12] The lay receiver and occasional receiver are defined in a footnote and receive only the briefest mention anywhere else in the chapter. For Hall's intents and purposes they are dispatched in an aside, discharged and forgotten. They are, of course, the only participants in the trade in stolen property who might adequately be described as "receivers."

It is Hall's intention, though, to change the emphasis in thought about the trade in stolen property from the reception of stolen goods to the buying and selling of them. With his typology Hall makes the change so directly and simply that the reader is likely to miss it. By defining "professional receiver" as "*dealer*," Hall effects two complete transformations instantly. Both are crucial. First, "receiver" is changed from a word which once meant "one who accepts or receives," to a technical legal term of no descriptive significance. Put differently, as a jurist and historian, Hall is stuck with the word "receiver." At the same time he realizes that

11. Ibid., p. 156.
12. Ibid., p. 156.

as long as it remains tied to its ill-formed legal and conceptual roots, it will impede the reorientation in thought he deems necessary. He therefore keeps the word out of historical obligation, but with "dealer" defines away the meaning it once had. In "professional receiver," "receiver" means nothing at all. Hall then is free to perform a second emphatic transformation: to saturate the conceptually empty "receiver" with "professional" and spend the remainder of his pathmarking chapter picking up the wealth of connotations which accompany it—rationality, organization, discipline, planning, status, and skills. The following paragraph is suggestive of Hall's impression:

> The amount of merchandise a [professional] receiver buys is affected by a number of factors: the condition of the market in general; the amount of capital which he has; the difficulty of securing the merchandise, which is determined by the measures that the industry concerned has taken to protect itself, rather than by the activities of the police; and the receiver's contact with potential buyers. Of all these factors, fluctuations in the general market are the most important conditioning forces upon the receiver's purchases, and consequently upon professional theft.[13]

There is no doubt but that Hall's typology, his emphatic transformation of "receiver," and the ideal descriptive section which followed them served his needs perfectly. They de-emphasized receiving stolen property and dramatized the skillful, rational techniques of the professional dealer. They gave the law a new image of the conduct it was designed to control and the criminal it had to contend with. Both images were highly critical of the concept of receiver in law, and both images suggested that substantively and administratively the law was lamentably inadequate to the task of controlling the skilled, professional, criminal dealer in stolen property. Unquestionably Hall was right.

However, on other grounds and for other purposes and perhaps in the long run for his own, Hall's typology and the elaboration which followed it are unsatisfactory. It bears reemphasis that Hall had no way of knowing what proportion of the traffic in stolen property passed through professional receivers. In spite of this lack

13. Ibid., p. 160.

of information (or possibly because of it) his images of lay and occasional receivers are unduly sparse and flat. They suggest nothing of the trade in stolen property among amateur thieves and dabbling dealers which thrives in bars, schools, offices, factories, and neighborhoods.

At the same time Hall did not take the amateur trade in stolen property seriously enough, he took the idea, the *image* of the professional too seriously. Hall, himself a professional, must surely have known that professionals, even learned ones, are not nearly as rational or disciplined nor perfectly formidable as they let outsiders believe they are. In the paragraph quoted above, which enumerates the factors affecting the amount of merchandise the professional receiver buys, the difficulty is not with what Hall says, but with what he does not say. There is no room in his analysis for other factors: the competence of the receiver, his business acumen, the attention he gives to his work, his industry or indolence, the condition of his health, his relationship with his wife, the intonation of his voice, or the quality of his (manipulative) smile. Hall's image of the professional is ideal. It admits no bungling, no stupidity, no laziness, no poor judgment, no misunderstandings, no pathos, and no humor.

Hall's omissions may in part be due to the sources of his information. The law enforcers, insurance investigators, prosecutors, and security agents he interviewed may have been outsiders to the receiver's world. Even if they were not, an elaboration of the human failings of those on the other side of the fence might have threatened their sense of their own professionalism or competence. It is one thing to account for a conviction or apprehension as a triumph of one's own superior professional skills, quite another to explain your victory as the plodding product of your opponent's bungling. However, Hall's too-perfect picture of the professional receiver derives more, I think, from his need for a characterization that would give him the greatest possible critical leverage in dislodging the awkward, inadequate, and antiquated concept of "receiver." In choosing "professional" he found an image suitable to his task, but unrestrained and unmodified, it forced too narrow, too disciplined, too neatly rational and technical an impression to capture the entire class of activities he sought to describe.

No metaphor should be taken literally, and all metaphors should be dropped once they have served the purpose for which they are essential. It ought not to be urged against lawyers that they are not artists.

THE CONCEPT OF "PROFESSIONAL FENCE"

At the present time, the data on the traffic in stolen property cannot sustain any typology which is true to those who participate in it. The concept of receiver is inadequate and awkward; while Hall's best image of the trade and its traders is inhuman. Any approach to the sociology of Vincent's place must take these critical limits into account.

With respect to those limits, the concept of "fence" has much to recommend it. Typologically, "fence" makes no claims and carries no obligations. Fences are part of the traffic in stolen property, but to discuss them does not preclude the possibility that superior categorizations are possible. Fences are obviously an important part of the trade in stolen property, but they may or may not be the most important part. Conceptually, fence is not tied to the legal heurisms that "receiver" is. It has never been part of law, but it has always been linked to it. Possibly most important of all, "fence" has survived in the common language and in the cant of thieves and fences for at least two centuries.[14] Its meaning is historically and socially fixed, and though subject to misuse, is acceptable to insiders. Moreover, the bits and pieces of literature which do make reference to the fence suggest connotations which are sociologically valuable.

What then are the criteria which distinguish the fence from other traders in stolen goods? Three, at least, govern its most ex-

14. The first reference to the verb "fence" noted in Eric Partridge, A *Dictionary of the Underworld* (New York: Bonanza Books, 1961, p. 235) is "Rowlands, *Martin Mark-All,* 1610." In a pamphlet by Charles Hitchen attacking Jonathan Wild, the noun form of "fence" is described as a word "in vogue" among thieves. *The Regulator; Or, A Discovery of the Thieves, Thief Takers, and Locks, alias Receivers of Stolen Goods, in and about the City of London* (London: Printed for T. Warner at the Black Boy in Pater-Noster Row, 1718), p. 19. Although the word is recorded in many sources between 1610 and the present, Partridge states that it did not become common slang all over the world until 1900.

pressive use. First, the fence must be a *dealer* in stolen property; that is a buyer and seller with direct contact with thieves (sellers) and customers (buyers), not simply a member of a burglary gang charged with selling what is stolen, nor a thief hustling his own swag, nor an "in-between man" or "piece man" trading on his knowledge of where certain types of property can be sold.[15] Second, the fence must be *successful:* he must buy and sell stolen property regularly and profitably, and have done so for a considerable period of time, perhaps years. Third, the fence must be *public:* he must acquire a reputation as a successful dealer in stolen property among law breakers, law enforcers, and others acquainted with the criminal community. He must arrive at a way of managing the full significance of that reputation.

So defined, "fence" is a satisfactory vehicle for thinking about the kind of trader in stolen property of which Vincent is historically and sociologically typical. I have chosen to add the adjective "professional" to stress certain characteristics which already inhere in the definition of fence: career, occupation, certain skills, and ability. In "professional fence," the word "professional" denotes nothing that is not already inherent in the concept of fence, but, in a way that is analytically harmless, suggests that certain features of the fence are more distinctive than others.

BECOMING A PROFESSIONAL FENCE

The theory begins with the person who will eventually manage to become a professional fence. Because achieving that status will require certain uncommon talents, it is necessary to begin with

15. "In-between man" is Hall's term, op. cit., p. 162. "Piece man" is mine, via a Federal Prison inmate from the New York City area who referred to himself as such. Both terms refer to someone who accepts merchandise from thieves and transfers it to the real buyer for a percentage or "piece" of the value of the goods. For his percentage, the piece man or in-between man is obliged, should he be identified by the thief, not to divulge the identity of the ultimate buyer. In the words of my informant, "Any big buyer is willing to give up points for protection." I believe that piece men or in-between men are usually specialists in one product line, probably trading on contacts they make within an industry. I have it on similarly bad authority that the equivalent of the piece man in the small trade–generalist fence industry is a "street man," someone rather like a number writer, who frequents certain areas and buys stolen property as an agent for a fence. Both are East Coast terms, and Vincent hasn't heard of either.

something more than an average, healthy, young man or woman. The reader has undoubtedly developed a sense of Vincent's character, but the following observation by Howson goes beyond what one could learn from our introductory sketch of Wild:

> Wild had no sensitivity, probably little creative imagination and, morally, he was an oaf. But he did have an abundance of what the eighteenth century called "Genius"—that is, ingenuity, cunning, resource, energy and that mysterious power we sometimes call "personal magnetism." He was able to manipulate thieves for so long because, I suspect, they felt he was really on their side, no matter how murderous his behavior. . . .[16]

Howson's characterization deserves particular attention because it is informed by an historian's interest in describing the personal talents at the source of an extremely influential historical career. While it is both evaluative and descriptive, its intention is analytical. His choice of "Genius" in its eighteenth century sense applies expressively to Vincent and is echoed in characterizations of fences by writers differently informed but in this respect equally informative.

Among those whose interest in the fence was corrective, some of the strongest contentions for the uncommon talents of the fence come from the first systematic American study of fencing ever published, *Criminal Receivers of the United States*:

> The burglar, the footpad, the sneak thief, the dishonest tradesman, equally depend wholly upon the cunning brains and well-perfected technique of the receiver to convert their booty into cash. The twentieth century fence is no fugitive Fagin, no shabby Mother Mandelbaum, but a resourceful operator, with connections both in the underworld and in the realm of seemingly honest business. He employs every known device to camouflage his calling.[17]

16. Gerald Howson, *Thief Taker General* (New York: St. Martins Press, 1971), p. 286.

17. Prison Committee of the Association of Grand Jurors of New York County, *Criminal Receivers of the United States*, subtitled: "Social and Economic Problems of the 'Fence'—Source of Organized Crime and Creator of Criminals" (New York: G. P. Putnam's Sons, 1928), p. 11. Mother Mandelbaum, alias "Marm" Mandelbaum, was born sometime around 1825.

While it would be unfair to accept "resourceful" and "cunning" from the Prison Committee of the Association of Grand Jurors of New York County without acknowledging that their use of these terms was self-serving as well as descriptive, the same qualities are identified by Howson and do apply to Vincent.

The characteristic of "personal magnetism" does not escape corrective impressions of the fence either, although since Fagin, its effect upon poor children has been a frequent theme. In his novel *A Child of the Jago*, Arthur Morrison describes Mr. Aaron Weech who is about to corrupt little Dicky Perrott:

> He was a pleasant man, this Mr. Aaron Weech, who sang hymns aloud in the back-parlour and hummed the tunes in the shop. A prosperous, white aproned, whiskered, half-bald, smirking tradesman, who bent and spoke amiably to boys looking sharply in their eyes, but talked to a man mostly with his gaze on the man's waistcoat.
>
> Indeed, there seemed to be something about Mr. Aaron Weech especially attractive to youth. Nearly all his customers were boys and girls, though not boys and girls who looked likely to pay a great deal in the way of refreshment, much as they took.[18]

Although one might be tempted to write off such literary treatments of the fiendish personal magnetism of the fence as creations of romantic literary imagination, documented cases of the Fagin myth survive even in the criminological imagination way beyond their time and explanatory capacities:

She weighed 250 lbs., was the "Jewish Mother" to hundreds of thieves, and has been called the most successful receiver of stolen goods in the history of New York City. Her success lasted from about 1860 until 1884 when she fled to Canada. She was not "shabby" however. Her home at 79 Clinton Street was decorated with elegant furniture. Marm "entertained lavishly with dances and dinners which were attended by some of the most celebrated criminals in America, and frequently by police officials and politicians who had come under the Mandelbaum influence." Herbert Asbury, *The Gangs of New York: An Informal History of the Underworld* (New York: Alfred A. Knopf, Inc., 1928), p. 215.

18. Arthur Morrison, *A Child of the Jago* (New York: Duffield and Co., 1896), pp. 65–66.

In one neighborhood in Boston there was a modern Fagin, called "The Lobster" by the children in the neighborhood. . . . For many years his ramshackle house has been the rendezvous for the boys and girls in the surrounding neighborhood, and he had displayed an aptitude that might well be termed genius, in discovering and developing the peculiar weakness of the individual child, and then twisting and further distorting that trait, till the child was prepared to enter upon a career of juvenile delinquency. With fiendish precision and ingenuity he had planned his illicit laboratory, carefully planting and fostering various vices and apportioning that iniquity to the individual child that best suited its characteristics.[19]

Descriptions of the personal magnetism of the fence vis-à-vis adults can also be found, but they are rarer. Christmas Humphreys says of the fence "Cammi" Grizzard: "Of middle height and somewhat portly build, his impudence and swaggering self assurance served to create a personality which dominated the small fry who hung about the 'Garden' [an area in London], and turned them when required into willing, if not able tools. To create the impression of settled opulence he invariably appeared with an enormous cigar beneath his blonde moustache or held in the diamond-studded hand with which he waved away objections to his flow of arrogance."[20] Similarly, Edward Crapsey describes William Brandon, "artist in evil" and professional fence of the 1870s in New York:

He proves his superiority over his more groveling fellows by his location, if by nothing else. While they are content to burrow in side streets or second class thoroughfares, he boldly establishes himself in the fashionable promenade and busi-

19. S. Drucker and M. B. Hexter, *Children Astray* (Cambridge: Harvard University Press, 1923), p. 77, cited in Edwin H. Sutherland and Donald R. Cressey, *Principles of Criminology*, 7th ed. (Philadelphia and New York: J. B. Lippincott Co., 1966), p. 209.

20. Christmas Humphreys, *The Great Pearl Robbery of 1913*, subtitled: "A Record of Fact" (London: William Heinemann, 1929), p. 8. A fascinating account by Barrister Humphreys of a single theft and attempt to sell what was stolen by Grizzard. Of most value is Humphrey's detailed description of the trial and conviction of Grizzard.

ness artery of the metropolis. And he declares his higher aims and methods in every other way—in his person, manners, and surroundings. . . . There was so much gentlemanly completeness in the presence of the man that it was difficult to imagine that he had ever stood at the bar of justice charged with the meanest of all crimes against property.[21]

It was the "gentlemanly completeness in the presence" of Brandon which Crapsey found so fascinating. And presence emerges as well in the less elegant, but no less complete, "Salt Chunk Mary," fence for Jack Black. He writes, "If I knew more of composition and writing and talking I might do justice to Mary, the fence, and friends of bums and thieves. It's an injustice to Mary . . . to try to crowd her into a few paragraphs or even a chapter. She should have a book."[22]

Without question, though, the fullest attribution of energy, presence, and personal magnetism in the literature of criminology belongs to "Ma" Mandelbaum:

> The energy of her character seemed to be all drawn down into the capacious, thick blubbered reservoir of her body, quiescent in reserve for things more vital than a handshake; and some of it welled up and shone forth in the rich geniality of her smile.
>
> "They call me Ma," she said expansively, "but I ain't their mother. Not the real one. But I'm a real mother, too. Four, Gott bless them. But to them," she waved her hand toward Mr. Pitney, "I am Ma because I give them what a mother cannot sometimes give . . . money and horses and diamonds. When they call me Ma I know they are happy!"[23]

Although one could continue to pick passages from the romantic and correctional literature on the fence that would buttress

21. Edward Crapsey, op. cit., p. 86.
22. Jack Black, *You Can't Win* (New York: Macmillan Co., 1926), p. 83.
23. Lewis E. Lawes, *Cell 202 Sing Sing* (New York: Farrar and Rinehart, 1935), pp. 485–86. Further information on Ma Mandelbaum, including a portrait of her, photographs of some of the lady thieves who worked for her (Old Mother Hubbard, Black Lena, Kid Glove Rosie, Sophie Lyons, and Queen Liz), and a drawing of one of her elegant dinner parties, appears in Herbert Asbury, op. cit., pp. 210–17.

notions of "ingenuity, cunning, resource, energy, and that mysterious power we sometimes call personal magnetism," the theoretical point intended here is quite modest and would not be advanced by doing so. Simply stated the point is this: unlike many forms of deviance that have been studied by criminologists, becoming a professional fence cannot be managed by just anybody.[24] Ability, energy, ingenuity, and certain persuasive skills are absolute prerequisites. Even though, as will be demonstrated below, there is a discernible institutional path to becoming a professional fence, the sociological forces alone are simply not strong enough to carry someone without such talents into the role. To be sure, talents are plastic attributes subject to growth and development in the course of a career, but the distinctive feature of becoming a professional fence that makes certain talents prerequisite is that errors of judgment, lack of effort, or failed persuasion, especially early on in one's career, can end it.

BECOMING A BUYER[25]

Although few people have the talent to become professional fences and fewer still actually do so, anybody can buy stolen property and an unknown, but probably quite large, number of people in the United States do. At the present time one can make no descriptive statements based on surveys of the mass of buyers of stolen property, but, analytically, three conditions are necessary for becoming one: capital, opportunity, and the willingness to do

24. Cf. John Lofland and Rodney Stark, "Becoming a World Saver: A Theory of Conversion to a Deviant Perspective," *American Sociological Review* 30 (1965): 862–875; Harold Sampson, Sheldon Messinger, and Robert Towne, "Family Processes and Becoming a Mental Patient," in *Deviance: The Interactionist Perspective*, ed. Earl Rubington and Martin S. Weinberg (New York: Macmillan Co., 1973), pp. 42–51; Howard Becker, "Becoming a Marihuana User," in his *Outsiders: Studies in the Sociology of Deviance* (New York: The Free Press of Glencoe, 1973), pp. 41–58; Martin Weinberg, "Becoming a Nudist" in Rubington and Weinberg, op. cit., pp. 277–90; and George Lee Stewart, "Becoming a John," *Urban Life and Urban Culture* 3 (October 1972); 255–74.

25. Throughout this section and the sections which follow it I have relied heavily upon David Matza's exegesis of Becker's "Becoming a Marihuana User" (see note 24) in his *Becoming Deviant* (Englewood Cliffs, N. J.: Prentice-Hall, 1969), pp. 109–42.

so. At this first stage in becoming a professional fence, a large amount of capital is not needed. The initial purchase of stolen property may be no larger than the everyday purchases a person makes, as in the case of the families who buy from Nora and Otis. This is not to say that having some money or, alternatively, suffering economic hardship may not influence a decision to buy stolen property, but rather that one can become a buyer of stolen property with only a very modest amount of money.

Given a modest amount of money, having the opportunity to buy stolen property and the willingness to do so are also necessary conditions, and they may complement one another. A willingness to buy may encourage the search for opportunities, and available opportunities may arouse the desire to buy.

Learning How To Buy

The potential buyer must first learn what he is being invited to do. After learning that, he must, if he does not know already, learn how to do it. In the case of an invitation to buy stolen property, he is being invited to buy something, a concept quickly comprehensible to almost everyone. *How* to buy something may be equally familiar to the potential buyer; the customers of Nora and Otis, for example, buy from them exactly as they would from any other cash-only, no-credit peddlers. Other types of buying, however, may involve complicated procedures of delivery and payment which may have to be explained to the potential buyer. Such procedures may even be the subject of negotiations between buyer and seller while the buyer is still evaluating his own willingness to buy. Although situations do arise in which potential buyers are mistaken or misled—as was the intent in Vincent's early hustling—no one buys stolen property willingly without first believing that he knows how to buy it.

Prerequisites of Purchase

The potential buyer of stolen property will be unwilling to do so unless he believes that he will be obtaining the merchandise offered for less than he would pay if he were buying through legitimate channels.[26] If the buyer believes that the seller is a thief or a fence, that belief alone may be sufficient to persuade him that the price asked is lower than he could ordinarily obtain. More sophisticated buyers may rely on their own knowledge of merchandise values, ask the seller for evidence, or, if possible, consult some external source of price information.

Secondly, the potential buyer must come to believe that he knows the effects of a decision to buy with respect to what he considers to be potential side effects of doing so. Such considerations are as varied as are the restraints civilized man has placed on his conduct. Buying stolen property is illegal, immoral, and often disapproved. Some potential buyers must consider many different side effects; others consider only a few. But all buyers come to believe that they will not get caught. This may appear fairly obvious, as it is to the customers of Otis and Nora; or the buyer may have to be persuaded by the seller (a task which Vincent sometimes performs); or the buyer may arrive at the conclusion himself after independent reflection. Frequently, I suspect, the potential buyer may also consider the effect of the knowledge that he has bought stolen property on family, friends, neighbors, and others who are important to him. For some people the problem of not getting caught includes not getting caught by significant others who would disapprove. Approving opinions may encourage a willingness to buy, while disapproving opinions may require hiding the merchandise or its illegitimate origins.

Of course, all judgments of the likely effects of buying stolen property are subject to revision after a purchase is made. The buyer may be damned, depressed, guilt-ridden, caught by the police, or ostracized by those he cares most about. He may also be cheated by the seller. Or he may have landed what he knows was a real bargain, to the envy of his friends, relatives, and neighbors. In any case, no one buys stolen property without believing (a) that he will be paying less than he would have to in the legitimate market, and

26. I exclude from this analysis those people who buy stolen property unseriously or pathologically. I have never heard of a case of someone's buying stolen property out of a diseased compulsiveness. There are some cases of buying stolen property as a titillating adventure; see the case of Vincent's doctor on p. 147.

(b) that possible negative effects of so doing can be avoided, ignored, managed, or endured.

One final decision on the part of the potential buyer is essential before he becomes an actual one. He must decide that he will enjoy having what he believes he is offered and what he assumes he knows how and why to by with impunity. Although people can and do enjoy property in many different ways, a dichotomous division of enjoyment is sufficient for our purposes here. Stolen property can be enjoyed either by consumption or exploitation.

BECOMING A DEALER

Learning how to enjoy stolen property by exploiting it, that is, by selling it at a profit as opposed to consuming it, will not necessarily lead to a person's becoming a dealer. The would-be dealer still must contend with the social and economic realities of getting into business. At this stage in becoming a professional fence, being willing begins to become different from being able.

The would-be dealer must ultimately confront and solve four problems that present themselves to anyone considering getting into business: the problem of capital, the problem of supply, the problem of demand, and the problem of distribution. How those problems are solved by the would-be dealer depends largely on the circumstances he finds himself in at the moment he considers becoming a dealer. Otis, for example, solves the problems of supply by making his own stolen goods. As this manufacture requires no raw materials and only minimal tools, he also solves the problem of capital at the same time. He solves the problem of demand by making only those goods stolen for which he knows there is a market, and Nora helps out with the distribution. Considered in this rather unorthodox fashion, Otis's solution of the problem of becoming a dealer must be regarded as quite efficient. It is, however, limited in a number of ways. The kind, quantity, and value of goods that Otis can sell are limited not only by his energies as a thief, but by the demands of his customers as well. There is little reason to believe that Otis will ever become more than a small-time peddler of stolen domestic goods. He has no capital and no contacts with other than domestic buyers, and his lack of ingenuity plus the tax of his addiction suggest that he will never develop any.[27]

Like Otis, Jonathan Wild also began his dealing in stolen property without capital and without contacts with well-heeled buyers. His system required only skill, ingenuity, resourcefulness, effort, personal magnetism, and contacts with thieves. The problem of capital was solved by having thieves hold the property until it was sold, and the problems of demand and distribution were solved first by a direct approach on information supplied by thieves, next by advertisement, and finally by opening up a lost-property office where buyers, by appointment, could contact him. As Wild's career demonstrated, the capacity of that type of system to expand was virtually unlimited. The modern dealers who have inherited Wild's system are the private investigators and security agents who recover valuable stolen property for insurance companies, private individuals, and industry by virtue of their cozy relationships with thieves, and who keep those relationships cozy by protecting cooperative thieves from apprehension.[28]

In contrast to both Otis and Jonathan, Vincent's development as a dealer in stolen property was linked at every critical point to the development of his business of selling legitimate property as if it were stolen. The drivers whom he had approached as buyers became his suppliers. The marginal and not-so-marginal merchants he met as a buyer proved willing to buy from him. The capital he raised in his shady as-if-stolen business fed the development of his business in the real thing. Vincent applied himself with ingenuity and energy to both enterprises, and in the long run the as-if business withered away.

The cases of Jonathan, Otis, and Vincent are examples of particular solutions to the general problems of capital, supply, demand, and distribution that every dealer in stolen property must solve. Otis's solution does not make him a dealer; he is only a seller and not a buyer. Both Jonathan and Vincent, on the other hand,

27. For a description of a middle-class dealer in stolen property who sells what an associate steals from Kennedy Airport plus whatever stolen property the dealer can manage to buy at bars, see Frank Emerson, "They Can Get It For You Less Than Wholesale," New York Magazine (22 November 1971), pp. 34–37.
28. Cf. Hall, op. cit., pp. 199–204.

managed to become dealers through effort, ingenuity, energy, and persuasiveness, and both began their criminal careers with almost nothing. However, the difference between being willing to become a dealer in stolen property and being able to become one need not always be bridged with great effort or great talent. The small merchant who buys stolen merchandise when the opportunity presents itself, places it on the shelves next to his legitimate stock, and sells it to the next customer who comes through the door has solved the problems of becoming a dealer. If the customer who walks through the door happens to be a detective, an informant, a thief, or the owner of the goods, however, he may be most willing but quite unable to solve the problems of becoming successful.

BECOMING SUCCESSFUL

In practice, becoming a successful dealer means working out a way of buying and selling stolen merchandise regularly and profitably without getting caught. Particular dealerships will require particular solutions to the problem of becoming successful. The successful dealer in jewelry must learn to do different things than must the successful dealer in stolen securities, automobiles, or general merchandise.[29] Any dealer could learn these skills from an experienced fence, but I suspect that fences' Fagins are even rarer than children's Fagins. A simple trial-and-error method of learning to become successful is also not a satisfactory way of explaining how the successful dealer learns to do the vast number of things he must. The successful dealer must not only learn what to do and how to do it; he must learn both things rather quickly and, in most cases, without a tutor.

If it has not already occurred, the problems of becoming a

29. There is summary material on specialist fences, especially silk and jewelry fences, in Hall, op cit., p. 204 et passim. The most detailed analysis of a big-time jewelry fence is Humphreys, op. cit. The most up-to-date information on large-scale specialist fencing of jewelry and securities is to be found in four volumes of testimony before a U. S. Senate Investigations Committee: U. S., Congress, Senate, Permanent Subcommittee on Investigations of the Committee on Government Operations, *Hearings On Organized Crime: Stolen Securities*, 92d Cong., 1st sess., 1971. All the fences called availed themselves of their rights against self-incrimination, but the testimony of Robert F. Cudak, a thief, is especially informative (pp. 208–74).

successful dealer will produce an attitudinal shift, a change in the would-be successful dealer's relationship to his environment, that will prove essential to solving the problems that produce it. In other words, becoming successful requires a certain attitude. The would-be successful dealer must realize that the problems of becoming successful fall on him directly and exclusively. They are his problems, and his alone. Only he can succeed or fail. If he is to be successful, he must make it so. As a dealer he might have bought and sold when the opportunity presented itself, but to become a successful dealer he must actively exploit his environment, and create and control his opportunities. When Vincent speaks of "wheelin' and dealin'," this is what he means.

So wheel and deal he shall, but how? The shift in orientation continues. The would-be successful dealer was brought to his active conception of himself with the problems of becoming successful. With those problems he surveys his environment. He looks around. He examines the ways in which goods are bought and sold, paid for and transferred. He develops, perhaps tacitly and perhaps overtly with a short pencil on a pad of yellow lined paper, the rudiments of a theory of what must be done: a hard look at his situation, an assortment of it, perhaps a re-assortment, a new familiarity informed by his problems. Like the cobbler who comes to know the world by its leather or the tailor who sees men in their clothes, the would-be successful dealer's occupation forces a new order and a new intimacy on his environment. Like the cobbler or tailor he works on his problems with his hands and his mind. And, if the pattern is simple, like good cloth or leather, the good racket that receiving is yields a bit even to the clumsy beginner. To decide to cut the labels out of coats, or to do it, is within the range of the most mediocre talent.

But unlike the cobbler or tailor whose fabric intimacy with the world may be ignored, forgotten, joked about, or discreetly savored, the would-be successful dealer's new intimacy is predatory. It is a means to his ends. It is to be exploited. Moreover, his predatory intimacy is dishonest. It is, by declaration, unconstrained by conventional faiths in what ought to be done or what one is supposed to do.[30] So liberated, with cunning, ingenuity, and effort, it may

30. I am indebted to Edwin Sutherland (*The Professional Thief* [Chicago: University of Chicago Press, 1937], p. 208) for the idea of predatory intimacy:

become ever so much more intimate with the possibilities of the environment than could the tailor with his cloth or the cobbler with his leather. That dishonest intimacy with the predatory possibilities of one's environment may take some time to develop, but with ability and effort it can be achieved rather faster than one might think. With its achievement comes a completed theory of dishonesty, the predatory suspension of faith, and the ability to see what ought not to be done in what others believe one is supposed to do.

In the general-merchandise business a simple survey of what most people believe one is supposed to do looks like this:

1. Possess various quantities of miscellaneous merchandise.
2. Possess receipts which cover possession of it.
3. Possess receipts and merchandise without being disturbed or disturbing others by possessing it.
4. Possess merchandise which is "distressed," i.e., damaged, disfigured, delabeled, not in its normal packaging, etc.
5. Possess merchandise in storage areas such as warehouses.
6. Possess means of conveying merchandise to and from buyers and sellers and to and from storage areas.
7. Possess catalogs, price lists, labels, cartons, packaging, and other such items useful in the course of business.
8. Buy merchandise at the best possible prices, taking advantage of profitable situations like production overruns, private sales, bankruptcies, and liquidations.
9. Sell merchandise at competitive prices and offer "bargains."
10. Employ others as assistants: family, friends, perhaps even those who for one reason or another are denied employment elsewhere and deserve "another chance."
11. Have drivers, buyers, sellers, and others regularly enter

---

While, as a pickpocket, he [the professional thief] may merely make physical contact with the clothes and pocketbooks of victims, as a confidence man he must enter into intimate associations with them. This intimacy is coldblooded. The feelings are expressed as by an actor on stage, with calculations of the results they will produce. He is like a salesman who attempts to understand a prospective customer only as a means of breaking down sales resistance and realizing his own objective of increased sales.

and leave one's place of business or storage areas with packages, samples of merchandise, deliveries, bills, receipts, checks, and money.

Such a list is, of course, an edited edition of Vincent's environment, what he had to work from in becoming a successful dealer. It is edited in two important ways. First, it is edited to display certain features of his business environment which one, with ingenuity, could exploit for the purpose of buying and selling stolen property successfully. Second, it is an outsider's list. It is a list of what goes on in the general-merchandise business which could be composed by someone familiar with the business, but that someone would not necessarily have to be a general-merchandise dealer. Undoubtedly a dealer could describe features of his business further and possibly, if Vincent is the dealer in question, exploit them further. Such exploitation is an application of the dealer's "ingenuity," a talent which must be given a specific meaning here.

Ingenuity

One misleading notion of the general-merchandise dealer's ingenuity is that he is able to buy and sell stolen property successfully because he knows the loopholes and subtleties of the laws prohibiting criminal receiving and is able to exploit these defects. He may, if caught, employ a lawyer who will aggressively search for legal weaknesses in the prosecutor's case, but by and large it is the dealer's explanation of what he did and why he did it which will get him off. The laws of receiving are weak, but their weakness is the product of the dealer's ingenuity, not the source of it.

What the dealer does know, better than his lawyer or anyone else, are the norms, conventions, participants, practices, and procedures in his business environment. It is from that source which his ingenuity springs. The ingenuity of the successful dealer is his ability to make his buying and selling of stolen property convincingly appear to be no different from what others in his environment normally and legally do. The suppositions on which he works are the conventions of his business not the subtleties of the criminal law. Vincent knows little about the criminal law, less than one might learn in half an hour with a law digest. His record indicates that he does not need to know more.

That many successful dealers, not only those in the general-merchandise business, do not need to know much about the criminal law follows from a proper understanding of ingenuity. It also follows from a correct notion of ingenuity that some types of successful dealers must have a highly developed predatory intimacy with the laws governing the practices and procedures in their business. For example, the dealer in stolen automobiles who ships them across state lines and re-registers them is likely to know a great deal about the laws and administration of the laws governing registration, title search, vehicle inspection, and vehicle transportation. However, the dealer in stolen automobiles may know nothing about these laws if he exports them to foreign countries. In that case he is likely to know customs inspection procedures, shipping regulations, etc.—those rules relevant to the ingenuity of the successful smuggler. Perhaps the paradigm case of the dealer's relationship to the criminal law is the case of Jonathan Wild. Wild initially needed to know the law against criminal receiving, later took advantage of the thief-taker's laws, and eventually had to adjust his business procedures to the restrictions of "Jonathan Wild's Act" (4 Geo. I, c. 11, sec. 4), which forbade recovering stolen property for a fee without trying to apprehend the thief. While such laws were the criminal laws against receiving, they must be seen as business law with respect to Wild. He was in the business of recovering stolen property and thief taking, and never pretended that he was in any other business.

The notion of ingenuity which suggests that the successful dealer must have an intimate knowledge of his business environment is not limited to knowledge of technical regulations, practices, and procedures. Ingenuity also generally implies a knowledge of the product that is traded. Thus the successful dealer in stolen jewelry is likely to be a jeweler, the successful dealer in stolen automobiles an automobile dealer, the successful dealer in stolen art an art dealer, etc. This is especially likely when the dealer deals exclusively in one type of product. A generalist fence like Vincent may enlist the aid of specialists when the need arises. Wild's case is also a model of product intimacy. As a recoverer of stolen property he learned from his thieves what he needed to know about the merchandise he was to return. As a thief-taker his products were thieves who "he was able to manipulate for so long because . . .

they felt he was really on their side no matter how murderous his behavior. . . ."

Ingenuity is also applicable to the norms and conventions of the successful dealer's environment. In some cases neither the product nor technical regulations nor business practices must be manipulated with ingenuity. A convincing assertion consistent with the norms of the dealer's business environment may be all that is necessary. Mary Owen Cameron cites an example of such conventional ingenuity:

"It works like this," he said, "a man comes into a neighborhood store with a lot of expensive books and equipment in his car. They're worth maybe $800–$900 wholesale. He says he's just closed up his store in Philadelphia. He's willing to sell the left over stock for what he can get out of it. The proprietor doesn't ask questions but shells out maybe $200 for the lot. He even gets a sales receipt signed with some phony name. He knows he's buying hot goods, but he thinks he's covered the legal side and stands to make a nice profit. He won't sell the stuff to just anybody, but he has some good customers he's known for a long time. They'll be glad to be let in on a bargain, and they won't ask any questions."[31]

In the practice cited by Cameron all the dealer must do is claim that he believed the thief's story. All the successful dealer must do in similar situations is claim convincingly that he believed the thief's story or, if no story is offered, offer a convincing one of his own. In Wild's case his claim that he was Thief-Taker General of Ireland and Great Britain, and those he had hanged to make it convincing, balanced perfectly his need for evidence that he really did try to apprehend the thieves from whom he recovered stolen property.

With the notion of ingenuity so elaborated, it now becomes possible to offer a systematic general theory of how the would-be

31. Cameron is quoting "the security official of a large chain of retail stores selling books and art supplies." She goes on to assert that although the quotation above deals with books and art supplies, most of the merchandise stolen by professional shoplifters is sold to small specialty retail shops. Mary Owen Cameron, *The Booster and the Snitch* (New York: The Free Press, 1964), pp. 57–58.

successful dealer learns the most important part of becoming successful, what he must do to avoid getting caught:

1. Getting caught means to be detected doing what one is
   not supposed to do. In the case of the dealer it is buying
   and selling stolen property.
2. In order to avoid getting caught the dealer applies himself to the problem of buying and selling stolen property
   in such a way as to make a convincing appearance that he
   is not doing anything different from what he ought to be
   doing.
3. He examines his environment for manipulable differences
   between what he plans to do (buy and sell stolen property) and what other believe he ought to be doing.
4. He decides to manipulate certain features of his environment: the product, some practices or procedures, and/or
   offer a dishonest account of his behavior consistent with
   the legitimate and conventional norms of his environment.

Having learned what he must do to avoid getting caught, the
would-be successful dealer in stolen property may find that forces
beyond his control prohibit him from buying both profitably and
regularly. This is particularly true if he has decided to become a
specialist dealer. The would-be successful dealer in fine art, for example, may buy and sell profitably, but may find that not enough
fine art is stolen to permit him to deal regularly. Similarly, the
would-be jewelry specialist may find that generalist fences like
Vincent and "occasional receiver" legitimate jewelers take up the
small regular trade, leaving him only with opportunities to buy
large quantities of very expensive jewelry which nonspecialists are
not prepared to handle. The would-be specialist in men's suits, on
the other hand, may find that he can buy small quantities of suits
regularly but not profitably, because thieves manage to sell them
to "lay receivers" at prices which are close to or equal to what he
would pay for them legitimately. Specialist dealers are generally
under economic pressure to deal in large quantities of their particular item. They are also likely to plan each highly profitable individual transaction days, weeks, or even months in advance.

The generalist dealer may find himself subject to quite different
pressures from the economics of theft. These pressures may permit
him to deal regularly but may tax his ability to do so profitably.

The advantage which the generalist dealer offers to generalist thieves is a ready market for those things which are commonly stolen. Like the department store or shopping center, his attraction is convenience. He is willing and able to buy most things that are stolen, often without special preparations. Two forces are likely to play upon him economically. On the one hand, there is a tendency for him to become oversupplied with particular items. On the other hand, he is under pressure to become more "convenient," that is, to handle a wider and wider variety of items. Because specialist thieves stealing large quantities of special items are likely to be working with specialist dealers, the unusual items that the generalist dealer is pressed to handle may be small amounts of items taken by chance by generalist thieves. Unless the generalist dealer has an unlimited number of buyers or develops other means of disposing of exotic merchandise, he must find ways of limiting what he buys so as to match his capacities to sell. The specialist dealer must also limit what he buys to what he is prepared to handle readily, but the intermittent character of his trade may make it possible for him to prepare to sell what he knows he is going to buy. Consider the account related to me by William Roberts, an ex-dealer on probation for receiving stolen goods, with regard to the pressures on a generalist fence to handle diverse merchandise:

In the beginning it went all right. I bought from the junkies in the neighborhood and sold what they brought me through my business. . . . That went on for a while and I made a lot of money. Pretty soon, one junkie tells another and he tells somebody else, and before you know it you have hundreds of junkies comin' down on you wanting to sell you everything. . . . I couldn't handle it, and it got to be that I was afraid to turn anybody down because I was afraid they'd dime on me [telephone the police]. After a while I knew it was just a matter of time. . . . I'll never forget the day it happened. I was getting in the [police] car, cuffs on my wrists, and two wagons here to haul the stuff away . . . when this junkie comes walkin' up the street pushing one of those supermarket carts with a fuckin' fruit scale on it . . . a big electric one. I probably would have bought it. . . . They took him away too. Now where the hell would I have sold a big fuckin' fruit scale?

The successful dealer in stolen merchandise, generalist or

specialist, may manage to deal with only a small number of thieves for his entire career. In such cases he is better considered a private buyer for those thieves, perhaps successful on his own terms, rather than a successful dealer as defined here. If he does let it be known to thieves, generalists or specialists, that he is willing to do business regularly, that declaration of interest is likely to become of interest to other thieves and, eventually, to the police. From this point on the successful dealer, in becoming a professional fence, will discover that what he must do becomes increasingly a question of what others may try to do with him.

BECOMING PUBLIC

The last step in becoming a professional fence is becoming public. If a dealer buys and sells stolen property regularly, many people will find out about it. Every thief who sells him something will know he is a fence. Many of his customers must be told they are buying stolen property. Other customers may suspect it because of his bargain prices; to encourage them to buy from him, the fence may tell them they are buying stolen goods whether or not that is the case. Sooner or later, for one reason or another, someone will tell the police. Becoming public—becoming known to thieves, customers, police, and others as a fence—is not entirely any successful dealer's own idea, but for every dealer who continues to buy stolen property regularly, learning how to become public is the last essential lesson in becoming successful.

The most consequential part of becoming public is becoming known to the police. This process will influence the way in which the successful dealer eventually becomes fully known to all his other audiences. Although the process can occur in many different settings and in many different ways, the most dramatic beginning is probably the most common. Getting investigated, searched, questioned, brought down, interrogated, lined up, fingerprinted, handcuffed, booked, photographed, celled, brought out, brought before, and bailed out is, of course, the unsettling bureaucratic experience of becoming officially and publicly known to the police as a criminal. The power of the state cannot be denied. It can, however, be taken in a number of ways.

As Matza has observed, the judicial act of signifying someone as deviant carries three different meanings.[32] The first is simply that of a name or label, a description which registers a person in some category. In the case of the dealer in stolen property the label is "receiver of stolen goods." The second meaning of the act of signifying someone deviant is derogation or "put down." To make this meaning quite clear, the Prison Committee of the Association of Grand Jurors added a little extra shabbiness to Mother Mandelbaum. The third and final meaning of the act of signification implies that the deviant exemplifies, represents, or "stands for" something. In order to examine the process of becoming public for the professional fence, it is necessary to examine how he must take in each of these meanings.

Registration

Once the process of registration has begun everything the dealer learned he must do to become successful acquires a new importance. He knew what he must do, but on the occasion of registration what is all-important is whether or not he did or can, in the face of inquisitors, do it. At least at initial occasions of registration, registrars may be unimpressed by the dealer's ingenuity. A statement that Vincent made in Chapter Five sets the preliminary context in which the dealer is likely to be asked to display his ingenuity:

A fence has to be tough, somebody who can take it without falling apart, if you know what I mean. Let's face it, the cops know you bought hot stuff and they think they got a good case. So you pull some bullshit which they know is gonna get you off, they're gonna get pissed.

The dealer's performance at trial must also be convincing. Vincent recalls rather proudly the judge's statement at his first adult trial for criminal receiving that he should either get a psychiatrist or an academy award for his performance. Vincent was convicted, in spite of his stellar performance, but he is proud of it because it was a new part in a script he had invented himself, and it was

32. Matza, op. cit., pp. 155–57. Matza's elaboration of effects of these component meanings of signification is different from my own, probably because we know different people.

played before a hostile audience. Since then, on a dozen or so different occasions, Vincent has perfected his courtroom acting technique so as to be able to perform perfectly and avoid conviction.

The most direct benefit that the fence derives from his ability to perform convincingly at ceremonies of registration is, of course, that he escapes the official label and the penalties which go with it, but this is not the only benefit. His ability may earn him a reputation for toughness in bureaucratic terms. That is, pinning a deserved conviction on him may mean a great deal of work with a low probability of reward. Vincent has added to this definition other impressions which are bureaucratically relevant. Among them is one which suggests that the work required to "get" him can be avoided. By buying only a portion of the large quantities of merchandise he is offered, he gives detectives the option of going after some less skilled buyer or dealer who may have bought the remainder of the merchandise.

Even if registration procedures are begun against him, and even if they are successful, the professional fence may use them to his own advantage. Within the criminal community, an arrest or conviction is normally considered to be prima facie evidence that a criminal's relationship with the police is not overly cozy.

Derogation

The criminal community is not the fence's only audience, however. Those who buy from him and those who live and work near him may still be concerned with the stigma or invidious moral evaluation, the "put down," implied by an arrest or conviction. How the fence deals with this meaning of signification, if it is within his capacities to deal with it at all, depends in part upon his circumstances.

On some occasions, an arrest or conviction may elicit a direct, more or less formal expression of censure and as a result may require a gross readjustment in the way one does business. For example, a parole officer convicted of buying stolen property from his parolees and selling it to friends or neighbors, to businesses, or to other officers, would without a doubt lose his job. Even an arrest for doing so would likely be intolerable to his employers. Although he might continue to deal without the cover of his official position, it would require re-organization of his business to do so. If their business was essential to their trade, a similar reorganization would be necessary by those who lose business licenses because of a conviction for buying and selling stolen property.

The stigma of an arrest or conviction may have even more damaging, if less direct, effects in other situations. An art dealer, for example, might find that certain customers or institutions would withdraw their patronage from the kind of person who would buy and sell stolen art. Or, an arrest or conviction may so threaten the credibility of the dealer that customers withdraw their trade because they believe that his advice or word cannot be relied upon.

Because Vincent is self-employed in a relatively unregulated business in which his judgments on the value of standard-brand merchandise can be easily verified, he has not suffered the effects of stigmatization or derogation as an art dealer or probation officer might. He does, however, experience an estrangement from legitimate society which he can only rarely overcome. Many of his "friends" are parasitic, willing to associate with him only for what they can get out of doing so. Others enjoy being around him because he lives a life which they find vicariously exciting but would be unwilling to lead themselves. For such people, knowing a real fence is one step better than reading about one or seeing one in a gangster movie. Vincent's constant companions, the "regulars" who virtually live in his store, are a motley collection of retired gangsters and hustlers too old to be actively criminal and too nostalgically criminal to become legitimate. Vincent finds their company comfortable but unstimulating.

Vincent reacts to his marginality in a number of different ways. Like Wild, he acts the gangster type when the situation calls for it. He is able to capitalize with his customers on his reputation as a fence, often selling perfectly legitimate goods as if they were stolen. But he is concerned with the appearance of legitimacy as well. He is not willing to take the "put down" of his signification as a fence. One interpretation of the motive for his civic and charitable activities (such as contributions to orphanages, churches, delinquency and recreation programs, political candidates' campaigns, police and firemen's funds, etc.) is that they create an economic link with legitimate society from which he is otherwise alienated. As I suspect is the case with many marginal men, Vincent finds refuge from his marginality, sometimes temporary, sometimes extended, in the love and company of certain women. Sometimes though, what appears to be refuge may only be more of the same:

I ain't braggin' now when I say this, Carl, but when it comes to bein' in bed with a woman I think I rank with the best of 'em. You know I can sometimes go for half an hour, maybe forty-five minutes without finishing, you know. If I want to do that I just set my mind to some deal I got goin' and I think about how to scheme it out. That way I don't think about what's happenin' an' I don't finish until I want to.

Exemplification

With respect to the police, the third and final meaning of signification, to stand for something or to be made an example of, is joined to the other two. Under the category of registration the police were left, in Vincent's terms, "pissed off" because the fence "pulled some bullshit" which frustrated their attempts at registering him. Although the fence's reputation in bureaucratic terms may amount to avoidable hard work at low reward, the relationship between frustration and aggression is not that simple. To be pissed off is to be pissed off. In those terms the fence is someone who deserves to be made an example of. He becomes a prime suspect for burglary and larceny investigations. Moreover, if he has a stable residence and place of business, he becomes a readily available prime suspect.

Thus, every time the police become aware of a theft of property they must investigate, the fence is likely to be one of the first persons approached.[33] This is especially the case when there is no

33. Though, of course, not the only one (witness this quote from Carl Werthman and Irving Pilavin, "Gang Members and the Police," in *The Police*, ed. David Bordua [New York: John Wiley and Sons, 1967], p. 70, as quoted in Matza, op. cit., p. 194):

Every time something happens in this neighborhood, them mother-fuckin' cops come lookin' for me! I may not be doin' nothing, but if somebody gets beat or something gets stole they always be coming right to my place to find out what's going on. [italics mine.]

evidence at the scene of the crime leading a detective to a particular suspect. One of the consequences of this regular contact between the fence and investigating detectives is that they get to know one another. The scenario of Vincent playing harassed-respectable-legitimate-businessman to a detective's officer-of-the-law-investigating-property-theft would soon become laughable to both performers. Reality must be introduced into the charade, and it is the experienced detective who can carry it in gently: "What's hot today, Vince?—Everything!" From that point on, given personal magnetism, the second meaning of signification, stigma or derogation, becomes a myth for outsiders. Vincent may be a "serious problem," but he is also "a nice guy."

The final meaning of signification is most subtle. It implies that by identifying the deviant as someone who is to be made an example of, the state brings the deviant into unwilling and unpaid service to it. In the case of the professional fence he must stand for the state's use of him as a regular suspect. Furthermore, there is considerable evidence that many fences become even more deeply employed by the state in giving it information about crimes and criminals.[34] Wild's system, the archetype for all professional fences, depended upon his maintaining a convincing balance between thief-taking and taking from thieves. But Vincent, unlike Wild, meets his obligations to the state by recovering stolen property rather than apprehending thieves. On those occasions when Vincent is offered exotic property (computers, military equipment, items of largely sentimental value, etc.) which he probably could not sell anyway, he buys it at his own expense, and then returns it to its owners via the police. That this behavior creates goodwill

34. Danny Ahern, *How to Commit a Murder* (New York: Ives Washburn, 1930), p. 62, puts the case most succinctly: "You can't trust all of them fences, because they are noted to me as rats." See also John Bowers, "Big City Thieves," *Harper's Magazine* (February 1967), pp. 50–54; Kellow Chesney, *The Anti-Society: An Account of the Victorian Underworld* (Boston: Gambit, 1970), pp. 187–89; Charles L. Clark, *Lockstep and Corridor* (Cincinnati: University of Cincinnati Press, 1927), pp. 17–19; P. Colquhoun, *A Treatise on the Police of the Metropolis*, p. 211; Clayton Ettinger, *The Problem of Crime* (New York: Ray Long and Richard R. Smith, Inc., 1932), p. 33; Jerome Hall, op. cit., pp. 199–204; Sheldon Messinger, *Professional Crime in West City* (Unpublished Manuscript, 5, July 1972), pp. 12, 24; and John Bartlow Martin, "Gene," in *My Life in Crime* (New York: Harper and Brothers, 1952), p. 67.

toward Vincent is undeniable. That Vincent, a businessman to
the end, manages to meet his obligations to the state with a
method of inventory control is obviously ingenious.

> But sure, e'er long, the Time will come again,
> When Watches shall be lost in Drury Lane;
> Snuff-Boxes, finely painted, miss their Way,
> And Rings, and Pocket-Books shall go astray;
> When *Phillis* at the Ball or Masquerade
> Shall loose a Present from some Lover made:
> Then you—unthinking Monsters!—you that now
> Exult at my unpitied Overthrow,
> Then you'll repent too late: you then in vain,
> Will wish to have your JONATHAN again!

*The Funeral Procession
of Jonathan Wild*[35]

---

35. Quoted in Howson, op. cit., p. 279. Its source is a print in the British
Museum: *Satirical Prints*, vol. 9, no. 1751.

Chapter 8

THE BIOGRAPHY OF A RESEARCH PROJECT

The real explanation, then, of how research was done involves a rather personal account of how the researcher lived during the period of the study.

William Foote Whyte,
Street Corner Society

My interest in studying the fence began sometime in April of 1967. At that time I was a senior at the University of Rhode Island attending a seminar in criminology with Professor Ralph England. For my semester project I had planned to replicate a study that required that I interview delinquent boys. I was refused permission to do so by the local institution, and found myself left with no final project for my seminar. With six weeks to go until the end of the semester, I went to Professor England for suggestions for an alternative to my aborted delinquency study. He suggested that I interview some police officers about fences. If my delinquency research had not been vetoed by the institution, and if England had not suggested the topic he did, I doubt that I would ever have considered doing the research of which this manuscript is the fruit.

The short piece of research I did for the seminar stayed with me through graduate school. With only four police interviews behind me, I considered myself something of an expert on fences, inasmuch as no one else knew anything about the subject. Such distortions are endemic among graduate students. Halfway through my graduate training I told people that there had never been a single sociological study of the fence.

Then I discovered Hall's *Theft, Law, and Society.* My hopes for being the pathfinder in research on the fence were crushed. But, I had too much invested in my reputation as an expert on fencing to let this stop me. I took some comfort in the fact that the first edition of *Theft, Law, and Society* was published in 1935, while the "reorganized and amplified" section on stolen property in the second edition was almost twenty years out of date. I assumed that I could add to Hall's analysis or at least provide more current information.

What made me think so was that, as far as I could tell, Hall had not in fact talked to any fences or thieves. He interviewed "public officials, private investigators, representatives of insurance companies, and other experienced persons."[1] Unless "other experienced persons" included thieves and fences, Hall wrote without benefit of their perspective. This seemed important to me because I had just read Polsky's *Hustlers, Beats, and Others,* and was persuaded by his argument that criminology needs information about crime from successful criminals, observed and interviewed in a natural setting.[2] Polsky also made finding talkative criminals sound easier than I had thought it would be.

I also had the notion that a case study of a fence, in addition to being interesting, would be a quick and simple dissertation. When I informally declared my dissertation topic in September of 1970, I assumed that it would be a simple matter of finding a fence and tape recording what he had to say. I should have known better. My naiveté sustained me for some fourteen months until I met Vincent.[3]

1. Jerome Hall, *Theft, Law, and Society,* 2d ed. (Indianapolis: Bobbs-Merrill Co., 1952), p. 156.
2. Ned Polsky, "Research Method, Morality, and Criminology," in *Hustlers, Beats, and Others* (Chicago: Aldine Publishing Co., 1967), pp. 117–49.
3. Ironically, I considered Edwin H. Sutherland's *The Professional Thief* (Chicago: University of Chicago Press, 1937) as the model of what I wanted to do with a fence. I did not know then that Sutherland and Jones had worked on *The Professional Thief* for almost five years. See Jon Snodgrass, "The Criminologist and His Criminal: The Case of Edwin H. Sutherland and Broadway Jones," *Issues in Criminology* 8 (Spring 1973): 1–17.

OFFICIAL CONTACTS AND OFFICIAL REFERRALS

Through the fall of 1970 and into the winter of 1971 I continued to read what literature I could find on fences. This included most of the references Hall had used and some historical materials he had not noted. I also began to arrange interviews with those who, in the course of their work, would be likely to come into contact with thieves. This meant police, security agents, criminal lawyers, crime reporters, and thieves themselves. All of these arrangements, which incidentally took a great deal of time because of the red tape involved, had two purposes: to prepare me for a case study of a fence, and to lead me to a willing subject.

I obtained permission to interview burglary-squad detectives in October of 1970, and in November of that year I managed to see officers in that division in order to arrange to do so. These were both Captains, who, after telling me I would never find a cooperative fence, referred me to a detective lieutenant. As it happened, I was introduced to the lieutenant at about a quarter to noon. It was clear that no researcher was going to keep him from having lunch with his squad, and it was also clear that this researcher would not be especially welcome to join them. We made an appointment to meet the following week at a less pressing hour.

When I arrived the following week at the appointed time, the lieutenant was nowhere to be found. No one in the squad room knew where he was. Four days later I managed to contact him again, and he explained that business required him to be "on the street." He said he was sorry that he had missed me. He also suggested that we postpone our work until the Christmas holidays were over. I agreed, and called him again in January.

When we talked in January we found that scheduling problems were going to make interviewing his detectives difficult. He explained that most of the men did paperwork in the morning at the office, and spent the afternoon "on the street."[4] As it happened, I taught classes in the morning and it was impossible for me to be at

---

4. I had worked with a municipal government law-enforcement agency before, and knew how "on the street" worked. By dividing the day so as to be in the office in the morning and "on the street" in the afternoon, it is usually possible to quit work early, because one goes home from the street without checking back at the office.

the station when the men were there. Consequently the lieutenant and I agreed to postpone my interviewing until June, when school was over and my schedule would be more flexible.

At the same time that I was negotiating for police interviews, I began a less systematic search for information and suggestions for a subject. This search began with an ex-homicide detective who, after twenty years on the force, had retired to become the head of a security agency. This man had been a consultant on a previous criminological research project, and it was through that researcher that I was referred to him.

The three interviews I had with this detective were candid and helpful. Not only did he know the criminal environment of the city very well, but he also knew and was willing to talk about his former colleagues on the police force. In sum, what he told me was that he believed that no fence could operate for any length of time without the cooperation of the police. He also said that it was his personal policy never to trust the detectives on the burglary squad, and added that he was thankful that he had never gotten assigned to that division while he was on the force. When I mentioned that I was having some difficulty in talking to detectives there, he suggested that I was getting "the royal runaround."

He also made a suggestion and a promise. The suggestion was of a fence who might be willing to talk to me—namely, "Knuckles" Jones.[5] Knuckles had been an informant for him years ago. Although he thought it unlikely that Knuckles would talk to me, he suggested that it might be worth a try. The promise the detective made was that if I were killed during the course of my research, he would see to it that my killer was brought to justice.

Polsky had never mentioned anything about *that* part of field work, but then it is unlikely that he had ever met Knuckles Jones. I checked newspaper files on Knuckles and gathered some background information on him. I decided that to go right out and talk to him, however, might be a bit rash.

Between January and May of 1971 I continued talking to security agents, crime reporters, criminal lawyers, and other public officials. Although the city I worked in was quite large, I found

5. This is a psuedonym, naturally. I assure the reader, however, that it is no more menacing than the real name I was given.

that most of the people in the crime control and criminal processing business knew one another. My interviews during these months
traced an informal network of friendships. An agent at one store,
for example, referred me to an agent at another, and so on.

Through friends who were themselves lawyers I managed to
interview three of the city's best-known criminal lawyers. Each had
a sizeable gangster clientele, and I hoped for referrals from them.
I explained to them that I thought I might be able to convince a
retired fence or one who was terminally ill to talk to me. I received
no suggestions from the first two lawyers, but the second one told
me that the third lawyer I was scheduled to see had been Knuckles
Jones's attorney for a long time.

I learned something about Knuckles from this third lawyer. According to him, Knuckles was a diabetic, an alcoholic, in his early
sixties, and currently in the hospital for minor surgery. The lawyer
did not think Knuckles would live another year.

I decided to try to take immediate advantage of what seemed
like a perfect opportunity. That same afternoon I called the hospital. I spoke with Knuckles, and mentioned the name of the ex-
homicide detective Knuckles had worked with for years. Knuckles
immediately said he "didn't know nothin' about no murders." I
emphasized that I wasn't a cop, wasn't interested in any murders,
and just wanted to talk to him a bit. He said I could see him if I
wanted to.

My strategy in trying to convince Knuckles to talk to me was
to offer him a kind of anonymous immortality in exchange for
information. To have someone want to write a book about you is
for most people, I suspect, flattering. I hoped to convince Knuckles
that he could have a book written about him even if the details
had to be changed to protect his true identity. The day after I
talked to Knuckles on the phone I visited him at the hospital.

I brought a copy of Sutherland's *The Professional Thief* with
me. I did this for three reasons. First, I hoped it would serve as a
precedent—as evidence that another criminal had seen fit to work
with a college professor in recounting the details of his occupation.
Second, I planned to tell Knuckles that if he had had as much experience as the newspapers claimed he had, he could, with my help,
produce a book as successful as Sutherland's. Third, I planned to
leave the book with Knuckles. Even if he was not convinced by the

first two reasons, getting the book back would give me an excuse for a second visit and another opportunity to talk to him.

Although I think the strategy was sound, it did not work. When I arrived I found Knuckles in a double room with only five or six feet separating him from a curious and attentive fellow in the next bed. Knuckles was in no shape to get out of bed, and confidential discussion was therefore impossible. I mentioned the name of the homicide detective to Knuckles, and he asked if he was "still in the business." I answered "no" and said that he was doing much the same thing, although he was in business for himself now. By phrasing his question as he did, without mentioning the "business" the detective was in, Knuckles was, I assumed, letting me know that he did not want his occupation advertised to his hospital roommate.

All during the time I talked to Knuckles the television was blaring. This meant that hushed conversation was impossible. Nevertheless, I did manage to describe in veiled phrases what I wanted. I showed Knuckles the book, but he declined to accept it. He said he wasn't well enough to read. I left, taking my copy of the book with me, and arranged to return a few days later when Knuckles might be feeling better.

When I returned to the hospital a week later, Knuckles looked worse than when I had left him before. He had had a second operation and was obviously in pain. I stayed no more than two minutes. The third time I saw Knuckles, another week later, he appeared much better. He said that the doctor was sending him home in two days, but that he would return the day after for more tests. He suggested that I see him then and perhaps, after the tests were over, we could go "drink a bottle of whiskey together" and talk about the book I wanted to write. I left that meeting with Knuckles under the impression that my problems in finding a subject for a case study were over.

I returned to the hospital on the day Knuckles had told me he would be back for tests. He never showed up; his doctor knew nothing about any tests; and his hospital roommate told me that Knuckles had left for a rest in Florida. I never saw Knuckles again after that hopeful third meeting in the hospital. For some time I entertained the interpretation that Knuckles had really intended to keep his appointment with me. I visited his home every week or so for the next three months. It was sealed up, and his neighbors confirmed that he had indeed gone to Florida. Knuckles stayed in Florida for about eight months. He died within the year.

I returned to further background work in June of 1971, under the impression that I still might be able to use Knuckles as the subject of my case study when he came back from Florida. I still had a number of police interviews to complete, or so I thought at the time.

Returning to police headquarters in June, I found my burglary-squad lieutenant as busy as ever. I hoped to get around his scheduling difficulties by waiting him out. While doing so, I planned to examine some official data on receivers of stolen goods.

I spent almost the first two weeks of June in the police station. During the first week there I conducted one interview. The lieutenant instructed one of his men to talk with me for a few minutes the first morning. The interview in fact lasted an hour and a half. On the fourth morning I appeared at the station house, the lieutenant told me that the detective I had talked to knew more about fences than the others in his squad and that I probably would not learn anything more from anyone else. I gave up trying to get through the lieutenant to the burglary-squad detectives at the station house, and for the next week spent my time looking through official records.

The official records I examined during the second week of June 1971 were investigation reports of arrests for receiving stolen goods. I had obtained a list of all the people who were arrested and charged with that crime during 1970. Importantly, my list comprised those who were charged only with the crime of receiving stolen goods. If at the time of arrest a person was also charged with some other crime (e.g., burglary, larceny, conspiracy), his name did not appear on my list.

The investigation reports included summary information about the arrest and basic information about the persons arrested. My list contained some four hundred names. During the second week in June I read and recorded the information available on the first fifty reports filed in 1970.

Not one of these reports described anything which even approached the character of a fencing operation. All of the reports described the receipt of fairly small items of property (such as a

camera, gun, lawnmower, or credit card), with the exception of a
few which dealt with stolen automobiles. The explanations given
for the possession of the stolen property were uniformly vague: "I
bought it from a man on the street"; "I never saw it before"; "I
bought it from a fellow I met in a bar"; etc.

It become obvious after reading the first fifty reports, that I
was not going to learn anything about fencing from the information contained in them. I now know why, and I should have
known better then. First of all, I needed the kind of close detail
about the day-to-day conduct of a criminal business that was not
likely to be captured in official summaries. Furthermore, I was
looking for information on successful professional criminals, who
are less likely to be caught than their amateur counterparts. Finally,
by choosing to examine the records of those who were arrested and
charged only with receiving stolen goods, I had succeeded in removing from my sample any major fences who did happen to be
caught during 1970. The reason for this is that an arrest of a fence
is an important arrest. The arresting detective is inclined to make
the arrest as serious as possible. Hence, it is standard police practice to add to the receiving-stolen-goods charge additional charges
of burglary, laceny, and occasionally conspiracy. These charges may
increase the leverage of the prosecuting attorney in negotiating a
guilty plea.

I might have used the list of arrests in 1970 on combined
charges of burglary, larceny, and receiving stolen goods. The problem with using this list, however, was that police practice in charg-
ing thieves and burglars is the same as it is for fences. They too
are usually booked on the triple charge of burglary, larceny, and receiving stolen goods. Thus, that category would include, in addition
to some reports of arrests of fences, literally thousands of arrests of
burglars and thieves. The payoff for examining all of those investigation reports simply would not have been worth the trouble. For
all these reasons, I quit reading investigation reports by the middle
of July, 1971.

I did manage to make some use of official records in tracking
down arrest histories of some of the fences I learned about during
my interviews. However, what I did find in this search is far less
interesting than what I did not find. Late in June of 1971 I applied
for the criminal records of twenty-five persons whom police officers,

district attorneys, crime reporters, and others in law enforcement or security had identified as fences. In order to hide my identity as the one who requested the records, I made the request through a friend in a nonpolice office of the city's criminal justice system. The office which made the request for me is fully authorized to do so and makes such requests daily. Of the twenty-five criminal records requested, only eight were forwarded by the police department. I was never able to secure the seventeen missing records, although I tried repeatedly to do so. In February of 1972 I made my last request for them. It was also the last time I met with any municipal official about my research.

I eventually cut off contact with government, justice, and police sources because I had begun to work with Vincent. I did not want false or unsettling information about me to be brought to him; I had many reasons to suspect that it might be if I continued my contact with official sources; and I was afraid of misinterpretation of my intentions by those officials who might communicate with Vincent. As it was, I explained to Vincent early in our acquaintance exactly what my work with the police and other public officials had been. I thought that the loss of official cooperation, such as it had been, was well worth what Vincent promised to give me.

CRIMINAL CONTACTS AND CRIMINAL REFERRALS

The path I took to meeting Vincent and securing his cooperation might well have been more direct than it actually was. However, the impediments I met in official circles and the relative lack of them among those whose careers were the concern of these officials prepared me splendidly for my work with him. I contacted Vincent for the first time in January of 1972. The events leading up to that contact begin on June 2, 1971.

As of that date I had spent a total of about two hours of my entire life talking to people whom I knew to be criminals. This estimate includes the total of forty-five minutes or so I had spent with Knuckles Jones in March of 1971, plus an hour and fifteen minute aggregate of nods, "hellos," "nos," "yes's," and lavatory directions I gave to probationers during a two-year research project I had once done. I suspect that my experience was about average for predissertation doctoral candidates. To further substantiate my relative innocence, I should add that as of June 2, 1971, I had never talked to anyone I knew to be a drug addict, nor had I spent more than fifty hours of my entire life talking with people who were black.

On that date I was, by prearrangement, to interview a black drug pusher at his home. I was assisted in making the arrangements by his probation officer (also black) who got to know me during my probation research and offered to help me with my fencing research. Now, generally speaking, I am not a very "groovy" person. I cannot use hip language, and if I do, it is quite apparent that I am out of my element. Fortunately, I knew myself well enough to know that I really had no alternative but to be what I am—a young college professor in his twenties. With a tape recorder in one hand and an entire brief case full of questionnaires in the other, my probation officer friend and I entered the pusher's home on June 2.

We were seated at the dining-room table by the wife of the man whom I was to meet. I knew his real name, but the sobriquet by which he was known to everyone else was "Sonny." We waited at the table for five minutes, during which time Sonny's wife called upstairs for him to come down. When he finally did, I was rather startled at his appearance. Sonny was six foot five inches tall and weighed over three hundred pounds. He sat down at the table and my probation-officer friend introduced us.

I explained in far too many words what I was doing and what kinds of questions I wanted to ask him. He looked at my officer friend, who nodded, and said he would answer my questions. I then asked if I could tape our interview, and again he looked at the officer, who this time spoke rather than nodded his approval. Sonny agreed to let me tape the interview, which lasted about an hour. Halfway through it the probation officer left. As he stood up to go he asked Sonny to take care of me, and Sonny replied that he'd treat me like I was one of his children. This was reassuring, but I noticed that after the officer left Sonny's answers became briefer and briefer. Finally he started to read a newspaper as I interviewed him, and my keen sociological eye told me the interview was over.

I thanked Sonny for his help and started to pack away my tape recorder. Sonny then looked up at me and asked if it would be any help if he invited four or five junkie thieves to his home so I could interview them too. I was amazed at his offer and enthusiastically responded that it would be of great help. Sonny said he would be glad to do it for me, and told me to call him back in a couple of days.

When I left Sonny that afternoon I could not understand what had happened to make him offer so generously to help me. I had used a tape recorder in my interview, and as if to be sure to chill my informant, I had taken notes at the same time. I had had enough questionnaires on the table in front of him to interview an army. I had asked him to repeat what he said often, because at that time I found it difficult to understand his urban-black patois. I was white, and obviously naive. By the end of what has to be regarded as one of the most poorly conducted interviews in history he was reading a newspaper while I was talking to him. Yet he offered to have me back to his home again and help me with my research. I believe I now know why Sonny offered to help as he did, but I should like to complete this account of my experiences with him before I suggest an explanation.

As arranged, I called Sonny back within a few days, only to find out that he had contracted pneumonia. Naturally this postponed our meeting. I waited three weeks to call again, and this time learned that Sonny had recovered from his pneumonia, but that a case of his had come to trial in the interim and he was now serving a two-year sentence in the state penitentiary. As it happened, this was the very same penitentiary at which I had arranged to interview thieves during the month of August. On August 2, 1971, I arrived at the prison, and the first inmate I called up to my office was Sonny.

When Sonny arrived he yelled to me from halfway down a hundred-foot corridor, "Hey, Carl baby, how the hell are ya?" As he walked toward me he pushed inmates standing in his way to the side, saying, "Sorry, shorty, I'm on the way to see my man, Carl." When he finally got to me he gave me a gentle hug and we went into the little office I had been given in which to conduct my interviews. Our conversation was warm, animated, and very cordial. An unknowing observer might have thought we were life-long friends reunited after a long absence. Sonny talked about his family. I talked about mine. We discussed my research, how it was coming and what I wanted to do here at the prison. Sonny told me to leave everything to him and that "if anybody gives you any shit, just tell ol' Sonny." Then he took me into the corridor and started to introduce me to inmates who were waiting for appointments with their caseworkers. Sonny said things like: "I want you to meet my old friend, Carl; he used to come over my house all the time when I was on the outside. He's a solid dude." "Hey, I want you to meet my man Carl. He's a college professor doin' some shit on fences. You know, like *The Godfather*. He's gonna be around here for a while." After Sonny introduced me to inmates in the corridor he took me around to the guards. His introductions of me to them were equally enthusiastic.

On my first morning at the prison I spent almost two hours talking with Sonny and getting introduced to people in the caseworkers' corridor. As new inmates came in, Sonny made it a point to tell them who I was and what I was doing. At lunch time Sonny and the rest of the inmates were obliged to leave the corridor, but Sonny made me promise to call him up again after lunch.

After lunch Sonny returned before I had a chance to send out a request for him. Inmates were not permitted to come to the casework area without being called and given a pass, but somehow Sonny managed to use his pass from the morning call and get there before I did. During the afternoon I explained to Sonny exactly the kind of people I wanted to talk to. He told me that he did not know any fences who were in the prison, but he did know a great many thieves, hijackers, and burglars. Sonny asked me for a copy of my questionnaire and also for some of my memo pads, on which my name and the name of the college where I taught were printed. When Sonny left me that afternoon, he made me promise to call him up first thing the next day.

I did call him up first thing the following day, and almost every day thereafter during the first two weeks of August. Each day he brought the name of a new inmate with him, whom I interviewed after I called him up and Sonny introduced us. I was never refused an interview by a referral from Sonny. I was never refused permission to tape record the interview, nor did I find any of the inmates I interviewed to be uncooperative. More often than not I had difficulty stopping an interview; I never had trouble starting one. I continued my interviewing through January of 1972, by which time I had collected twenty-one interviews at the prison. All of these interviews were tape recorded, and while most lasted about two hours, some totaled over six hours and had been taken in three or four sessions.[6]

My success in interviewing at that prison was intially due to Sonny's referrals. However, neither Sonny's original cooperation and continued enthusiasm nor the willing participation of the many inmates I interviewed can be completely accounted for by the strength of his referrals. In one especially dramatic example of eagerness to participate, I found an inmate talking about fences into my tape recorder after I had left the room. Why was it that I found the response I did?

First, some of the more grotesque expressions of interest in talking to me, like indignation over not being interviewed and talking into my tape recorder when I was out of the room, were undoubtedly a response to the boredom of prison. Against the bleakness of prison life even a slightly interesting chat with a college professor can become an exciting and sought-after relief.

Also, I think that Sonny had translated what I was doing into terms that the people I was to interview could understand and relate to. By telling everybody I was doing a book about fences "like *The Godfather*" he made the nature of my inquiries acceptable. One inmate even made a concerted effort to invest money in my book.

Primarily, however, I think that I received the reponse I did because I offered to most of those I talked to a rare, and gratifying, opportunity to speak with authority on one of the few subjects about which they could actually do so. Most of the thieves I interviewed were relatively uneducated and, since they were in prison, at least temporarily unsuccessful. The opportunity to educate a

6. I interviewed every day during the first two weeks and three days during the fourth week of August 1971. Between September and December I interviewed for an entire day once a week. Because of complications imposed by the prison routine I was never able to complete more than one interview per day. I also found as I went along that I had incurred obligations to those I had interviewed to visit with them when I returned. I often received little notes from unknown carriers I passed in the corridors asking me to call up someone who had remembered some things about fences that he had forgotten to tell me in an earlier interview.

college professor and participate in his research by giving opinions, anecdotes, descriptions, and accounts of their experiences was a reinforcing experience. (On one occasion I was stopped on the way to lunch by an inmate who was rather indignant that I had not called on him to participate in my research.)

The cooperation I received was further enhanced by my status as a writer and college professor. I was a legitimate-society type, with a suit, tie, briefcase, tape recorder, questionnaires, engraved memo pads, and a voice and vocabulary to prove it. My interest in the inmates was uniformly taken as complimentary, and my remembering their names and joking with them as we passed in the main corridors was, I suspect, flattering. I was not interviewing Sonny or any of the inmates to help, rehabilitate, proselytize, or chastise them; rather, I was interested in their careers and their opinions, and I needed their knowledge. I believe that all of the errors I made in my initial interview with Sonny helped in the long run to gain his cooperation. Those errors may have been disastrous interviewing techniques, but at the same time they bespoke my identity clearly enough: "Here is a college professor writing a book who wants to talk to you to find out the real story."

Throughout my interviewing experience, both in prison and out, I found that my role and the status attached to it were critical features of the interviewing situation. I am almost willing to say that in single-contact interviews they overrode everything else. I should add that although I use the word "status" to describe the fact that what I am was viewed as prestigious by some of the inmates I interviewed, this in no way means that my key to success in interviewing inmates was to "lord it over them." I can think of nothing else which would have more quickly destroyed the kind of cooperation I sought. The idea was not to rub the inmate's nose in my status, but rather, through my interest in his experience and need for his expertise, to allow my status to rub off on him.[7]

7. In considering the sociological dimensions of the interview situation in which I found myself, which was largely defined for me by the way Sonny saw fit to present me to his fellow inmates, I have come to realize that the methodology literature has recognized this status effect, but has often regarded it as an impediment rather than an advantage. Indeed, it can be an impediment if the interviewer is not careful. For example, I would imagine that if one were interviewed about one's sexual experiences by Dr. Kinsey, one might feel a special obligation to live up to his expectations and provide him with

My success in interviewing at the state penitentiary was not duplicated at the federal prison where I spent the third week of August. At that institution I had no inmate like Sonny to vouch for me, and all of my interviewees were selected by prison case-workers. Of the twenty-five inmates I interviewed at that institution, only three were helpful and cooperative. However, the type of inmate I interviewed there was also quite different from the inmates I interviewed in the state prison.

My federal-prison interviewees were all of a much higher class of criminality. Some had organized-crime connections, and all were white. All had been imprisoned for receiving large quantities of stolen goods from interstate shipments. Many were fairly well educated, and many owned businesses or were otherwise apparently well off. I was flatly refused by eight inmates, and many others were friendly but evasive. Clearly, not only was I suspect at the federal prison, but I also had far less relative status to offer inmates there. The three inmates who did choose to talk with me had all turned state's evidence at the time of their trials. They probably assumed they had something to gain by talking with me, and as they had already "finked," they knew they had nothing to lose.[8]

FINDING VINCENT

I had planned that my prison interviews would serve only the purpose of collecting information about fencing as thieves themselves understood it. Although I realized that their impressions would reflect their biases, I hoped that their perspectives would

---

the kind of information he was looking for even if the truth had to be stretched to do so. In such an interview situation the interviewee's status might well be at stake because of the great status inequity and the particular means by which that inequity can be resolved. I do not think that the situation that was constructed for me had "demand characteristics" of that intensity attached to it. See Robert Rosenthal, *Experimenter Effects in Behavioral Research* (New York: Appleton-Century-Crofts, 1966); Raymond L. Gordon, *Interviewing: Strategy, Techniques, and Tactics* (Homewood, Ill.: Dorsey Press, 1969).

8. I later learned that two of the three inmates who chose to cooperate with me thought I was an FBI agent when they first met me.

function both as preparation for my case-study interview and as a cross-check on what my case-study subject told me. I assumed that asking for information about particular fences would be futile, given what I understood to be the criminal's code on such matters. In fact, in the introduction to each interview I explained that I was not interested in names, dates, or anything else that could get anyone in trouble.

I soon found that names would come up naturally and that trying to avoid using real names often involved an awkward substitution of a fictitious name for the real one. Furthermore, after interviewing nine or ten experienced thieves, I found that I could often tell what fence they were talking about by the descriptions they gave or the locations they mentioned. When I thought I knew the fence an inmate was describing, I would say something like, "Hmm, that sounds like Swaggi," or Jones or Big Leo, or whoever I thought it was. If I was right, the thief was always impressed. It showed him I knew what I was talking about. If I was wrong the thief would usually correct me with, "No, it ain't him, it's _____." Once I had established who the fence was that the inmate was talking about, I could ask more detailed questions about that particular fence's business.

It was my good fortune to find four thieves who had worked extensively with Vincent. I interviewed each of them before I met Vincent, and before I knew that he would become the subject of my case study. It was one of these thieves who suggested that Vincent would be the ideal subject for me. This thief's nickname was "Eyeball." Vincent had given the nickname to him.

Eyeball was a package thief; he specialized in theft from mail and delivery trucks. When a driver left his truck unattended Eyeball would enter by breaking the lock with a small crowbar he carried in his sleeve. It seems that Vincent was the one who taught him to survey the contents of the truck and select ("eyeball") the more valuable packages. Vincent had also served as Eyeball's parole sponsor, providing him with a patently legitimate employment while he actually earned his living by stealing. In order to fulfill his parole requirements to the satisfaction of his parole officer, Eyeball spent a good deal of time in Vincent's store.

Eyeball knew Vincent well and, unlike many thieves, knew about Vincent's operations after the goods had been given to him. Eyeball had watched Vincent deal with other thieves and also knew details about Vincent's personal life, and he was willing to talk about what he knew. Eyeball believed that Vincent had set him up for the arrest which led to the sentence he was serving when I met him. However, he acknowledged that while he was in prison Vincent had been good to his family, and that "In spite of what he done to me, I still can't help but like the guy."

My interviews with Eyeball concentrated largely on Vincent. Eyeball had dealt with other fences, but his long experience with Vincent and the extent to which he was familiar with Vincent's operation were unusual. It was Eyeball's idea that I make Vincent the subject of my case study.

He would be the ideal man. The old guy, he's a likeable old guy. That's what messed me up. And the reason I would suggest him is because, you know, he's wise enough and knows that you couldn't do him no harm. You understand? Yaaa.

If it was I, you know, I would write him a letter and ask him, you know. And see what kind a reply he gives back. And he's the type of person that will reply back. Ya, I'd try him.

And like I say, he may be just about givin' up. As for hisself and him bein' the type of dude he is, I think he might go for that. I'd try him. You know, write him a letter and express to him.

You got your college stationery and give him a light rundown on, you know, where you been and talked to a few people and them who's done business with him. And that you're writin' a book an' you put it on the same line as The Godfather.

He knows you couldn't harm him in any way, you know. You're interested an' it's fascinatin'. I think he'd come in, yaaa. I'm damn sure. You can't loose nuthin' but an eight-cent stamp an' that's for damn sure.

An if he's goin' through what he expressed, you know, about goin' away and just takin' it easy, this would be somethin' for him to do. Yaaa. 'Cause he swears he can't stand it no more: "Aw, Jesus H. Christ, I'm gonna die here, right here [in the store]." That is the way he expresses hisself. "I can't stand it. Hell, I got

*all the money I can use." You know, this is him. Ya, I'm damn
sure he'd come in.*[9]

I did exactly as Eyeball told me to. I wrote Vincent the following letter on college stationery:

30 December 1971

Dear Mr. Swoggi: [sic; see note 10, p. 216]

We have never met. Since I know something about you,
I ought to tell you something about me. I'm first of all a
professor of sociology and criminology at Beaver College. I
teach criminology, theory, research, etc. I've published some
articles and for the past two years I have been writing and
researching a major book. The topic of the book is the professional receiver of stolen goods. It can and will be an important and interesting book.

I have read everything ever written about the "fence."
Most of it is junk. Fencing is an old occupation. The first
time the word fence was used in print was 1610. Since then
there have been some very famous fences both real and
fictional. I wouldn't suppose you had ever heard of Jonathan
Wild, Moll Cutpurse, or Isaac Solomons, but they were all
major fences in the 18th and 19th centuries in England.
Many real fences throughout history have been men with
amazing abilities and almost giant characters. Such men,
though, are few and far between.

There is surely an art to being a fence and there are but
a very few great artists left. I have some suspicion that the
art and character of fencing is dying or changing. There are
certainly a lot of nickel-and-dime hustlers and pushers who
will pick up swag for peanuts but they are not true professionals or artists of the caliber that the occupation of fencing
has known.

---

9. This is a transcription of Eyeball's comments. The melody and color
of his speech are absent in this typed transcription. Translation of spoken
words into written words is a genuine methodological problem for the sociologist. Meaning is extremely fragile, and it is ever so easily damaged in translation. I shall have more to say later about how I handled this problem with
Vincent.

During the past two years I have talked with close to a hundred thieves. The majority of them have been at the state prison. To date I have almost 50 hours of tape recorded interviews, stories, and anecdotes about fences and fencing.

I am not a cop. I can keep things confidential and there are quite a few guys who can give me "references." (Tommy Blue was the man who suggested that I write to you before I try to see you. Eyeball sends his regards.) Eyeball didn't give me any information that might be harmful to you. For one thing, I'm not interested in anything of that sort anyway.

Let me try to tell you what I am trying to write about. First, I want to try to describe the style and quality of the professional fence. How does he live? What does he do? Who are his friends? What kinds of people does he deal with? How does he handle them? Second, what kind of man must a fence be? Actor, businessman, artist, or hustler? What skills must he have? Why does he choose and stick with his business? Third, I'd like to know how the business has changed, both in the past ten or twenty years and since it began in the seventeenth century. Is amateur competition greater today than ten years ago? Is the old time fence a thing of the past? Do unprofessional thieves make for unprofessional fences? And fourth, I'd like to write about the fence as a "criminal without victims," a man whom thieves, the neighborhood, and his customers are glad to have around, a man with no direct victims.

I am not interested in any details which could get anyone in trouble. Names, dates, specific crimes, specific places, specific people are of no interest to me. If I were a cop, I'd have to warn you of your rights before talking to me. Since I tell you that I am not a cop and will not make any such warning, nothing that you say to me could be used against you. Also, as you are aware, there is a statute of limitations on receiving. It would be just as helpful to talk about things the way they were three years ago as they are today.

To be honest with you I'd like to write your biography.

It could become a classic book. I'll call you during the first week of January. Please don't turn me down without letting me take you to lunch and tell you more.

Sincerely yours,

[Signed]

Carl Klockars
Professor, Sociology and Criminology[10]

I sent a copy of The Professional Thief with the above letter for the same reasons that I had done so with Knuckles Jones. I attached to the book a handwritten note on personalized college stationery which read, "This is what I want to do with you."

THE FIRST MEETING WITH VINCENT

As I had promised in the letter, I called Vincent at his store a few days later. The conversation was brief, but Vincent said he was interested. "Come to the store anytime that's convenient," he said. I suggested lunch the following day.

When I arrived at the store Vincent was not there. The man behind the counter (who I later learned was his brother Tony),

10. There are a number of errors in this letter. Some are intentional and others are not. First, I misspelled Vincent's last name. This was unintentional. Second, I am not a Professor of Sociology and Criminology; I am an Assistant Professor of Sociology. I misrepresented myself here on the assumption that Vincent would not be familiar with academic rankings or customary disciplinary divisions. Third, I had not read everything ever published about the fence and much of it is not junk. I thought the claim would strengthen the impression of my seriousness. Fourth, I had talked to many thieves, but one hundred was an exaggeration. Sixty would have been a more reasonable estimate. Fifth, the description of what I wanted to write about as well as the whole tone of the letter is slanted toward the most complimentary aspects of fencing. Sixth, the statement that because I did not warn Vincent of his rights nothing he said to me could be used against him is totally false. I don't know where I got that idea. Although I later discussed most candidly the dangers Vincent might face in permitting me to write his life history, Vincent never brought this error in the letter to my attention. Had he picked it up, it might have been a disastrous error, impugning both my competence and my credibility.

asked me if I was the college professor. I answered that I was, and noticed that two or three of the regulars standing in the store also knew that I was expected. Within a few minutes Vincent returned. I introduced myself, and he suggested we go into the back room, where we could "talk private."

Vincent said he had been thinking about my proposal and had talked it over with some friends, one of whom was a judge. "The judge's advice was to do it," Vincent said, " ' 'cause there's nobody can say anything bad about you.' " Vincent said he liked the idea, but wondered if I was planning to use real names in the book. I told him no, and added that I would also change dates, places, and descriptions so that no one would know it was he.

Then Vincent started to tell me about his life: his years in the orphanage, his gifts to children, his work as a hustler, his deals as a fence. For more than an hour Vincent talked. Two or three times he would pause and say, "Oh, there's so much." Then, as if to prove it, he'd talk more. Frankly, I was overwhelmed. I had expected caution. I had expected to have to persuade Vincent. Instead, he was trying to persuade me.

He succeeded, and we planned to meet a few days later at his home to begin work. As I was leaving the store the telephone rang. When Vincent answered, I moved away to let him talk privately. After a few seconds he signaled me to come close to the phone, and held the receiver so I could listen. The man on the other end of the line was trying to sell him 1500 pairs of hot shoes. Vincent asked for samples. My role as a nonparticipant observer had begun after I had known Vincent for little more than an hour.

I still do not know why Vincent consented to my offer that first day. My letter was persuasive and, I think, established my credentials to Vincent's satisfaction. Perhaps Vincent simply wanted something new to talk about; perhaps he considered having a college professor write a book about him flattering; perhaps he was proud of his success and skill and wanted to talk about it. I have asked Vincent why he chose to work with me. He always says that he wanted to help me out if he could. As time went on, both helping me and enjoying our meetings did apparently figure into his motives. I have no best hypothesis, and sometimes Vincent's explanations of his own motives are quite unsatisfactory.

THE INTERVIEW ROUTINE

Between January of 1972 and April of 1973 I interviewed Vincent once and occasionally twice a week. With the exception of the first few meetings, my weekly visits began in the late afternoon when I arrived at Vincent's store. I would watch him do business for an hour or so, and after he closed, we would go to dinner at a modest Italian restaurant. During dinner Vincent would recount the events and deals he had participated in since last I saw him. As we got to know one another better, Vincent would, in a relaxed fashion, review with me his options on pending deals and ask for my opinion on how he ought to proceed.

Although I always tried to pay for dinner and even claimed, "My grant will cover it," Vincent always took the check, saying, "I made more money than you today. When you make more than me, then you can pay." From the restaurant we would drive to Vincent's home; there, in Vincent's consideration, the "real" interviewing would begin. This was signaled by my opening my briefcase and taking out my notebook and pencils. Vincent's part in the ritual was to settle in his large recliner chair and light his cigar. Quite often the topic with which we would begin was carried over from our conversation at dinner.

By ten-thirty Vincent would usually grow tired; he started his day at five-thirty every morning except Sunday. Occasionally an especially productive interview would keep us going until midnight, but usually I would leave by eleven. As I drove home I would dictate my comments, recollections, and impressions into a small, battery-operated tape recorder. The lateness of the hour, the amount I had drunk during the interview and at dinner, and my attention to driving all took their toll on the quality of these comments. I was usually home in a few hours and always too tired to review my interview notes. This task was postponed until the following morning.

On occasion the routine as I have described it was broken by having a visitor at dinner, making a side trip after dinner for business purposes, or making a visit during the evening. Once or twice we ate at Vincent's home, where he prepared dinner with my assistance; once or twice his daughter made a special Italian dinner for us. But for fifteen months the pattern remained virtually the same: an hour at the store, two hours at dinner, three to four hours of "real" interviewing, and an hour of variable-quality dictation. In sum, I spent roughly four hundred hours watching, listening to, and talking to Vincent over a period of fifteen months.

THE INTERVIEW STRATEGY

The problems of what to ask Vincent and when and how to ask it governed my choice of an interview strategy. I assumed that, despite his enthusiasm and cooperation as evidenced by his open-ness at our initial meeting, he would have to learn to trust me before he shared the most sensitive details of his life and occupa-tion with me. Consequently, I chose to interview him about the least sensitive areas of his life first. For the first three of the fifteen months I worked with Vincent, our "real" interviews were focused only on his prefencing years: his family, his school, his years in the orphanage, his street hustling, his marriage, and his years in Mid-City.

Gradually, my weekly visits became a part of Vincent's life. I got to know his daughter, some of his customers, his former wives, his girlfriends, and the regulars at the store. His daughter, who like many Italian daughters made it her responsibility to look after her father, liked having him spend time with me. A few times she asked me if I would arrange for my interview visits to fall on nights when she would be away from her father and no one else would be there to keep him company. Had Vincent known of these requests, he would have strongly resented his daughter's meddling.

Vincent enjoyed the time we spent together. I listened care-fully to him when he spoke, and wrote down what he said. I asked him questions and was interested in him. I ate with him, drank with him, learned from him, invited him to my home, brought him cakes my wife had baked, brought my family to his store, drove him in my car, visited him in the hospital, sent him birthday cards, and showed him my son's baby pictures. I came to like Vincent and he knew it. As time went on we became good friends.

The strategy of putting off interviewing Vincent about his criminal conduct paid off in ways that I had not anticipated. Not only was Vincent's trust and confidence in me increased, but I also became more familiar with the people who were part of his business. During dinner, when Vincent talked about the day's or week's events, I came to understand the working principles of his world. These experiences saved me from asking distracting questions when the interview topics were more critical.

I think it is also fair to say that during these less sensitive and less important first few months of interviewing, I learned how to interview Vincent. I learned when I should talk and when I should listen. I learned which of his facial gestures betrayed boredom, and which caution, enthusiasm, or puzzlement. I also developed little skills like postponing my note taking for a few seconds so that Vincent would not know which details of his story I was writing down. Generally, I found that I could communicate my interest in and enthusiasm for a topic very quickly to Vincent, and once I got him started on a subject he would talk for remarkably long times at a stretch. Vincent makes his living by talking, and he loves to talk about his business, his deals, the characters he meets, and himself. In many ways he was an ideal subject.

By April of 1971, I had interviewed Vincent about his early years and the events leading up to his arrest in 1951 (the pre-fencing years). Between April and August of 1971 we talked about fencing. Then, in the first week of August, we started the whole process over again; reviewing what he had told me during the last six months. I began to write the first draft of the manuscript in August, and to do so, needed Vincent's testimony to fill in gaps in my interview notes. In August I met with Vincent seven times. Each time I brought a dozen or so pages of manuscript for him to read to me aloud, and each time I interviewed him about the events which chronologically followed what he had read to me.

This system had two important advantages. First, it let me check the reliability of Vincent's accounts. I could compare what he told me this second time with what he had told me five or six months earlier. If he had lied to me, even Vincent could not remember his lies six months later.[11] In fact, I found only the most minor discrepancies.

Second, it permitted me to check how accurately I had captured Vincent's language and phrasing. Both Vincent and I agreed quite early in our work together that tape recordings of our interviews would have been a security risk. I made detailed notes on what Vincent said; I also developed a sensitive ear for the style of his expression. I believe that by having him read aloud what I had written as quotations from him, I satisfied reasonable demands for accuracy. When Vincent stumbled over a line or phrase, it would usually mean that I had not quoted him properly, and I would change it by having him retell the incident.

There are some extremely subtle problems in using quotations as I have throughout the manuscript. One, which I mentioned earlier in this section, is the problem of translation of spoken words into written words. In that translation, tone dynamics, silence, rhythm, gesture, and many other expressive components of the spoken word are lost. A second problem is that as people begin to share a history of assumptions and common understandings, much of their dialogue can be understood only if the reader also shares these understandings.[12] In quoting Vincent as extensively as I did, I faced both these problems repeatedly.

The second problem was less difficult than the first. Vincent thinks and remembers anecdotally. He is terrible at the kind of careful generalizations which characterize academic analysis, and it took some time for me to realize the difference between his

11. I make this claim cautiously. Vincent has a system for lying that is remarkable:

> You see, when I make up a story I figure it out so clearly and plant it so strong in my mind that I actually believe it myself. Like say I'm gonna tell the police that a certain guy sold me some stuff. Now I think of a guy I know, maybe it was somebody I knew twenty years ago, and I really think hard about him: the kind a clothes, his hair, the shape of his face, every detail. Now when I get through tellin' the police every little thing about the way this guy looked, they gotta figure it really happened. You know you do that, there's nobody gonna trip you up on your story 'cause it's like it really happened, which I actually believe when I do that.

12. Harold Garfinkel's detailed analysis of this problem appears in his *Studies in Ethnomethodology* (Englewood Cliffs, N.J.: Prentice-Hall, 1967), pp. 38–44.

cognitive style and my own. Vincent thought nothing of saying "all your criminal lawyers are crooks" and then proceeding to describe two or three exemplary lawyers he has known. Fortunately, anecdotes are complete units in themselves, and, unlike everyday dialogue, do not assume understandings which would make direct quotation unintelligible. This made quoting Vincent quite easy. The reader will recall that the vast majority of quotations in this manuscript are stories with a beginning, middle, and end, the latter most often a punchline which makes Vincent's point. That is the way Vincent thinks about things.

The problem of translation was more difficult. Vincent is a wonderfully expressive talker. He accompanies what he says with gestures, smiles, and changes in voice tone which are fully part of the words he uses. I am sure that as I wrote up my interview notes on the days after our meetings I added phrases and sentences to Vincent's discourse which he had not actually said. These phrases and sentences were necessary to restore the meaning and sense which was lost in transferring Vincent's spoken words to the written page. I do not mean that I added carelessly, nor can I point to any particular phrase which is mine and not Vincent's. I am sure that phrases I did add were characteristic of Vincent's expressive style, as every quotation I attribute to him has his personal read-aloud approval. I confess that what I have written is not tape-recorder accurate, but at the same time I believe the quotations I attribute to Vincent convey what he said and meant better than would a transcribed recording.

PROBLEMS OF METHODOLOGY

Reliability and Validity

Although the interview strategy itself provided a check on the reliability and internal validity of Vincent's testimony, it was not the only check. The question of the truth of Vincent's testimony is quite critical; hence, I should like to review some of the ways in which I was able to cross-check what I was told and encourage truthfulness.

1. **The Interview Strategy.** As I have mentioned above, the interview strategy itself provided a check on the internal validity of Vincent's account. By interviewing Vincent twice about everything I reported, and having the second interview separated by as much as seven months from the first, I was relatively certain that if Vincent had lied, he could not have repeated his lies exactly as he had many months earlier.

Also, the interview strategy was such that I already knew a great deal about Vincent's criminal occupation before I began to systematically interview him about it. Our dinner conversations (which Vincent never considered part of the real work on the book) provided me with detailed accounts of the operations of Vincent's business. These accounts, which I continued to get throughout the fifteen months I met with Vincent, could be compared with what Vincent told me in the more thorough, "real" interviews.

Finally, the interviews were taken weekly over a period of fifteen months. It would have been virtually impossible to sustain some kinds of false impressions over such an extended period of time.

2. **Corroborative Interviews and Review of the Text.** Because I found myself welcomed by Vincent's friends and family, I was able to interview some of them systematically about Vincent. Vincent's daughter read much of the text and offered her opinions on it. Others talked with me in a casual way and supported what Vincent had told me about them. The reader will remember, too, that in addition to talking to Vincent's family and friends, I interviewed a number of thieves and other experienced persons before meeting Vincent. Four of the thieves and possibly some of the other persons had done business with Vincent.

3. **Historical and Sociological Coherence.** Although the literature on fencing is meager, Vincent's descriptions square with what is available. Furthermore, his accounts are believable sociologically in that they do not defy reasonable normative expectations.

4. **Complementary Methods.** In addition to interviewing Vincent about his business, I watched him work at it. I observed his dealings with thieves, customers, and others.

5. DOCUMENTS. I managed to secure some documents which corroborated Vincent's testimony. These included newspaper articles, orphanage records, probation records, and many miscellaneous documents which Vincent himself showed me. Among these personal documents were letters, photographs, bills, sales receipts, stock certificates, and licenses. I also saw merchandise and money.

6. A FINAL PRESS FOR AUTHENTICITY. In the course of interviewing Vincent I developed some techniques which seemed to encourage truthfulness. I explained to him a number of times that I would need proof for much of what he told me. This, I said, was not because I did not trust him, but because I would have to tell sociologists and criminologists I had proof for everything I put in the book. I also told him that the book would be read by some very sharp people, people who knew the business very well. If they detected exaggeration or misrepresentation in any part of the book, then the whole book would be discredited. Vincent wanted the book to be a success very much, and this reasoning seemed to discipline his enthusiasm.

I imagine that anyone who was having a book written about him would want that book to reflect his best side. Vincent was no exception. On occasion I could tell that he was exaggerating, or adding details which he thought would make good reading. When I sensed that this was happening I sometimes feigned boredom or tried to change the subject. Once and only once I came down very hard on Vincent for what I knew to be a lie. There were some very tense moments that evening. Vincent knew I had him, but he would not admit it. The evening ended with my elaborating on the possibility of the book being discredited. Vincent got over the tension of that evening quicker than I did. When I called him the next day to apologize for getting angry at him, he told me to forget it and that I was still his best friend.

Anonymity and Confidentiality

One final matter merits discussion in this review of the methods of my research. It is the problem of protecting Vincent from law enforcers and other interested persons who might wish to discover his identity. As I explained in my introduction, I have changed names, dates, places, and descriptions of events with this purpose in mind. I am convinced that from the evidence in the text Vincent's true identity cannot be established. But, of course, that is not an entire solution to the problem.

At this time there is no legal protection for the criminologist who has done this type of research. He could perhaps be subpoenaed and forced to testify to investigating committees and grand juries under threat of imprisonment if he refuses. I do not anticipate that this legal situation will change much, nor am I sure that it ought to. Knowing Vincent the way I do, I can well imagine the way he or others with similarly ingenious criminal imaginations could subvert the intent of the most carefully written shield law.

On at least half a dozen separate occasions, Vincent and I discussed what I would do to protect his identity and what the dangers might be to him or his family were he discovered as the subject of my study. Our agreement was that since Vincent had so much at stake, he would have the final say on anything that I wrote in the life history chapters. Some parts of his business could not be described. Vincent never asked me to remove anything I had written from the text; I knew what he would have objected to and simply did not include it in the life history section. This process did not compromise the theoretical analysis, in which I was able to add what was necessary from historical sources and interviews with others.

Furthermore, I made it clear that I would talk if I were forced to, rather than go to jail. I explained to him that if he were subpoenaed, he too could face the alternatives of talking or jail. I added that I would not say more than I was forced to, and that I did not think it would be wise for him to do so either.

Throughout the months I spent with Vincent many people knew what I was doing. This group included my colleagues on the faculty, my family and friends, the granting agency which supported my work, and some of the police and security agents I had talked to early in my research. Eyeball knew I was going to contact Vincent, and many thieves knew I was looking for some fence to work with. Unfortunately, the number of people who knew not only that I was working on a case study of a fence but that the subject of my case study was Vincent was not under my control.

Although I had strongly urged Vincent not to say anything about our working together, he just could not resist a little advance publicity. He always introduced me as the college professor who was writing a book about him. Vincent told FBI agents, detectives, judges, reporters, and most of his good customers about the book. In January of 1973, he told me, "You know, the word is out about the book now. Ya, a guy came in the store today, haven't seen him in years, said he heard they were writin' a book about me. I told him it was true, but the book was only gonna be for colleges out West."

By April of 1973, Vincent was telling me about his plans to sell the book, autographed for a small charge, in his store. He also developed a scheme to call all of the bookstores in the city in order to create a demand for the book. Vincent also began to think that a movie about him would be good and that a second book ("We can get the women in that one.") would be a sure seller. All of this made me uncomfortable about my care in covering up details which could identify Vincent.

I mentioned to Vincent in April that I thought having him die at the end of the book might be a way to take the pressure off him from those who might want to find out who he was. Vincent, naturally, thought this was a terrible idea. He suggested that at the end I have him getting on a boat to go back to Sicily, and then, if I could find somebody to write a second book (I had explained to Vincent that I was a sociologist, not a novelist, and could not write the kind of book he had in mind), it could be called *Vincent Returns*.

In as many ways as I knew how, I tried to disabuse Vincent of these dreams and schemes, but he stuck with them. Half of the time he knew he was dreaming, but half of the time he did not.

As I have come to know and like Vincent, I have often found it difficult to judge as severely as I should the harmful things he has done and continues to do. Perhaps that bias has entered some of the pages of this life history. I invite criticism on this count, but only from those who have been close enough to the kind of world I have tried to describe to distinguish between my bias and the assumptions of everyday life which prevail there.

BIBLIOGRAPHY

Ahern, Danny. *How to Commit a Murder*. New York: Ives Washburn, 1930.

Asbury, Herbert. *The Gangs of New York: An Informal History of the Underworld*. New York: Alfred A. Knopf, 1928.

Association of Grand Jurors of New York County, Prison Committee. *Criminal Receivers of the United States*. New York: G. P. Putnam's Sons, 1928.

Barnes, Robert Earl. *Are You Safe From Burglars?* Garden City, N.Y.: Doubleday and Co., 1971.

————. "The Fence: Crime's Real Profiteer." *Reader's Digest*, September 1973, p. 155.

Becker, Howard. *Outsiders: Studies in the Sociology of Deviance*. New York: The Free Press of Glencoe, 1963.

Black, Jack. *You Can't Win*. New York: Macmillan Co., 1926.

Borrow, George. *Celebrated Trials*. Vol. 2. New York: Payson and Clarke, 1928.

Bowers, John. "Big City Thieves." *Harper's Magazine*, February 1967, pp. 50–54.

Bryan, James H. "Occupational Ideologies and Individual Attitudes of Call Girls." *Social Problems* 13 (1966): 441–50.

Burke, Kenneth. *A Grammar of Motives.* New York: Prentice-Hall, 1945.

———. *Permanence and Change.* New York: Bobbs-Merrill Co., 1965.

———. *A Rhetoric of Motives.* Berkeley and Los Angeles: University of California Press, 1969.

Cameron, Mary Owen. *The Booster and the Snitch.* New York: The Free Press, 1964.

Chandler, Frank W. *The Literature of Roguery.* Vol. 1. Boston: Houghton Mifflin Co., 1967.

Chesney, Kellow. *The Anti-Society: An Account of the Victorian Underworld.* Boston: Gambit, 1970.

Clark, Charles L. *Lockstep and Corridor.* Cincinnati: University of Cincinnati Press, 1927.

Clinard, Marshall B. *The Black Market.* New York: Rinehart and Co., 1952.

Colquhoun, P. *A Treatise on the Commerce and Police of the River Thames.* London: Printed for Joseph Mawman, 1800.

———. [A Magistrate] *A Treatise on the Police of the Metropolis.* London: Printed by H. Fry for C. Dilly in the Poultry, 1796.

Crapsey, Edward. *The Nether Side of New York.* New York: Sheldon and Co., 1872.

Defoe, Daniel. *The King of the Pirates, Including the Life and Actions of Jonathan Wild.* New York: The Jenson Society, 1901.

Dillenberger, John, ed. *Martin Luther.* New York: Doubleday and Co., 1961.

Drucker, S., and Hexter, M. B. *Children Astray.* Cambridge: Harvard University Press, 1923.

Emerson, E. Frank. "They Can Get It For You Better Than Wholesale." *New York Magazine*, 22 November 1971, pp. 34–37.

Ettinger, Clayton. *The Problem of Crime.* New York: Ray Long and Richard R. Smith, Inc., 1932.

Fielding, Henry. *The Life of Mr. Jonathan Wild The Great.* Oxford: Basil Blackwell, Publisher to the Shakespeare Head Press of Stratford-upon-Avon, 1926.

Finestone, Harold. "Cats, Kicks, and Color." In *The Other Side*, edited by Howard Becker. New York: The Free Press of Glencoe, 1964.

Friedman, Albert B. "The Scatological Rites of Burglars." *Western Folklore*, July 1968, pp. 171–79.

Fuller, Ronald. *The Beggars' Brotherhood.* London: George Allen and Unwin, 1936.

Garfinkel, Harold. *Studies in Ethnomethodology.* Englewood Cliffs, N.J.: Prentice-Hall, 1967.

Glazer, Nathan, and Moynihan, Daniel P. *Beyond the Melting Pot.* 2d. ed., rev. Cambridge: M.I.T. Press, 1970.

Goffman, Erving. *Stigma: Notes on the Management of Spoiled Identity.* Englewood Cliffs, N.J.: Prentice-Hall, 1963.

Goldin, Hyman E.; O'Leary, Frank; and Lispus, Morris, eds. *Dictionary of American Underworld Lingo.* New York: Twayne Publishers, 1950.

Gordon, Raymond L. *Interviewing: Strategy, Techniques, and Tactics.* Homewood, Ill.: Dorsey Press, 1969.

Hall, Jerome. *Theft, Law, and Society.* 2d ed. Indianapolis: Bobbs-Merrill Co., 1952.

Harney, Malachi L., and Cross, John C. *The Informer in Law Enforcement.* Springfield, Ill.: Charles C Thomas, 1960.

Hayward, Arthur, ed. *Lives of the Most Remarkable Criminals.* Vol. 1. London: George Routledge and Sons, 1927.

Hill, Matthew Davenport. *Suggestions for the Repression of Crime.* London: John W. Parker and Sons, 1837.

Hitchen, Charles. *The Regulator; or, A Discovery of the Thieves, Thief Takers, and Locks, alias Receivers of Stolen Goods, in and about the City of London.* London: Printed for T. Warner at the Black Boy in Pater-Noster Row, 1718.

Howson, Gerald. *Thief-Taker General.* New York: St. Martin's Press, 1971.

Humphreys, Christmas. *The Great Pearl Robbery of 1913.* London: William Heinemann, 1929.

"The Informer Privilege: What's In A Name." *Journal of Criminal Law and Criminology* 64 (1973): 56–66.

Irwin, William Robert. *The Making of Jonathan Wild.* New York: Columbia University Press, 1941.

———. *The Newgate Calendar.* New York: Capricorn Books, 1962.

Jackson, Bruce. *A Thief's Primer.* London: Macmillan and Co., 1969.

Landesco, John. *Organized Crime in Chicago.* Part 3: Illinois Crime Survey. Chicago: Illinois Association for Criminal Justice, 1929.

Lawes, Lewis E. *Cell 202 Sing Sing.* New York: Farrar and Rinehart, 1935.

Life and Death of Mrs. Mary Frith, commonly called Moll Cutpurse,

The. London: Printed for W. Gilbertson at the *Bible* in Giltspur Street without Newgate, 1662.

Lofland, John, and Stark, Rodney. "Becoming a World Saver: A Theory of Conversion to a Deviant Perspective." *American Sociological Review* 30 (1965): 862–875.

Mainwaring, George. *Observations on the Present State of the Police.* London, 1822.

Mandeville, Bernard De. *An Enquiry into the Causes of the Frequent Executions at Tyburn.* Los Angeles: Clark Memorial Library, 1964.

Manning, John, ed. "No Money Down." Philadelphia: Publication of The Model Cities Consumer Protection Program, vol. 1, no. 3, p. 3.

Martin, John Bartlow. *My Life in Crime.* New York: Harper and Brothers, 1952.

Matza, David. *Becoming Deviant.* Englewood Cliffs, N.J.: Prentice-Hall, 1969.

———. *Delinquency and Drift.* New York: John Wiley and Sons, 1964.

Maurer, David W. *The Big Con.* New York: Pocket Books, 1949.

———. *Whiz Mob.* Gainesville, Fla.: Publication of the American Dialect Society, 1955.

McHugh, Peter. "A Common Sense Conception of Deviance." In *Deviance & Respectability*, edited by Jack Douglas, pp. 61–88. New York: Basic Books, 1970.

Merriam, Charles Edward. *Chicago: A More Intimate View of Urban Politics.* New York: Macmillan Co., 1929.

Messinger, Sheldon. *Professional Crime in West City.* Unpublished Manuscript, 5, July 1972.

Mills, C. Wright. "Situated Actions and Vocabularies of Motive." *American Sociological Review* 5 (1940): 904–13.

Morrison, Arthur. *A Child of the Iago.* New York: Daffield and Co., 1896.

Partridge, Eric. *A Dictionary of the Underworld.* New York: Bonanza Books, 1961.

Pike, Luke Owen. *A History of Crime in England.* Vol 1. 2d series. London: Smith, Elder and Co., 1876.

Polsky, Ned. *Hustlers, Beats, and Others.* Chicago: Aldine Publishing Co., 1967.

President's Commission on Law Enforcement and the Administration of Justice, Task Force on Assessment. *Crime and Its Impact—An Assessment.* Washington, D.C.: Government Printing Office, 1967.

Price, Carroll S. "Sources of Information." *Police*, March–April 1960, pp. 47–51.

Pringle, Patrick. *Hue and Cry*. Great Britain: William Morrow and Co., n.d.

———. *The Thief-Takers*. London: Museum Press, 1958.

Radzinowicz, Leon. *A History of English Criminal Law and Its Administration from 1750*. 2 vols. New York: Macmillan Co., 1957.

Roselius, Ted, and Benton, Douglas. *Marketing Theory and the Fencing of Stolen Goods*. Report prepared for the National Institute of Law Enforcement and Criminal Justice, Law Enforcement Assistance Administration, U.S. Department of Justice, August 1971.

Rosenthal, Robert. *Experimenter Effects in Behavioral Research*. New York: Appleton-Century-Crofts, 1966.

Ross, H. L. "The 'Hustler' in Chicago." *Journal of Student Research* 1 (1959): 13–19.

Rubin, Theodore Isaac. *In the Life*. New York: Ballantine Books, 1961.

Sampson, Harold; Messinger, Sheldon; and Towne, Robert. "Family Processes and Becoming a Mental Patient." In *Deviance: The Interactionist Perspective*, edited by Earl Rubington and Martin S. Weinberg, pp. 42–51 New York: Macmillan Co., 1973.

Schur, Edwin. *Labeling Deviant Behavior*. New York: Harper and Row, 1971.

Scott, Sir Harold, ed. *The Concise Encyclopedia of Crime and Criminals*. London: Rainbird, McLean, 1961.

Scott, Marvin B., and Lyman, Stanford M. "Accounts." *American Sociological Review* 33 (1968): 46–62.

Shover, Neal. "Structures and Careers in Burglary." *Journal of Criminal Law, Criminology, and Police Science* 63 (1972), pp. 545–49.

Simmel, George. *The Sociology of George Simmel*. Edited and Translated by Kurt Wolff. New York: The Free Press, 1964.

Skolnick, Jerome. *Justice Without Trial*. New York: John Wiley and Sons, 1969.

Slim, Iceberg. *Pimp: The Story of My Life*. Los Angeles, Holloway House Publishing Co., 1967.

———. *Trick Baby: The Biography of a Con Man*. Los Angeles: Holloway House Publishing Co., 1967.

Smith, Richard Austin. "The Incredible Electrical Conspiracy." *Fortune*, April 1961, pp. 132–80.

Snodgrass, Jon. "The Criminologist and the Criminal: The Case of

Edwin H. Sutherland and Broadway Jones." *Issues in Criminology* 8 (Spring 1973): 1–17.

Stewart, George Lee. "Becoming a John." *Urban Life and Urban Culture* 3 (October 1972): 255–74.

Sutherland, Edwin H., and Cressey, Donald R. *Principles of Criminology*. 7th ed. Philadelphia and New York: J. B. Lippincott Co., 1966.

Sutherland, Edwin H. "Is 'White Collar Crime' Crime?" *American Sociological Review* 10 (1945): 132–39.

————. *The Professional Thief*. Chicago: University of Chicago Press, 1937.

Sykes, Gresham, and Matza, David. "Techniques of Neutralization." *American Sociological Review* 22 (1957): 664–70.

U.S., Congress, Senate, Permanent Subcommittee on Investigations of the Committee on Government Operations. *Hearings on Organized Crime: Stolen Securities*. 92d Cong., 1st sess., 1971.

Von Hentig, Hans. *The Criminal and His Victim*. New Haven: Yale University Press, 1948.

Weber, Max. *The Protestant Ethic and the Spirit of Capitalism*. New York: Charles Scribner's Sons, 1958.

Weinberg, Martin. "Becoming a Nudist." In *Deviance: The Interactionist Perspective* edited by Earl Rubington and Martin S. Weinberg, pp. 277–290. New York: Macmillan Co., 1973.

Westley, William A. *Violence and the Police: A Sociological Study of Law, Custom, and Morality*. Cambridge: M.I.T. Press, 1970.

Whibley, Charles. *A Book of Scoundrels*. New York: E. P. Dutton and Co., 1912.

Williamson, Henry. *Hustler!* Garden City, N.Y.: Doubleday and Co., 1965.

INDEX